POVERTY IN THE SOVIET UNION

By the same author

Class and society in Soviet Russia (1972)
Soviet government, a selection of official documents on internal policies (1974)
Privilege in the Soviet Union (1978)
Soviet sociology, 1964–1975, a bibliography (with T. A. Jones, 1978)
Education in the Soviet Union (1982)

POVERTY IN
THE SOVIET UNION

The life-styles of the
underprivileged in recent years

————————— ⁕ —————————

MERVYN MATTHEWS
University of Surrey

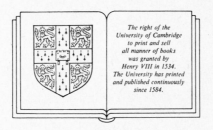

The right of the
University of Cambridge
to print and sell
all manner of books
was granted by
Henry VIII in 1534.
The University has printed
and published continuously
since 1584.

CAMBRIDGE UNIVERSITY PRESS

CAMBRIDGE

LONDON   NEW YORK   NEW ROCHELLE
MELBOURNE   SYDNEY

Published by the Press Syndicate of the University of Cambridge
The Pitt Building, Trumpington Street, Cambridge CB2 1RP
32 East 57th Street, New York, NY 10022, USA
10 Stamford Road, Oakleigh, Melbourne 3166, Australia

© Cambridge University Press 1986

First published 1986

Printed in Great Britain by the University Press, Cambridge

British Library cataloguing in publication data

Matthews, Mervyn
Poverty in the Soviet Union: the life-styles
of the under-privileged in recent years.
1. Poor – Soviet Union – History – 20th century
2. Soviet Union – Economic conditions – 1918–
    305.5′69′0947   HC340.P6

Library of Congress cataloguing in publication data

Matthews, Mervyn.
Poverty in the Soviet Union.
Bibliography.
Includes index.
1. Poor–Soviet Union. 2. Soviet Union – Social
conditions – 1945–   . 3. Cost and standard of living –
Soviet Union. I. Title.
HC340.P6M38   1986   305.5′69′0947 86–993

ISBN 0 521 32544 7 hard covers
ISBN 0 521 31059 8 paperback

To Mila, Owen and Emily

CONTENTS

——————— ·◌· ———————

PART II

PREFACE

———— ✦ ————

In recent years poverty in the industrialised nations of the world has attracted considerable interest. The problem has become a distinct branch of academic research, using most of the social disciplines to investigate cause and effect. All the more striking, therefore, is the fact that the study of poverty in the Soviet Union should have been relatively neglected. The problems of poor people in that vast land have received far less attention than they deserve.

The reasons for this are fairly straightforward. Public discussion of poverty as such is virtually banned in the USSR itself, and even specialist Soviet writers cannot easily broach it. The Soviet Union claims for itself exemplary social development, and outside observers have perhaps been a little too ready to believe that Soviet reality bears little blemish of this kind. Travel and residence restrictions on foreigners mean that the poor are relatively inaccessible for purposes of observation anyway. Constant Soviet propaganda about rising living standards, not to mention some hefty improvements in real terms, have tended to deflect attention to other topics.

In any case, the sociological disciplines as practised in the West have, in our view, underperformed in this particular sphere. Political scientists find little of interest in a social group which is excluded from the power game, and has little measurable impact on matters of governance. Economists seem to concentrate on macrodevelopment and mean values. Their work in any case has been inhibited by the highly unsatisfactory nature of Soviet income statistics, and the imponderables of the 'second' economy. Sociologists tend to rely on survey materials and suffer most from the inaccessibility of the subject matter. Recent studies concerned tangentially with poverty have been disappointingly arithmetical, or stopped at any reality beyond the wage-packet. Such material as *is* available has been subjected to systematic analysis and synthesis.

My own study cannot possibly fill so large a gap in Soviet studies (personally perceived though it may be). To do so would require a longer and more detailed appraisal than I attempt here, and would, I think, need to be a coordinated effort by many hands. My main hope is that the pages which follow will encourage the appearance of broader and more systematic studies of those social groups which have derived least material benefit from Soviet-style socialism.

My approach may be summarised as follows. The first chapter of the study, after a brief discussion of poverty in general, proceeds to review the historical background to Soviet poverty, and the manner in which it has been investigated inside the USSR. The story is carried up to the late seventies, and inevitably treats such matters as consumer goods policy, accepted definitions of poverty, Soviet statistical practice, and the stringency of the censorship. Having argued that poverty not only existed in the late seventies, but was in fact widespread, I go in Chapter Two to ask what socio-occupational groups were most likely to experience it. Their configuration, not surprisingly, bears a fair resemblance to what one finds in bourgeois societies: but specifically Soviet characteristics, in so far as they can be discerned, are dealt with in some detail. Chapter Three is devoted to the essentials of the poverty life-style, my aim being to describe, with some statistical backing, the likely diet, clothing and housing of a poor urban family. I explore, in so far as it is possible, the standards achieved by the late seventies, and their relationship to national averages. Shortages of data and the complexity of the patterns involved preclude detailed comparison with other countries.

Up to this point the study is concerned with fact rather than theory, and with marshalling ascertainable information. The chapters that follow, though sequential upon the first three, are more conceptual than factual. Information on the topics covered is generally more scanty, and the topics themselves are of a more abstract nature. Where hard fact is lacking, I have endeavoured to indicate likely parameters, and suggest how poverty may fit other aspects of Soviet reality. Chapter Four begins by exploring the relationships between poverty and education, or more specifically, the advantages and disadvantages of the Soviet school system for poor people. The same approach is adopted with regard to medical facilities and legal services. The third part of the chapter deals with the impact of poverty on people's use of time, recreation and holidays.

No account of the poverty problem would be complete without reference to the constitutional status of work, and to the social security system, of which the poor are supposed to be the primary beneficiaries. In Chapter Five I have attempted to demonstrate the social implications of labour in the USSR as a right and a duty. I then move beyond the glib concept of state security as a 'transfer payment', to consider how far it may actually alleviate poverty. Here a more chronological approach has proved possible, and the story may be traced through the secretaryships of Khrushchev and Brezhnev. This is one of the few dimensions of poverty which have received detailed attention from western scholars. At the same time the relevance of social security should not be exaggerated: it is essentially a palliative, necessitated by the inability of the authorities to remove a long standing social evil.

In Chapter Six I explore the question of how the poor are involved in (or, more accurately, excluded from) the political process. Low standards of living have, of course, always influenced political development, in that successive leaderships have needed to take some account of the consumer for economic planning. But the political system, being highly centralised and unitary in character, scarcely allows the poor a voice; it also seems to admit them unwillingly to the centres of power. The resulting situation undoubtedly requires comment. I have supplemented our own ruminations on this theme by Appendix 1, containing unofficial documents in which the poor, or people closely connected with them, express uncensored views on poverty in the USSR.

The last chapter of the book touches upon two of the most thorny aspects of all. The first is social mobility into and out of the poverty state, one dimension of which is the much-commented notion of a 'poverty trap'. The second is the degree to which poverty exists in East Europe, and how far it may be compared with that in the USSR itself. A postscript reviews the present Soviet plans for the alleviation (if not eradication) of poverty, and the prospects for living standards in the immediate future. Mere enumeration of all these aspects suggests how much research will be required to analyse them in detail.

The reader will, I hope, forgive a number of references to my earlier work, especially on Soviet social structure. I have long held the view that the extremities of any society are more interesting than its midriff.

The 'average' man is by definition close to mediocrity, and evokes little intellectual excitement. Some years ago I endeavoured to define a Soviet 'elite', and having done so, wrote a book about it. The present study may to some extent be regarded as parallel in intent: in fact, some curious similarities between the Soviet elite and the Soviet poor will become apparent as the study unfolds.

The sources of information which I have used also require comment. Soviet statistical handbooks, unlike those put out by the US and many other governments, do not recognise poverty as a quantifiable phenomenon, and provide little data which is of direct relevance. However, works by individual scholars have dealt quite competently with the problem of 'minimum' family budgets, while sociological studies based on sample populations, and papers published by individual institutes, often throw a side-light on low income groups, without explicitly admitting as much. Handbooks for enterprise managers sometimes reveal exceedingly low wage rates. I have devoted some time and effort to locating and analysing works of this nature.

Yet given the difficulties of the topic, more information was needed. My work on elitism showed that a great deal could be learned from recent Soviet emigres. In 1982 I was fortunate in being able to launch a small survey of emigre families who had been relatively poor before they left the USSR, and some of the results of this work have been used to suggest answers where official sources fail. The questionnaire was in fact designed to elucidate facts about poverty life-styles that would otherwise be quite beyond the reach of investigation. A brief account of the undertaking is given in Appendix 2.

My own experience of poverty in the Soviet Union is limited, but not altogether lacking. As a foreigner resident in Moscow in the 1960s, I was fortunate (if that is the right word) in having acquaintances who were indeed poor, and who lived in near-slum conditions. Hopefully such observations as I was then able to make 'in the field' have ensured a fair degree of realism in my interpretation of more current material. For what I have written, including, no doubt, some oversight or error, I take full responsibility.

Writing this book has required substantial help from other quarters. I must thank the Trustees of the Leverhulme Foundation for granting me a Research Fellowship to begin work in the spring of 1982, when on sabbatical leave. The US National Council for Soviet and East European Research in Washington then provided substantial financial backing for the emigre survey, and for much of the travel which the research entailed. The University of Surrey provided a small research grant in the early stages, and excellent computer facilities later on. Dr Lawrence Eisenberg of the Frederic Burk Foundation of San Francisco State University ensured exemplary administrative backup for the earlier work done in the USA. Professors Abram Bergson, G. Grossman, Bernice Madison, H. Rigby, V. Treml and Mr K. Bush made many valuable suggestions for improvement; Professor Murray Feshbach's work on Soviet demographic trends again proved invaluable, while Dr Michael Ryman found some useful medical data for me. I wish also to thank Professors Adam Ulam and Marshall Goldman of the Russian Research Centre, Harvard, for the opportunity to devote the last three months of a Mellon Fellowship at the Centre to revision and completion of the manuscript. Finally, a special word of appreciation is due for the labours of Miss Rose Benedetto, Mrs Treacy Curlin, and Mrs Joan Prain, who typed endless drafts with great promptness and accuracy.

PART I

I

IS THERE POVERTY
IN THE SOVIET UNION?

———————— ⁓ ————————

The problem of poverty has over recent years remained a subject of debate throughout the world. The governments of richer countries express continuing concern about it, while the poorest countries, where dire need is common, are objects of intensive study. The fact that the population of the world is now wealthier than it has ever been, means that the plight of those who have fallen behind is more obvious. Governments in a position to help feel a greater compulsion to do so. Nevertheless, some types of poverty seem well-nigh intractable, and destined to burden mankind for decades, if not generations, to come.

A glance at some 'basic indicators' of poverty by the World Bank reveal the enormity of the gap between rich and poor.[1] Of the 125 countries listed, 38 of those categorised as 'low income' had a per capita Gross National Product of less than a dollar a day; all 18 'industrialised' and 'capital-surplus oil exporting' countries were, by contrast, all in the 9 to 40 dollar range. GNP is not a particularly good indicator of personal well-being, but it is very convenient for purposes of comparison. We may note at this point that the Soviet-type states of East Europe were in the 5 to 15 dollar range.

Although many people in the world are obviously poor, views on where the threshold of poverty lies vary greatly. In the poorest countries only a small minority of the population may be above it, but even the richest countries harbour a poor. Rich governments usually maintain units for monitoring poverty in their own societies, and run expensive systems of social security to help the needy. While poverty in the poorest countries may be 'absolute', and life-threatening, that found in more fortunate lands is best thought of as

3

relative deprivation against a respectable mean. We commonly find situations in which groups at the bottom of the income scale in one land are rich beyond the wildest dreams of average, or well-to-do citizens in another. By and large, defining poverty is easiest when the condition is acute.

Given the great variety of poverty situations, it is expedient to preface our study of the situation in the USSR by considering two extreme types, on the safe presumption that such poverty as exists there may be located somewhere between them. In the report just mentioned, an *absolute* poverty line was set at the 45th percentile of per capita income distribution in India, a country already fifteenth from the bottom of the listing (Bangladesh, Ethiopia, Nepal, Burma and Vietnam were the largest states below it). Four dominant characteristics were distinguished in poverty of this type. The first and pre-eminent was nutritional difficulty.[2] Generally, the poorer people are, the greater proportion of their income goes on food; those in absolute poverty may use up the equivalent of 80% or more for this purpose. There is an unhealthy reliance on starchy foods (mainly simple grains), and a deficiency of protein, vitamins and other nutrients. Malnutrition, the impairment of physical or social functions, and easy vulnerability to famine are commonplace. The second problem is that of health. Poor people in undeveloped countries often live in primitive conditions, and lack facilities for basic personal hygiene. Public health standards are low or non-existent, epidemics are common, age-specific death rates, particularly among infants, are high, and life-expectancy is limited.

Thirdly, there is commonly a problem of high fertility since socio-economic restraints on family size are few, and contraception is unavailable or unwanted. Rapid population growth need not necessarily be bad in certain circumstances, but once an optimum level has been surpassed, it may well generate poverty. There are more mouths to be fed, and more children requiring care and attention. Mothers have to leave productive work for appreciable periods, clothing and shelter become more difficult to provide.

The fourth major problem is education. It would seem that the worst aspects of poverty may be alleviated, at least in the long run, by equipping people with the skills they need to help themselves, beginning, of course, with reading. This opens their minds, not only to more effective methods of food production, but also to improved hygiene and birth control. Indeed, in the broadest sense, education may be regarded as *the* ultimate factor in poverty control. It must, however, intermesh with progress on other fronts. There is no point in teaching a child to read if there are no books or newspapers in his village, or technical appliances with which to use the knowledge gained.

The popular response to extreme poverty conditions varies. Feelings of apathy and hopelessness may alternate with fierce resentment. Most governments have come to regard it as shameful. Explanations are invariably sought in political theory (with exploitation as understood by Marx, common amongst them), but more subtle analysis may implicate traditional cultures, the abrasive policies of the world's economic giants, or inadequate local resources, etc. Philosophical justification may be sought in teachings on the ephemeral nature of wealth, and the over-riding importance of spirituality.

Poverty in the richer lands inevitably assumes quite different forms. Life-threatening deprivation is virtually unknown; the main problem is not so much an overall absence of the means of sustenance, as one of 'unfair' distribution. The definition of a poverty line, or threshold, becomes ever more complex. In countries where there is a relatively open press, it may also be a matter of considerable public debate.

The USA, with a per capita GNP of 9,590 dollars, offers an exemplar of 'industrialised' poverty. It became a matter of major concern in the early sixties, when the US Council of Economic Advisors adopted the general rule that families with annual incomes of less than 3,000 dollars should be considered to be 'in poverty'.[3] This figure alone illustrated the gap between American poverty and the varieties experienced in undeveloped countries. This definition was soon superseded by another, in which the core element was the cost of a food plan considered by the Department of Agriculture to be nutritionally adequate within national eating patterns. Non-food costs were estimated on the basis of a 1955 Food Consumption Survey at twice those of the food basket for families of three or more, so food was to absorb one-third of family income. A higher multiplier was used for one and two-member families. Since 1964, the Statistical Abstract of the United States has regularly carried basic tables on the number and characteristics of 'poor' families.[4] As for the relationship of poverty to average well-being, the 1964 threshold for a four-member family came out at 42% of median family income. By 1979 the figure had fallen to 32.8%, and by this measure 11.6% of the population was recognised as being in poverty. It is not surprising, given the approximate nature of these statistics, that considerable variations were proposed around them. By 1983 certain changes in categorisation, and adverse economic conditions, had raised the proportion of people so registered to 15.2%; but estimates of the contingent then ranged from 35.2 million to 23.7 million, depending on how the major forms of state assistance – food stamps, medicaid, and public housing – were assessed.[5]

Beyond the matter of costing, deficiencies in nutrition, clothing and housing remain, of course, central to the poverty situation in the USA, but are assessed with regard to the supplies and services normally available in the social context. The poor tend to be slum dwellers, and lack adequate medical provision, social hygiene and sanitation, which leads directly to poorer health patterns. Transport may be a problem for them in both urban and rural environments, especially if fares are not publicly subsidised. Thus it was found that the largest family expenditure amongst the American rural poor in 1973 was on transportation, which absorbed no less than 29% of income. The poor are less likely to observe local norms of school attendance, obtain training, or enjoy average job opportunities. Hence the common correlation between family poverty, low-paid, unprestigious jobs and unemployment. Work problems and deficient socialisation would seem to explain higher than average rates of involvement in crime. Immigrants from other lands, Negroes, Hispanics and native American Indians are prominent amongst them, or to put it in another way, certain ethnic groups have significantly higher poverty rates than the American whites. The poor tend to predominate in certain states, large cities and rural areas; but in terms of absolute numbers, urban poverty comes to predominate over rural poverty.

The fact that the poor are a minority, and eligible for well-known types of national or local assistance, means that they have come to be regarded as a group apart, with its own subculture, needs and responses. They endeavour to make their plight public, and gain some influence in national policies through the media or recognised political channels.

There would seem to be little doubt that the Soviet Union has its own poverty problem. Although it fits into the richer end of the spectrum (with a per capita GNP of 3,700 dollars per annum, or just over ten dollars a day in 1980) its large heterogeneous population and uneven pattern of economic growth would seem to make some degree of poverty well-nigh inescapable. One would expect Soviet poverty typically to resemble that of industrialised lands, but with its own national and societal peculiarities. Soviet reality in fact supplies much evidence to support this contention. We shall begin our consideration of it with a brief review of living standards, insofar as they can be perceived since the October 1917 Revolution. The story of poverty in twentieth-century Russia still awaits telling in a detailed and systematic manner.

LIVING STANDARDS FROM LENIN TO BREZHNEV

Before the onset of the First World War at least two-thirds of the population of Russia were peasants, living mostly in primitive conditions. The working class was poor, even by Western standards, and many of its members retained strong ties with the land. A contemporary, but very approximate estimate of the per capita national income in Russia in 1913 was 414 dollars, as against 1,548 in the UK and 2,063 in the USA.[6] Thus it may be said, without belittling economic progress of previous decades, that poverty was both common and severe. Only the most favoured sections of society escaped it.*

The war itself involved enormous losses of life, property and territory and greatly exacerbated economic difficulties. The Bolsheviks came to power with an ambitious programme of measures designed to ensure social justice and improve the lot of the poor, both in town and village. But the Red Terror, Civil War, crude redistributive policies and the famine of 1921 prostrated an already poor country. Industrial production fell by half, and agricultural output by at least a third. Hyperinflation rendered the Bolshevik guarantees of a minimum wage and social security (at least for state workers and employees) virtually meaningless. By the spring of 1921 the Bolshevik leadership was forced to the realisation that its initial economic policies had been disastrous. The efforts to banish 'capitalist exploitation' had all but destroyed the wealthier classes without benefiting

---

* The difficulties of generalising on income and consumption levels (not to mention the problems of international comparison) prevent firm conclusions, and much of the data we shall give here is indicative only. The principal information gaps, from the early twenties at least until the mid-fifties, include (1) the absence of reliable official statistics (2) the Soviet-specific patterns of expenditure (with high-cost clothes, low-cost housing, 'free' education, etc.) (3) the difference between legal, 'free' and black market prices (4) the absence of a proper measure of inflation (5) the absence of figures for the distribution of incomes and (6) the large, and partly impenetrable peasant economy.

more than a tiny proportion of the poor. The Tenth Party Congress, held in March 1921, brought the inauguration of the New Economic Policy, or NEP, which implied a more conciliatory attitude towards the 'middle' and 'rich' peasants (or kulaks), a modest restitution of private enterprise, and palpable relaxation of political pressures.

The twenties, by and large, were a period of restoration and growth. Economists who have delved into the relevant statistics maintain that by about 1927 both agricultural and industrial output had regained their pre-war levels. This implies that living standards had done the same; but from a Western standpoint the Soviet Union continued to be a very poor nation. The International Labour Office statistics on the purchasing power of wages in terms of food, which are perhaps the best available, showed that by this time the average Russian worker earned about one half of the UK, and a quarter of the USA rates respectively. These proportions probably exaggerated the well-being of the Soviet people as a whole, because wages in Moscow (on which they were based) were higher than in the provinces, and workers were better off than peasants.

Given all the unknowns, changes in the *distribution* of income are even more difficult to estimate. It is, however, clear that the dispossession of the 'exploiters' left no condition of equality. A new differentiation was early promoted in workers' wage scales, so as to reflect output, skill and the economic importance of any particular job. At the same time the vagaries of location, climate and effort ensured considerable differentiation among the peasants.

During their first decade of power the Bolsheviks changed the social composition of the poor, subtracting some elements and adding others. In the countryside, the richer peasants fled, taking their expertise with them, while some of the poorest benefited from association with the new regime. But Party influence was extremely limited and most peasants' daily lives were not, as yet, profoundly affected by the administrative and titular changes going on above. Official policies undoubtedly had more impact in the towns. Many workers were advanced to positions of administrative trust and responsibility, while the condition of others was alleviated. The ranks of the urban poor were, however, swelled by numerous families from the former 'exploiting' classes, families which had lost their earners in military action, war invalids, orphans and many others. There are still people alive in Russia who can tell lurid tales of those years. An old lady once related to us how she and her family, who had been mildly affluent before the Bolshevik take-over, were twice evicted from their home, and found themselves without shelter in the street.

The abandonment of NEP, accelerated industrialisation, and the enforced 'collectivisation' of agriculture which Stalin promoted after 1928 brought even more widespread social change. The years up to 1939 saw the working class grow (according to Soviet estimates) from around 12 to 33 million, mostly as a result of immigration from the villages. The white-collar workers, or 'employees', increased as a social group from 9 to 30 million. Over the same period the peasantry and the associated group of individual 'craftsmen' shrank from about 117 to 85 million, and was confined almost entirely to the new collective farms and cooperatives. Private enterprise (apart from peasant cultivation of private plots) was almost entirely suppressed. In December 1935 Stalin made his famous speech declaring that the exploiting classes had been finally vanquished, and that the era of 'socialism' had begun.

The 'Great Change', as it was called, had highly deleterious effects on living standards and inevitably intensified poverty. Industrialisation meant emphasis on heavy industry and neglect of consumer goods. The working conditions of the masses deteriorated. The rapid enlargement of the urban population created demands for housing which were simply not met. In the countryside, many peasants killed their livestock and/or destroyed their implements, rather than surrender them to collective use. The kulaks (often the most competent families in the village) were finally 'suppressed'. There was a sharp fall in agricultural production, and another famine which took years to overcome. Estimates of real wages show that (despite a possible late improvement) by the end of the decade those of the Soviet worker had fallen by between 20% and 50% against 1928.[7] Agricultural output is thought to have risen by about 15% over the same period, but the notorious system of 'obligatory deliveries' and state taxes deprived the peasant of benefit, so his income lagged significantly behind that of workers and employees. As for the international dimension, ILO figures suggest that by 1937 Soviet workers were earning only about a quarter as much as their British counterparts, and less than a seventh as much as Americans.

Renewed emphasis on income differentiation widened the gap between rich and poor. The social security benefits, though real enough, were meagre, and the post-revolutionary concept of a minimum wage was ignored. The ranks of the urban poor were swelled by migrants, mainly young men, from the countryside. The peasants in the villages found themselves working harder for a smaller return. The prison camp population, following the 'wrecker' trials of 1929 and the purges of the mid and late thirties, is thought to have risen to something between 3 and 7 million. Conditions in these establishments often amounted to slow death by overwork, starvation or exposure. A former inmate, for example, who spent twelve years in Siberia, told us that she and her workmates survived only by eating some of the more digestible food supplied for the animals in their care.

The Second World War, which the Russians entered only after the German attack of June 1941, dealt another devastating blow to living standards. Between 1941 and 1942 the invaders occupied territory up to a line stretching from Leningrad to the Northern Caucasus. The industry left in areas under German rule seems to have come to a virtual standstill, and there was a catastrophic drop in agricultural production. Official sources claim that 70,000 villages and hamlets, together with a large proportion of the urban housing stocks, were destroyed. The direct population losses alone are thought to have amounted to at least 20 million souls. To talk about 'living standards', let alone 'poverty', in such circumstances is almost meaningless. However, by 1948 recovery was well under way, and estimates of the real wage for that year vary between 45% and 60% of the 1928 figure. The next few years saw further improvement, and by 1954 comparable estimates ranged from 80% to 124%. Agriculture (which may serve as a rough measure of peasant income) may have regained its 1940 level by the beginning of the fifties. The ILO indices showed Soviet workers' purchasing power in 1951–2 to be 28% and 18% of that of the British and American workers respectively.

The components of the poverty life-style were no doubt much the same as had developed after the Revolution – frequent food shortages, scarce, low quality consumer goods, high prices, long queues, inadequate housing etc. But the social composition of the poor changed again. The urban poor became more numerous as urbanisation proceeded and the peasantry was syphoned off for non-agricultural labour. The losses of men in military operations, and the mass imprisonment of returnees, meant once again that many families were reduced to one-parent status, and many children orphaned. Invalids were an all too common sight. The movement of younger people to the towns meant that the village was left with a larger proportion of elderly people, and since most farms were both poverty-stricken, and responsible for keeping them, their plight was often dire. When Stalin died in March 1953, he left a society which still had a massive poverty problem.

The two decades which followed saw the steadiest rise ever recorded in the living standards of the Soviet population. Both of the leaders who sought Stalin's mantle – Khrushchev and Malenkov – seemed to have a keen awareness of the people's material needs. The supremacy of investment in heavy industry, could not, of course, be questioned; but Khrushchev, who soon won the power struggle, attached special importance to improving food supplies (which demanded a kinder policy towards the peasantry), increasing low wages, improving housing, and upgrading social security benefits. From the mid-fifties onwards the peasants obtained guaranteed advance payments for their labour in the collective fields, the abandonment of the 'residue' system (whereby they were paid only after the farm had met all other obligations), a reduction of state impositions on their income and, by 1965, a completely new system of state pensions. In 1956 a minimum wage of 270–350 roubles a month, depending on the branch of the economy, was introduced for workers and employees. This minimum seems to have been generally observed, and was raised to 60 new roubles (600 at the old rate) in 1968.[8] In 1956, too, workers and employees were granted minimum pensions of not less than 30 roubles, together with improvements in other rates. As a result of these new policies per capita consumption, according to careful American estimates, rose by something like 40% between 1955 and 1965, and reached approximately 30% of the US level.[9]

The increase in well-being achieved under Khrushchev had its disappointing features. Given the low starting point, it was hardly great enough; the needs of the consumer remained firmly subordinated to those of the state, and the improvement was somewhat erratic. In any case, it was soon slowed by a marked fall in the overall rate of economic growth.

Nevertheless, the proportion of people 'in poverty' fell significantly. A few estimates of wage and income distribution published in the late sixties reflected not only a general rise in well-being, but also a markedly more egalitarian distribution. As we suggested a number of years ago, by the middle of the decade, a third or more of the Soviet working class were then living below an acknowledged 'poverty

threshold'. The Khrushchev years saw poverty (in that sense) cease
to be the fate of an overwhelming majority to become that of a sizeable
minority.[10]

What social groups were most vulnerable? By and large, the new
wage and income policies underpinned the old socio-occupational
framework, and the people who had been at the bottom before
remained poor. Industrialisation had continued apace; the working
class, which numbered 105 million by the time of the 1959 Population
Census, increased to 139 million in 1970, while the peasant numbers
fell from 66 million to about 50 million. This presumably meant a
larger poverty contingent in the towns and a somewhat smaller one
in the villages. There were fewer pensionless elderly, particularly in
the countryside, fewer war invalids and fewer orphans, as time
wrought its change on the human frame. In terms of life-styles, poverty
retained its long-term 'deficit' characteristics, albeit in milder form.

The Brezhnev leadership, instituted in October 1964, showed a fair
degree of concern with the problem. The existing investment priorities
were mostly retained; but living standards continued to edge upwards,
and some of the Soviet figures are (at first sight) quite impressive. Thus
the average wage for workers and employees was said to have
increased from 97 roubles in 1965 to 169 roubles in 1980. Over the
same years the real income of the peasantry, including an allowance
for produce from the private plot, apparently rose from 51% to 89%
of that of workers and employees.[11] The state minimum wage, which
is also of direct relevance, rose from 60 roubles in 1968 to 70 roubles
by 1977. The social security coverage of the more needy groups in
society – pensioners and large or deprived families – also underwent
improvement. Official figures showed rises of 200% to 300% in retail
trade and the output of light industry.[12] Meanwhile the official price
indices for comestibles and basic consumer durables, rents for state-
owned accommodation, and payments for most public amenities, rose
very little.

Yet these figures, on the whole, produce too optimistic an impression
of the Brezhnev years. More detailed wage data showed that after 1967
two important categories of earners – the low-grade non-manuals and
specialists – experienced a distinct and ominous levelling-off in their
earnings (a phenomenon rarely revealed in Soviet statistics). Foreign
observers generally believe that in the late seventies and early eighties,
partly as a result of harvest failure, average living standards faltered
or even fell. A set of estimates prepared by Professor G. E. Schroeder

suggests that the annual per capita growth of consumption in fact dropped from an average of 2.9% between 1971 and 1975 to 2.1% in 1980. Food consumption was thought to have increased by 1.6% annually between 1971 and 1975; 1% between 1976 and 1980; but only 0.3% in 1980. Services, including health and education, grew by 3% annually between 1971 and 1975, but only by 2.6% in 1980.[13] A slowdown of this magnitude might be of little significance in conditions of adequacy or abundance, but the Soviet Union had achieved neither.

Moreover, the declared increases in trade and consumer goods production might be less impressive than would appear at first sight. They represented the response to a pent-up demand, and low levels of expectation; the quality of such goods is poor, implying a short life; and the figures conceal a bad 'mix'. Thus, although official statistics show adequate supplies of large items (like radios, washing machines, vacuum cleaners, etc.) no figures are available for hundreds of small items (cooking utensils, toiletries, stationery, hardware, etc.) known to be in deficit. A significant part of the output of light industry must go to satisfying the needs of the armed forces, estimated at around 5 million, anyway. Ironically, the improvements in the money incomes of peasants and agricultural workers must have increased the rural demand for consumer goods, causing greater shortages in the towns. A startling growth in the level of personal savings suggests an increasing discrepancy between money income and the availability of goods to spend it on.[14]

The struggle for higher living standards in the Soviet Union has therefore enjoyed varying degrees of success at different times. Economic performance compares unfavourably with that of many capitalist lands which have also known economic and social disaster. By the late 1970s, according to Professor Schroeders and Edwards, Soviet per capita consumption was still only 34.4% of the US level, or 52.2% and 59.1% of that of West Germany and the UK respectively. The fact that these gaps have widened somewhat subsequently does not augur well for the alleviation of poverty in the USSR.[15]

POVERTY AND FAMILY BUDGET STUDIES

By the time the Bolsheviks came to power, Russia had already acquired quite a respectable history of investigation into people's living standards. The first known studies, dating from the late eighteenth century, were designed to elucidate the social and economic benefits which the individual peasant might gain from the enlargement of landed estates. Not surprisingly, such work was descriptive rather than statistical in orientation. Budget studies in a more precise sense, involving the itemisation of incomes and expenditures of small numbers of families, were started in the 1870s, after the serfs had been emancipated and the local government offices had begun to collect statistics on a regular basis. The same decade saw the first serious investigations of working people's nutritional norms. By the 1890s sampling methods came into use, permitting a higher level of representativeness.[16]

Coherent analysis of workers' budgets was carried out in St Petersburg by the Menshevik economist S. N. Prokopovicz in 1908. This work was followed, in the course of a few years, by studies in Moscow, Kiev, Baku and other towns, while statistics provided by the official Labour Inspectors allowed some generalisation of the results. The Soviet economist, I. Ya. Matyukha, has in fact claimed that during the four decades preceding the Revolution some 4,500 workers' and employees' budgets, and over 11,000 peasant budgets, were compiled, making Russia unique in such a statistical endeavour.[17]

Such studies could not but reflect the acute deprivation characteristic of the land. Prokopovicz, for example, concluded that the average workers' wage, at 250 roubles, was only about a half of what was needed to keep a family. Most workers arrived from the village whilst in their 'teens, remained single, and led an unsettled existence. When their physical powers no longer sufficed for factory employment, they returned to the village and were replaced, not by their own children, but by a new generation of erstwhile peasants. The main exceptions to this pattern were workers who managed to acquire a skill, and earn higher wages.

After the Revolution the new leadership had good reason for maintaining the tradition of budget research. During their first chaotic years of Bolshevik power there was a need to monitor sharp changes in the living standards of the social groups most likely to support the regime. In the longer term, a planned society required the regular collection of social statistics. Lenin himself had delved deep into the economics of living standards under the tsars, with the gratifying aim of showing how bad they were. When the new leaders started to administer the economy, they found that such information was needed for such purposes as compiling 'state balances'; establishing a minimum or subsistence wage for the working class (as promised in the RSFSR 1918 Labour Code); assessing the rationing systems designed to counter famine; monitoring changes in the social configuration of the peasantry; and promoting the long-term aim of overall social control. Budget studies could also be used to supplement other processes of economic measurement.

The specific mention of such a wage in the Labour Code gave the investigation of family budgets an almost constitutional justification. In 1918 standard 'minimum budgets' were worked out by a number of town departments of the Commissariat of Labour and by the trade unions, primarily for industrial workers. The budgets varied greatly in content and itemisation, according to the ideas of individual compilers; but the main problems of compilation were practical, rather than conceptual. The cost of many items, particularly foodstuffs, varied greatly according to whether they were bought at state prices (by means of a ration card), or on what was then called the 'open market'. On the other hand, chronic shortages and the inexorable march of inflation soon made nonsense of most statistical data. The cost of a day's food in European Russia on the open market apparently rose from 21 roubles in January 1919, to 326,100 roubles in April 1922.[18]

In any case, such exercises could not but reveal a striking gap between any acceptable minimum and current earnings. Early in 1918, an unskilled worker in Petrograd was said to earn 280 roubles a month, whereas the cost of his food reached 601 roubles and 50 kopeks. Since the worker had to eat, the gap was usually bridged by help from relatives in the village, the barter of personal possessions or theft of state property. The supply situation in the provinces was probably worse than in the capital. As the economic crisis deepened, economists found it expedient to replace the assessment of a subsistence minimum with that of a selection of food items only. Data available for the spring of 1922, when the worst was over, showed that the average wage in most test areas still varied between 70% and 130% of the cost of such a selection. Only in the mid-twenties did rising living standards enable budget calculations to be expanded again to include non-comestibles, and some better quality food.

The first attempts to collect and analyse family budgets after the Revolution were evidently made in Petrograd in May 1918 and Moscow in October of the same year. The conduct of the surveys was, however, greatly impeded by social conditions, particularly hyperinflation and the public's unwillingness to participate. The Red Terror stalked the land, and form-filling, as everyone knew, could have unwanted consequences. The return of questionnaires was extremely low, and never appears to have led to any worthwhile results. At any rate, despite all the difficulties, some fifteen studies of workers' and employees' budgets were said to have been made in large towns of European Russia, the Ukraine and Central Asia; and by 1922 no less than 12,000 budgets had been collected.[19]

The All-Russian Statistical Conference of November 1922 concerned itself specifically with family budget studies, and made certain over-riding stipulations about their development. Such studies were to 'elucidate the average standard of living of the worker, trace deviations observable in different layers of the social classes, and different areas, and map changes observable over previous years'. From 1923, urban budget studies were turned into an annual exercise, covering one or two months in the autumn, while continuous monitoring was organised in some localities. The families chosen for the purpose were visited by an authorised 'statistician', who checked their income and expenses, and compiled a list of their belongings. After 1931 the investigation of industrial workers' budgets was extended throughout the USSR, and by 1940, 12,000 workers' families, and 8,000 budgets of engineers, technical and white-collar families were said to be covered.[20]

The peasants continued to be a problem in their own right. The need to distinguish a 'village poor' which would ally itself to the Bolshevik cause had been imperative from the beginning, and an effort was made to include peasant households in the 1919 economic survey. The fact that only 600 households responded was another measure of the extent to which the operation failed. Regular budget surveys were, however, started amongst the peasants in 1923, with a coverage of 9,000 households, and by the end of the decade over 20,000 were being monitored annually. As far as we have been able to ascertain, very few of the results were published in tabular form, though they did generate some authorised studies.

The peasant budgets could not but have shown massive poverty; farm-size being a fair indicator. By 1925, for example, no less than 51% of the peasant family holdings comprised less than five acres, while holdings of as little as ten acres or more (only 11% or so of the statistical total), were categorised as 'well-off' or 'rich'.[21] The slow improvement in peasant well-being revealed as the years went by was balanced by increasing economic differentiation between households. The larger and more efficient one pulled ahead, starting a trend which was to serve as a dreadful justification for the dispossession of millions during the collectivisation drive. When this came (in 1929) it caused widespread disruption of peasant society and a cessation of budget surveys. However, in the longer term, the relatively close administration of the farms simplified such work, and the number of family budgets monitored grew from a reported 5,740 in 1932 to over 21,000 in 1940.[22] The extent to which Soviet statisticians concerned themselves with setting subsistence minima for the peasant is difficult to elucidate since the central government had effectively repudiated responsibility for peasant well-being; they could have been under no great pressure to do so.

The Second World War brought all survey work to a halt except, apparently, in some of the eastern regions of the country. It was started again on a regular basis in 1951. The families first selected for investigation included those of workers and employees, industrial specialists, teachers, and medical personnel. Within a few years railway personnel and collective farmers were added. The importance attached to the information obtained may be gauged from the growth of the sample. In 1961 the number of budgets stood at 24,000, of which about half were drawn from peasant families. By the early seventies a figure of 62,000 was achieved, and this seems to have proved adequate for longer term purposes, since it is still, at the time of writing, quoted in the USSR statistical year books.[23]

Our account of budget investigations contains reference to publishing restrictions, a matter which requires further comment. Lenin had, of course, introduced state censorship only a day or two after the Bolshevik coup, and this was quickly elaborated to form a detailed code which included economic information. Even so, the subsistence minima, in the form of 'budgetary indices', or budgetary selection costs, were for some years made known by regular notices in the press, and there was a fair amount of published scholarly analysis.

This practice was, alas, to be suspended as Soviet life became increasingly Stalinised towards the end of the decade. The Five Year Plan entailed restrictions on the publication of the basic economic indices, and by the mid-thirties even major economic data were unavailable. In 1930 the Central Statistical Administration lost its identity, insofar as it was merged with the USSR State Planning commission, and a number of leading research institutes were closed.

Analyses of family budgets ceased to appear both for the country as a whole, and for the localities, after 1928. It is not therefore surprising that the standard Soviet works have hardly anything to say about the massive body of data collected by this means since. The material currently available amounts only to a few guarded treatments by Soviet scholars, and the two or three aggregated tables published annually in statistical year books since 1973.[24]

On the other hand, a little information on the actual sampling procedures has been provided in a number of sources, including the International Labour Office, and a summary of them may form a fitting conclusion to our review.[25] The selection of families is said to begin with the designation of survey areas, and, within them, 'typical' enterprises. The personnel of these enterprises are then grouped according to their skill and wage ratings, and individual representatives of each group chosen on a mechanical basis. A comparable practice is followed for collective farms. The use of the place of employment – rather than of residence – for information gathering accords with other Soviet practice and ensures a fuller response. Respondents' families are required to keep records of their domestic income and expenditures, both in money and in kind. To judge from the accounts available, particular attention is paid to food purchases; some check on the accuracy of nutritional entries is possible through wage and canteen documentation.

The completion of the individual questionnaires is monitored by 'statisticians', each of whom has responsibility for between twenty and thirty families. All are visited twice a month and their entries checked against known prices of goods and services. The statistician deals with inconsistencies in individual questionnaires, while more general problems are the responsibility of local inspectorates. However, the anonymity of returns is supposed to be absolutely assured. According to the account published by the ILO, this information is used 'to carry out calculations on a variety of subjects, such as the volume of consumption, production for (personal) use, and the various balance sheets of the national economy'. It was also necessary 'for planning, state administration, and scientific research work'. We have found no overt reference to the use of budget studies for monitoring the needs of the poor.

THE 'KHRUSHCHEV' MINIMUM BUDGETS

The Khrushchev leadership, fettered as it was with the taboos of the Stalin years, deserves credit at least for reactivating the analysis of family budgets, and permitting calculation of new subsistence minima. The word 'poor' was still banned for this purpose but 'underprovisioned', (*maloobespechenny*), served instead.

In the mid-fifties a number of research institutes, including the Moscow Research Institute of Labour, the Institute of Food Studies of the Academy of Medical Sciences, and the Housing Institute of the Academy of Construction and Architecture, were instructed to assess and cost the basic consumption requirements of a contemporary urban family. This involved both re-examination of studies done in the twenties, and new research. By 1958, as part of the framework of the 1959–65 Seven Year Plan, several variants had been prepared. Some improved versions, together with an argued exposition of the calculations behind them, were finally published in a small book by the Soviet scholars, G. S. Sarkisyan and N. P. Kuznetsova in 1967.[26] This exposition attracted considerable attention amongst analysts at home and abroad; and it has not, as far as we are aware, been substantially superseded, despite the passage of so many years. Although not above criticism, the budgets as published can still be used as an acceptable yardstick for assessing the poverty threshold in Soviet towns.

The first variant covered the minimum monthly needs of an urban family comprising a husband, a wife, a 13-year-old boy and an 8-year-old girl in the mid-sixties. It was costed, in terms of official parental earnings, with due allowance for state subsidies and services, at 51 roubles and 40 kopecks per head. We discussed this budget in another context many years ago; it is reproduced, together with 'prospective' and 'rational' variants, in Table 1.1.

As may be seen, the new minimum budget was strongly characteristic of an advanced industrial society and made fair allowance for the accoutrements of urban living. At the same time it reflected many specific constraints of Soviet reality. Food purchases took up 56% of outgoings (indicating a high level of need), but they would have fallen proportionately if certain other budgetary items had been costed at capitalist rates. Housing and communal services, on the other hand, came out at only 5.4%, partly because they were state-subsidised, and partly because provision was low. The tiny sums allowed for furniture and household goods presumably covered wear and tear, but not

Table 1.1. *The Khrushchev minimum family budgets*

	'Current minimum'		'Prospective minimum'		'Rational'	
	roubles	(%)	roubles	(%)	roubles	(%)
Food, including bought meals	28.8	55.9	34.0	51	52.5	34.3
Clothing, footware	10.8	20.9	13.4	20.1	33.3	21.7
Furniture, household goods	1.2	2.6	2.5	3.8	7.0	4.6
Toiletries of all kinds, medicines	0.7	2.2	1.2	1.7	4.3	2.8
Cultural goods and sports ware	1.1	1.3	1.2	1.8	5.6	3.6
Tobacco	1.4	2.7	0.4	0.6	0.9	0.6
Alcoholic drinks			2.2	3.4	5.1	3.3
Expenditures on non-food items and savings			0.2	0.3	7.0	4.5
Sub totals	44	85.7	55.1	82.7	115.6	75.4
Housing and communal services	2.8	5.4	3.4	5.1	6.8	4.5
Holidays, various services	0.7	1.4	3.3	4.9	8.7	5.7
Cinema, theatre, other cultural needs	0.9	1.7	1.4	2.1	5.2	3.4
Hairdressing, baths, laundry	1.2	2.3				
Transport, post, telegraph	1.2	2.3	2.5	3.7	12.0	7.7
Membership fees,	0.6	1.2	0.7	1.0	5.0	3.3
Other expenses			0.3	0.5		
Sub totals	7.4	14.3	11.5	17.3	37.7	24.6
Totals	51.4	100.0	66.6	100.0	153.3	100.0

Source: Sarkisyan and Kuznetsova, pp. 66, 125, 166.

capital costs. In any case, they betokened fairly spartan accommodation. No outgoings were entered for medical and educational needs, as these were provided 'free' by the state; neither was there any entry for personal savings. The budget contained unrealistically low figures for alcohol and tobacco consumption (2.7%), while public spectacles and holiday services were presumed to be almost free (which they were not). The inclusion of a nominal sum for 'membership fees' reflected the exigencies of life in a collectivist society. The budget, as proposed, implied a meagre level of provision within the framework of Soviet reality. Its main conceptual inadequacies lay in ignoring any illegal payments made to obtain deficit goods; the higher prices charged in collective farm markets; and also in understating important culturally-determined expenditures, particularly on alcohol.

The costing of this budget at 51.4 roubles, nevertheless raised an embarrassing problem when compared with the income levels of the day. In 1965, the *average* wage, net of standard income tax, and union dues, was only 87.8 roubles, or 175.7 roubles for two earners.[27] Yet the statistical family of two working adults and two children required an income of 205.6 roubles (i.e., 4×51.4) to reach the stipulated subsistence level. No data were provided for single persons or families of different sizes, but Sarkisyan and Kuznetsova's figures clearly implied that even an *average* urban family would still be way below this level, despite the improvements in living standards over the preceding decade. We have shown elsewhere that perhaps a third of all urban workers were at that time living below the poverty threshold, so defined. The proportion of disadvantaged among service and low grade white-collar personnel, not to mention the peasantry, was certainly larger.[28]

The 'prospective' or longer-term minimum budget, which Sarkisyan and Kuznetsova also discussed in detail, is no less revealing. True, the authors carefully avoided saying when it could be implemented; Khrushchev, but a few years previously, had cause to regret a precise dating for the advent of communism. Their argument indicated, however, that they had set their sights on the seventies, and this budget is still the best measure available for the end of the decade. The prospective budget was supposed to reflect the improved opportunities which 'expanding production would bring for broadening the circle of minimal essential needs, whose satisfaction requires a higher family income'. This curious formulation suggested that the improved supply of goods and services would both prompt and satisfy new expectations among the less fortunate citizenry.

In terms of content, the prospective budget, requiring a per capita income of 66.6 roubles, was but a modest advance on the current one. As may be seen from the third and fourth columns of Table 1, the diet became a little more costly, but fell to 51% of total expenditure. Outgoings on clothes and housing likewise increased somewhat in absolute terms, but diminished percentage-wise. This still left a strong 'poverty' configuration. No separate provision was made for hair-dressing, public baths and laundry (the reasons being unexplained), but there was a small entry for 'expenditures on other goods, and savings'. Prices were presumed to be stable. Curiously, the biggest increases, proportionally, were for holidays, transport and communications, tobacco and alcohol. Perhaps the consumption of these items was thought to be unduly restricted in the first variant so that some increase could be permitted without negative consequences. In terms of relevance to the average wage, the prospective budget required two net earnings of 133.2 roubles, which about equalled the gross wage reached by 1976; we shall have more to say about this in the next section.

The 'rational' family budget raised its own thorny problems. It was costed at no less than 153.3 roubles per capita, just three times the first minimum budget. Unfortunately, the long-term trend in wage rates would suggest that the achievement of this goal was a very long way off. Between 1960 and 1970 the absolute growth was about 41 roubles, and between 1970 and 1980 – about 47 roubles, bringing the average wage up to 168.9 roubles in the latter year. Should anything like this pace be maintained (a questionable proposition in itself) rates sufficient to cover the rational budget would hardly be reached in less than three decades. If an example of objective Soviet scholarship is to be sought in this sphere, we need look no further.

A second problem concerned the concept of egalitarianism. The recognition of rational *norms* in conditions of plenty implied considerable social homogeneity. How far, in such circumstances, were individuals to be allowed 'irrational' divergencies, freed from the exigencies of supply? The compilers circumvented this dilemma by claiming that the rational budget would become viable *before* the advent of true communism, which would ultimately find its own ways of limiting insidious economic differentiation.[29]

The rational budget is also of interest insofar as it reflects an ideal consumption pattern for Soviet man. Against a threefold increase in total expenditure, his diet is to be greatly improved, and to cost almost twice as much as in the first minimum budget; but it is to absorb considerably less of all expenditures. Outgoings on clothes are to be increased by a factor of three, those on furniture by a factor of five, holidays – twelve, public spectacles and culture – six, transport and communication – ten, and membership fees – nine. The amount spent on tobacco and alcohol is to be more than doubled, but savings and 'other expenditures' are to rise to 7 roubles per capita. The improvements in economic well-being are, it would seem, intended to promote not only more developed leisure pursuits, and a broadening of cultural horizons, but also greater personal comfort of a suspiciously bourgeois character.

THE EXTENT OF POVERTY IN THE LATE SEVENTIES

Our consideration of Soviet living standards so far leaves no doubt that in the late seventies they were, by envied capitalist standards, still exceedingly low. The poverty threshold of 66.6 roubles per capita, as stipulated in the 'prospective' budget, may be taken as a yardstick and set against the little data available on income distribution so as to arrive at some assessment of the extent of poverty in a Soviet context. Given the scarcity of information, anything more than a general assessment is out of the question.

Let us begin with the evidence of a number of sociological surveys which, though bearing on other matters, have provided income distributions for the respondents. The samples are often quite large, and designed to be representative for divers stated purposes. We would like to emphasise that *all* the income distributions which we have so far located in survey returns contained poor people; those we have chosen by way of illustration here were selected solely for their detail and apparent reliability. Let us comment upon each of them in turn, beginning with the urban studies.

The first (case 1 in Table 1.2) is taken from an investigation of consumption patterns among families in different income brackets by the economists S. A. Aivazyan and N. M. Rimashevskaya in 1978.* This was evidently part of the continuing Central Statistical Administration study of 62,000 family budgets. The authors did not name the two towns to which their figures related, or even provide dates, so we can only assume censorial intervention. Data covering 346 families in one of the towns, however, can be recalculated to show a 'poverty contingent' (respondents with a per capita income of less than 60 roubles a month) of about 23%. A study of marital stability in Moscow in the years 1977 and 1979, based on samples of 100 and 388 families, showed that 15% and 12% of them were below the same threshold (cases 2 and 3). There was no indication that these samples had been over-weighted with poor people so to demonstrate a poverty–instability correlation.

A set of income distributions for families of different sizes in Estonia, which has one of the highest living standards of all Soviet republics, showed no less than 18% of all 'full families with children' to have per capita incomes of under 60 roubles (case 4). The range here was

* The sources of the studies listed here may be traced from Table 1.2 and the bibliography.

Table 1.2. *Incidence of low-income families in various sociological surveys*
(Selected cases)

Case number	Location	Year	Total number of respondents	Proportion in lowest income bracket (%)	Lowest per Capita income bracket [a]
1	(Not stated)	1978	346 families	23.0[b]	0–60
2	Moscow	1977	100 families	15.0	0–60
3	Moscow	1979	388 families	12.0	0–60
4	Estonia	1978	600 families	18.0	0–60
5	Odessa	1976	(not stated)	16.2–22.6	0–50
6	Tuva	1977	1,564 respondents	56.9	0–70
7	Novosibirsk	1975	578 families	35.0	0–50

[a] Roubles per month.
[b] Our calculation.
Sources: 1, Aivazyan and Rimashevskaya, pp. 120ff; 2, *Sotsiologicheskie issledovaniya*, No. 3, 1981, p. 107; 3, *Ibid*; 4, Kelam, p. 186; 5, *Sotsiologicheskie issledovaniya* No. 3, 1978, p. 191; 6, Boiko, p. 179; 7, Ryvkina, p. 291.

from 5% for married couples without children to 28% for incomplete (i.e., one-parent) families. A labour survey conducted in four districts of Odessa in 1976 (case 5) revealed that between 16.2% and 22.6% of the inhabitants had per capita family incomes of 50 roubles or under; Odessa is not, of course, considered to be a particularly poor town.

A detailed socio-economic survey covering 1,564 persons living in the Tuva Autonomous Republic (on the Mongolian border) invites particular attention. All respondents were Tuvans, a Turkic people akin to the Uigurs, and the study was designed to provide a social assessment of townspeople of this nationality. The results (case 6) showed that 56.9% had per capita incomes of 70 roubles or less (in fact, 18.6% of them received under 40 roubles). Per capita family income was also given, rather unusually, by branch of employment, and we reproduce this data separately in Table 1.3. As may be seen, the poorest people were employed in agriculture, forestry, trade, catering, transport, communications, housing and public amenities, – a pattern, as we shall see below, which was fairly common throughout the Soviet economy. It is noteworthy that the average wage of urban Tuvans was reported to be around 131 roubles, against a current figure

Table 1.3. *Per capita monthly income in the Tuva ASSR* (% *distribution*)

Branch	Income (roubles)		
	0–40	41–70	71 and over
Industry	14.9	38.8	46.4
Construction	24.1	38.0	37.8
Agriculture and forestry	42.3	40.2	17.5
Transport, communications, trade and catering	28.1	34.7	37.3
Housing and public amenities	31.2	45.5	23.3
Health services	12.7	36.7	50.6
Education and culture	10.0	41.2	48.8
Administration	10.9	39.1	50.0
Other	4.0	12.0	84.0
Total (100%)	18.6	38.3	43.1

Source: Boiko, p. 179, adapted. The income groups have been simplified; the figures for 'Transport, communications' and 'Trade, catering' branches, which had nearly identical distributions, have been amalgamated and averaged. The '71 and over' column includes a small proportion of undisclosed incomes.

Workers in 'agriculture and forestry' were presumably town-based, and travelled out daily; in 1980 the largest town, Kyzyl, had only 70,000 inhabitants.

of 155 roubles for the USSR as a whole. But the situation which obtained in that distant corner of the globe must have been typical of many small towns throughout the country.

An indication of poverty in the Soviet village may be obtained from a series of eminently respectable investigations of life styles in the Novosibirsk oblast in the early and mid-seventies.[30] The last of these, covering the families of 578 workers, white-collar employees and peasants (case 7), provided a figure of 35 % for persons receiving 50 roubles or less, reflecting the traditionally lower standards in the countryside. The results of these studies were thought to be broadly representative of Western Siberia and the Soviet Far East – indeed, one author claimed that the Novosibirsk village was comparable, in terms of income, with villages throughout the RSFSR.

Manipulation of economic (as opposed to sociological) data gives less impressionist results, but is also fraught with problems. The 66.6 rouble threshold may, for instance, be modified for officially-admitted inflation and income tax, and set against the average wage for 1979. Inflation, as reflected in Soviet price indices, would have raised the family poverty threshold by a little over 4%, to 278 roubles for a family of four, which in turn required a net income of 139 roubles on the part of each of two earners. (Some economists would certainly claim that more allowance should be made for inflation, but we would argue that the commodities most needed by poor families were least affected, and we would anyway prefer a cautious estimate.) In 1979 the average wage, as registered in official statistical handbooks, reached 163.3 roubles, or approximately 145.3 roubles net of income tax at about 10% and union dues of 1.6 roubles. Two working parents would at this rate have taken home some 291 roubles, so the 'safety margin' between two average wages and two 'poverty wages' (the 278 roubles needed to be earned for our four-member family to reach the poverty threshold) was only 13 roubles, or 3.25 roubles per head. To put it another way, the poverty wage for a statistical family of this type was still about 95% of the net average wage.

A comparison with the US figures is not without interest. The US poverty 'cut-off' level for a non-farm family of four in 1979 was, as we have noted, only 32.8% of the median income, and indicated that 11.6% of the population was in poverty. There is, furthermore, little doubt that the US threshold, so defined, was in real terms a third or more higher than the Soviet one. It was thus more inclusive, and if applied to the USSR would have covered a majority of the Soviet labour force.[31]

The same Soviet figures provide another indication of the extent of poverty if set against a putative wage distribution. In most economies, of course, wages tend to be distributed unequally. When drawn on a graph they form an asymmetric curve, the right hand tail of which, stretching far along the horizontal axis, shows the distribution of higher earners. If the poverty wage is marked off as a point on the horizontal axis, the area under the curve to the left of that point may be taken to represent the proportion of all earnings less than that wage.

The problem of analysis with the USSR lies, of course, in the shape of the curve. No recent national curves are available and there is no obvious substitute. But various curves may be tried, depending on the proclivities of the analyst, so as to provide various possible solutions. The assessment of income (as distinct from earnings) raises further problems. The only Soviet curves to come to our notice which allowed the construction of rudimentary, but apparently genuine wage distributions for all workers and employees were published by the economist, M. Loznevaya, in 1966.[32] These have certainly been somewhat remoulded since, yet still form, in our opinion, the most tolerable starting point for a hypothesis. The three hard, or relatively hard, figures we have at our disposal are the average gross wage (163.3 roubles in 1979); the current official minimum of 70 roubles, which may be augmented by, say, 10% to allow for creep and bonuses; and the net poverty wage of 139 roubles, as estimated above, which equalled 154 roubles gross. If these figures are set against gross earnings, as distributed under one of Loznevaya's curves, and the horizontal axis tentatively recalibrated to accommodate the declared growth wage, we find that about 58% of earners got less than the poverty wage.

This, however, is only part of the hypothesis. The returns from our emigre survey suggest that in the lower income groups, on average, some 12% of net earnings came from unofficial sources (legal and illegal).* If we recalculate the gross wage which the earners in a four-member family needed so as to surpass the poverty threshold, *presuming that such secondary earnings existed*, we arrive at a lower figure of 135 roubles.[33] This amount, measured under the same curve, excludes a smaller area from under the left-hand side, and reduces the poverty contingent to about 41%. The difference between the two percentage figures reveals the extent to which sturdy private endeavour reduces poverty, and alleviates the problem for the state authorities.

Certain other distribution data suggest that this figure is about right. The rudimentary wage curve which may be derived from the Tuva sample we have just mentioned gives 64% and 53% receiving less than the poverty wage (depending on whether allowance is made for unofficial earnings at the rate proposed). But the standard of living there was (to judge from the local average wage) some 10% below the national average of the USSR for that year. An ungradated curve available for rural wage-earners in the Novosibirsk oblast in 1977 gave corresponding figures of 63% and 34%, suggesting that there were fewer people at the bottom of the distribution.

So much for the evidence. There are, in fact, good reasons for regarding our hypothetical figures as too conservative. The Soviet figure for inflation, as we have noted, is probably too low, even at the bottom of the market, while the level of secondary earnings, based on

---

* In the absence of authoritative Soviet sources, we regard this survey as an acceptable indicator of the life styles, attitudes and motives of a sizable section of the Soviet poor. Reference will be made to it on several occasions in the ensuing pages. See Appendix 2 for a brief account of methodology and content.

a Jewish emigre sample, may be overstated. Total peasant earnings were said to be 11% lower than those of state employees, while agricultural workers, comprising 10.4% of the non-peasant labour force, were certainly among the lowest paid. Although life is different in the village, this strongly implies that the proportion of people in poverty in rural areas was higher than in the towns.

A startling, but authoritative pronouncement that Soviet monthly salary data, as published, are inflated, since they include a sum for annual 'holiday pay', has been made by the Soviet economist V. Perevedentsev. Writing in the journal *Zhurnalist* in August 1974 he declared explicitly that the official figure of 135 roubles given for 1973 (part of the main, on-going series for the USSR) meant a pre-tax cash payment of only 126 roubles, as nine roubles were held back to cover leave. Obviously, any allowance for this practice, if built into our figures, would somewhat increase our estimates of the extent of poverty. Although we could not, in the circumstances, bear the onus of re-interpreting all the Soviet wage figures used, the implications of this point are considerable. In any case, if asked to suggest some general magnitudes, we would hypothesise 'poverty contingents' of up to two-fifths of all workers and employees' familes, and rather more of the population at large. The history of poverty in Soviet society makes these proportions seem reasonable

One further point needs to be made in conclusion. Evidence of low income in the seventies, though ample, should not be considered without regard to the constraints of Soviet reality. Widespread shortages of food and consumer goods mean that many essentials cannot be purchased at all, or only at inflated prices, and this must push the real, as distinct from theoretical, poverty thresholds firmly upwards. Perusal of official data, such as we have attempted here, is essential if we are to arrive at a fair estimate; but to concentrate solely on the arithmetic of official releases can lead to unrealistic conclusions.* The analysis to which we now proceed endeavours to embrace all of the more important elements in the situation.

---

* Examples of such conclusions are to be found in McAuley: *Economic Welfare in the Soviet Union* (1979). The author examined much of the older official data, but failed to understand numerous aspects of Soviet economic reality.

2

WHO ARE THE
SOVIET POOR?

———————— ·◇· ————————

Poverty in any land can only be considered with reference to the people afflicted by it. We shall now review the social and occupational groups whose per capita income is low enough to make poverty, as defined in Chapter One, highly likely for them. The social groups comprise families whose income is inadequate to cover dependent members, certain categories of pensioners and self-supporting indi-viduals. The occupational groups, on the other hand, contain toilers whose jobs would not ordinarily pay enough to lift a family out of the poverty state. This means, in effect, that we need to review most common occupations in the lower reaches of the wage structure.

We shall consider as 'low-paid' only persons who are mature, and have achieved at least something like an average qualification in their chosen trade. Virtually all young workers and employees, not to mention apprentices and learners, are poor when they start: but they may expect to be well-paid in later life, so we shall, on the whole, omit them from our generalisations.

Since censorship restrictions prevent the publication of wage and income distributions, either by branch of the economy, or throughout the country as a whole, we must limit ourselves, in most cases, to illustrating published wage rates, or (when available) pensions and other per capita payments. It is worthy of note that the failure of the authorities to publish more than a smattering of data from the 1979 population census greatly complicates estimation of the size of the groups of people involved. We shall begin with a brief outline of how wages are fixed in the Soviet economy.

THE STATE WAGE SYSTEM

Since the Soviet state prohibits private hire of labour for productive purposes, all employed persons, except those who sell personal skills or services, are deemed to work for the state or authorised cooperatives. The trade unions are politically impotent, and have little real say in the organisation of labour. The central authorities therefore exercise legal, if imperfect, control over all employed persons' rates of pay.

The workers (who may be defined as persons directly involved in production, or in closely associated processes) are the largest occupational group. In 1890 they numbered some 79 million souls, and were engaged in some 6,000 officially defined jobs. Workers must know at least one trade (*professia* in Soviet parlance) which enables them to do one or more jobs; individual skills are supposed to improve as time goes by, allowing promotion through qualification scales, each step of which has its corresponding 'wage tariff'. Payment may be by piece-work or on an hourly basis.

In recent years the number of steps, or *razryady*, has in most scales been reduced to six, though there are eight in non-ferrous metallurgy and machine building. The more menial jobs do not give access to the higher and better-paid *razryady*: drivers, for example, have a three-class scheme.

The wage system has long suffered from significant distortions. Any particular job may be difficult to define, and different rates of pay may be set for one and the same thing at adjacent enterprises. There is said to be a tendency for managers to employ workers somewhat below their skill level, partly because the number of highly skilled personnel may be greater than the number of posts available, and partly because this practice reduces labour costs. Basic rates are usually supplemented by incentive bonuses, adjusted to attract workers into otherwise unpopular jobs, or encourage effort. The assessment of bonus payments is a constant problem for labour economists: overpayment of them in the late 1970s was said to have provoked an upward revision of work norms. Authoritative comment on the level of bonuses is somewhat contradictory, but in industry they seem to have varied between 15% and 40% of the basic wage. A figure of 19% has been quoted for state agriculture.[1] Generally, there is little doubt that bonus schemes are relatively less beneficial to low-paid employees, who may get a lower percentage on their basic rates, and therefore fewer extra roubles in their pay packets.

The differential between the lowest and the highest steps in the basic wage scales is of some relevance to the study of poverty, partly because changes in it may reflect official policy on egalitarianism, and partly because it is one of the few things which can be ascertained with some degree of certainty. The gap certainly narrowed under Khrushchev, but broadened again during the later Brezhnev years. By the mid-seventies differentials were running at 1:1.86 in the extractive industries and forestry; 1:1.71 in heavy industry and textiles; and 1:1.58 in the sewing and food-processing industries and mechanised sectors of agriculture.[2] Such a range may seem modest, and favour the lower-paid, but as we have already mentioned, there is nothing sacrosanct about it.

Soviet 'employees', as distinct from workers, are paid by salary rather than wage. Employees include all non-worker and non-peasant occupations, from menial service staff through office workers to middle-grade technicians and high-grade specialists. The low-grade jobs usually have only two (closely related) rates of pay, one junior and one senior. The salaries, unless paid by productive enterprises, are not subject to bonus supplementation, but service personnel in such enterprises may be transferred to 'wage-related' scales, like workers. The salaries of high-grade specialists, on the other hand, are much more differentiated, varying not only by seniority, but also by the size of the enterprise or organisation. Some ministries have as many as six categories for managerial staff, and offer bonuses as well. Intermediate, middle-grade posts usually have only two or three-step scales. The worst-paid workers and employees are most likely to be found, in the USSR as elsewhere (a) in the traditionally neglected industries and branches of the economy (b) in manual or (c) unskilled or low-skilled jobs, and (d) in small towns and rural, rather than urban localities.

Remuneration for peasants is considered to be so distinct that it is dealt with not in the state labour code, like other wage systems, but in the collective farm charter itself. For many years the peasant suffered from the iniquitous 'residue' system, under which he was paid for his work in the collectivised fields, in money or in kind, only *after* harvesting, and *after* the farm had met all other financial commitments. Most peasants were heavily dependent on the produce from their small private plots to stay alive. Since the mid-fifties the system of payment has been gradually brought closer to that of the industrial (and particularly state farm) pattern. Collective farms may now pay their manuals a monthly wage with a six-step scale, supplemented by a

Table 2.1. *Low-paid branches of the economy, 1981*

	Total number employed (millions)	Average pay, workers (roubles, monthy)	Average pay, employees (roubles, monthly)
All industry	30.7	190.2	148.2
Food processing	[2.7][a]	167.0	137.4
Light industry	[4.8][a]	155.2	133.0
State agriculture	10.3	153	123
Trade and catering	4.7	140.7[b]	
Education	9.3	136.7	
Health and Social services	6.2	128.5	
Culture	1.3	112.8	

[a] Bracketed data are estimates.
[b] Including supply services.
Sources: *Narodnoe khozyaistvo SSSR 1922–82*, pp. 399, 405, 475. *Vestnik statistiki*, No. 8, 1982, p. 79. L. S. Sbytova, p. 59.

production bonus, while all the farm service and white-collar personnel receive salaries, albeit at lower rates than are paid for comparable jobs in the state sector.

LOW-PAID BRANCHES OF THE ECONOMY

The Soviet economy embraces at least fifty-seven separate industries, but few labour statistics are available for them. More general figures on earnings by branch of the economy, however, come out every year, and these show an expected and very stable, gradation among them. The best rates are paid in the extractive, energy-producing and heavy industries. As may be seen from Table 2.1, in 1981 averages below this were paid in the ten branches of light industry, (i.e., textiles, footwear and garment production) and the nine branches of food processing. Were figures available, we would expect to find 7 to 8 million people employed in these sectors. Low paid also were personnel in state farming, trade, and catering. Education, public amenities and health likewise paid poorly; toilers in the 'cultural' sphere did worst of all.

Each branch of the economy, of course, contained posts yielding relatively high salaries. Nevertheless, it is relevant to note that the low-paid branches as defined here, employed in all well over 30

Table 2.2. *Workers in manual jobs (1980/1) (millions)*

All branches of 'material production' including	'over 40'
Industry ('about' 40%)	11.8
Construction ('over' 50%)	4.7
Agriculture ('over' 66%)	7.1
Trade ('over' 66%)	3.2
Other sectors, (residual)	13.2

Note: All figures were given in approximate terms, or as fractions. The absolute figures in this table are our estimates on this basis.
Sources: S. A. Kheinman, Vol. 2, p. 48; *Narodnoe khozyaistvo SSSR, 1922–82*, p. 402.

million people, or something approaching a third of the non-peasant labour force.

MANUAL WORKERS AND SERVICE PERSONNEL

Manual and unskilled jobs are still to be found in very large numbers throughout the Soviet economy. By 1980 there were still some 40 million people employed in unmechanised jobs in 'material production' (Table 2.2 provides a partial breakdown). Two low-paid categories are usually distinguished amongst them. Firstly, there are 'assistant workers', who are said to be not directly involved in the production process, but perform unskilled supportive functions for those who are. Many such workers are described as 'labourers', or 'riggers'. They numbered about 2 million in industry alone at the time of the 1975 labour census and have apparently become more numerous since.[3] It seems that they were almost all men. According to figures published in 1977, their highest basic rate was 90 roubles a month, depending on working conditions. Labourers working alone, on indoor jobs, earned least, and those in brigades handling exports were said to earn most.

The second category comprises 'junior service personnel', who do menial jobs unconnected with material production, in all types of enterprise and organisation, and who cannot aspire to the appellation of 'worker'. The main occupations here are cleaners, janitors, doorkeepers, watchmen, heating attendants, messengers, etc.[4] Although these people are sometimes, for statistical purposes, listed as 'employees', together with higher-grade white-collar staff, they

Table 2.3. *Low-paid service jobs*

Post	Basic salary
Cleaner Watchman }	75–80
Warehouse personnel Storeman }	80–85
Dvornik (sweeper)	75–80
Driver	75–90

Note: Salary figures in roubles per month, for personnel in the 'non-production' organisations in the service sector of the economy.
Source: A. N. Ershov and A. F. Yurchenko, pp. 324, 328, 330.

should in no circumstances be confused with them. A recent authoritative article on labour problems states that 'the proportion of loaders, cloakroom attendants, sweepers, cleaners, washers, etc., among workers' stood at 15.4%, and had not fallen over the years 1970–9.[5] This, apparently, is a combined figure for assistant workers and junior service personnel, and would yield a total of something like 12 million. The basic wage rates for junior service personnel in trade, catering and the state agricultural sector ranged from 70 to 85 roubles (Table 2.3). It is unlikely that the rates for similar kinds of jobs in industrial and productive sectors were a few roubles more, and that some were supplemented by incentive payments. Such detail, however, is not revealed in the statistical sources available.

OFFICE STAFF

Any industrialised state requires large numbers of office staff to function. At the time of the 1970 Population Census the Soviet Union had around 5 million employees of this type, and statistics available since would suggest a significant increase.[6] Yet office work, for various reasons, has always been disparaged in the USSR. Equipment is often primitive; stationery is a deficit commodity; and even photocopying has been inhibited by fears of illegal use. Only offices belonging to prestigious organisations would appear to have been adequately modernised.

It is not surprising in the circumstances that secretarial and associated staff should be badly paid. The basic salaries offered in

Table 2.4. *Low-paid office posts*

Post	Basic salary	
	(Junior)	(Senior)
Clerk (filing, general or accounts)		
Secretary, typist		
Copy machine operator	75; 80	80; 85
Cashier		
Draftsmen		

Source: A. N. Ershov and A. F. Yurchenko, p. 328, Salary figures in roubles per month.

non-productive organisations, trade, catering, as published in 1981, varied from 75 to 85 roubles (Table 2.4). Office staff in agricultural organisations, certain state committees, and construction did a little better, and got from 75–95 roubles.[7]

Although no other data are at present to hand, it would seem that rates of this kind were fairly standard for comparable staff in most, if not all, branches of the economy. In some enterprises, again, they may have been subject to enhancement by bonus; but the evidence we have on the sums paid, and the thrust of the regulations, suggest that such extras were rare and limited in amount. Evidently, office work was for those who preferred relatively protected working conditions to higher remuneration.

Rates of pay of the order earned by low-grade manuals, service personnel and office staff were clearly far from ensuring a satisfactory standard of living for those with families and dependents: indeed, one may well ask how they managed at all. There are a number of partial explanations. Many of them (as we shall see in a moment) were women, and probably provided only a second wage in the family. Some did second jobs simultaneously. Others were casual employees, young people prepared to earn little until they could find employment more to their taste, or manual workers seeking less demanding, if worse-paid jobs. Some of them were pensioners, who were attuned to low pay, or who could not subsist on their pensions alone. This still left a large number of permanently low-paid people with full family responsibilities. If any improvement is to be posited in their lot over the longer term, it will have to come from changes in the occupation structure, and growth of training facilities. The number of people wanting to do the most menial jobs will probably fall, while continuing difficulties of attracting labour may prompt the authorities to improve the rates of pay. It is, of course, precisely these categories which have been protected by the state legislation on the minimum wage.

LOW-PAID PROFESSIONALS

In most countries the acquisition of a university degree or its equivalent leads, usually after some years, to well-paid work, provided that work is available at all. In the USSR many specialist jobs (out of a total of 12.6 million in 1981) carry unexpectedly low salaries. They are mostly to be found in the generally lower-paid sectors of the economy and in enterprises where the opportunities for supplementary payments are restricted. The list in Table 2.5, compiled from a number of branch handbooks, speaks for itself.

The salaries listed were those offered by various agricultural agencies in the RSFSR, catering and cultural enterprises, and the state school system. As may be seen, scales starting at around 90 roubles, and ending significantly below the average wage, were common. The fact that these sectors were amongst the worst paid in the economy does not mean that such salaries were unknown elsewhere. The sectors together employed at least a quarter of the labour force; similar professions are practised throughout the economy; and many of the rates paid elsewhere would vary only by a few roubles. A doctor working in a prestigious rest home belonging to the USSR Ministry of Construction, for example, could not expect to earn a much higher salary than colleagues doing the same job in rest homes of more modest standing. Thus figures quoted in 'branch' handbooks are much more generally applicable than might be supposed at first sight. The fact to be emphasised is not that such specialists may start off on a low wage, but that long years of service need hardly raise them above a poverty life-style.

In view of this one would expect many of the country's 17.2 million middle-grade posts – those which lie beneath the specialist level, but are generally above the manual and service levels – to afford modest remuneration as well. Such evidence as we have indicates that this was the case (Table 2.6).

Table 2.5. *Low-paid specialist posts*

Posts	Basic salary (Roubles, monthly)	Sector	Principal conditions of service
1 Engineers of all types 2 Economist 3 Legal advisor 4 Stock-manager	95–130	Trade (Catering enterprises)	According to category (1–4)
5 Engineers of all types 6 Agronomist 7 Veterinary surgeon 8 Book-keeper	105–145	Agriculture (various production enterprises)	Not specified in tables
9 Doctor	100–170	Agriculture (various Health Service institutions)	5–30 years service
10 Librarian	100–125	Agriculture (cultural institutions)	According to years of service
11 Club and culture organisers	90–137	Agriculture (cultural institutions)	According to years of service
12 Teachers	80–137	Education (general schools)	According to duties and years of service
13 Teachers	90–164	(Nursery and special schools)	According to duties and years of service

Notes: All the salaries listed are basic, and specified for degree holders. Salaries for posts 1 to 4 are taken from a handbook issued by the USSR Ministry of Trade in 1981; those for posts 5 to 11 were listed by a variety of agricultural ministries, mainly in the RSFSR, for 1981; the remaining rates (12, 13) were approved by the State Committee for Labour and Wages and the Trade Union Council in November 1967. The documentation is complex and here we attempt only to illustrate the lowest scales.

Sources: Posts 1–4, A. N. Ershov, A. F. Yurchenko, Section X. Posts 5–11, M. F. V'yaskov and others, pp. 24, 75, 78, 202, 203. Posts 12, 13, A. I. Shustov, V. I. Budarin, p. 278.

WOMEN WORKERS AND EMPLOYEES

It has long been evident that Soviet women in general earn less than men. Although discrimination between men and women doing the same job is constitutionally forbidden, and equal pay provisions are automatic, the socio-economic mechanisms which both protect and limit women's labour in bourgeois societies are no less operative in

Table 2.6. *Low-paid middle-grade posts*

	Posts	Salary
1	Technicians of all types	80–100
		80–150
2	Medium grade veterinary personnel	80–150
3	Laboratory assistants	75–85
4	Teachers, nursery personnel	65–128
5	Nurses, midwives	89–91
6	Ward attendants	98–80
7	Library workers (medium grades)	85–100
8	Club workers (medium grades)	80–100
9	Orchestral musicians (employed in dance halls, restaurants)	70–85
10	Artists, second class	70–110

Note: All salaries listed are basic and specified for persons with secondary special and general education only.
Sources: Posts 1, 3, – A. N. Ershov, A. F. Yurchenko, Section X. Posts 1, 2, 7, 8 – M. F. V'yaskov and others, p. 25, 75, 78. Posts 4 – A. I. Shustov, V. I. Budarin, p. 278. Posts 5, 6 – N. I. Malov, V. I. Churakov, p. 241 (average sums). Posts 9, 10 – N. P. Savinov, p. 51. See Table 2.5 for comment on these sources.

the USSR. From a Soviet manager's point of view, women are often less desirable employees than men. Women cannot legally be used for many dangerous or arduous jobs (though they may often be seen working as simple labourers). There are restrictions on what they can lift, and they cannot be used for night work. They can claim advantageous pension provisions, and are highly likely to stop working so as to have children, a messy function which imposes extra obligations on employers. Beyond this, some inequality undoubtedly stems from womens' involvement with the home and family, or a genuine lack of interest in competing with men at the workplace. We have little reason to assume that Soviet women share the aims and objects of the more strident feminist organisations in the West.

Generalised Soviet data, which may be used to compare men and womens' earnings in any given enterprise or group of families, are hard to come by, but indirect indications of lower earnings among females are numerous. For instance, a group of 862 working women respondents in a survey conducted by Professor Gur Ofer and a team of researchers in Israel, centring on the year 1973, revealed that wives in full-time employment earned on average only 59% as much as their husbands. The comparable figure for our own emigre sample was

71%. In terms of occupational structure women still predominate in the lower-paid sectors of the economy. According to a note in a recent statistical compilation, these included trade and catering (83% female), health and social security (82%), education (75%), and culture (74%). It will be noted that all of these branches fit neatly at the bottom of the listing given in Table 2.1. Women were also said to be numerous in the food-processing and garment-making industries.[8]

It would appear, however, that they also tend to find themselves in lower skill, and therefore wage, categories than men within any given sector. Figures collected in the course of a study of 11,000 workers in twenty-two enterprises of the RSFSR between 1969 and 1972 showed that whereas in the baking, meat, milk, processing and textile industries they lagged behind the men by 0.1 to 0.9 of a wage category, the gap in machine-building was 1.4 categories. The same source showed that women took longer to rise in the pay scales.[9] At the time of the 1970 Population Census 75%–85% of service personnel, and 60% of Soviet office staff were women. Women have long predominated amongst low-paid specialists: thus although, in 1980, they occupied 59% of all middle and high-grade jobs, in medicine and general school teaching, two of the lowest paid 'specialist' branches, the proportions of females were 68% and 72% respectively.[10]

In a family situation, of course, women would tend to benefit from their husbands' higher earnings, their own wages being regarded only as a secondary source of well-being. Clearly, outside the family situation, employed women would be more likely than men to find themselves in poverty situations. Elderly women whose pensions were necessarily based on lower earnings would be particularly disadvantaged.

SECONDARY EARNINGS AMONG THE URBAN POOR

If a person does not earn enough to ensure a reasonably satisfactory standard of living, his natural impulse is to earn more, even though full-time employment may place severe constraints on his time and surplus energy. What sources do poor people find? The survey which we recently conducted among emigre families (see Appendix 2) provides indications evidently unobtainable elsewhere.

Overtime at one's place of employment – which might appear to be the obvious answer – is not widespread in the Soviet economy,

except in the agricultural sector. Managements are reluctant to pay
the official overtime rates, and hidden labour reserves evidently make
it unnecessary. Thus although the wage of respondents in the sample
was low (averaging a modest 99.9 roubles gross, or 91.3 roubles net
of tax and union dues) only 15 % of them worked overtime, and then
only for about an hour thirty minutes a week. In about half of these
cases, overtime was either not recognised as such by the managements,
or involved voluntary duties which were unpaid. Payments, when
made, averaged about 20 roubles a month. The main reasons which
respondents gave for doing overtime were: financial need, the
requirements of the job itself, or the insistence of the management;
the reasons for not working overtime were the impossibility of finding
any, the pressures of normal work, and lack of time. Only 5 % of the
respondents took on regular second jobs, which averaged six hours a
week and brought in about the same amount of money. These sums
were helpful enough in any given family, but when averaged across
the sample accounted for a relatively insignificant 3.5 roubles of
monthly earnings.

Work of an officially approved character is not, however, the only
way of earning money in the USSR. There is no doubt that a
significant proportion of the country's wage-earners supplement their
income by involvement in the so-called second, or black economy.
Respondents to our survey exhibited a marked propensity to earn
money from illegal activities at the work-place, or from undeclared
work outside it. (Many private earnings, though quite legal in
themselves, entail heavy rates of taxation and are for this reason
illegally concealed.) Some 19 % admitted to various forms of 'fiddling'
at work, and 36% reported repair jobs, cleaning, teaching, and
various other service activities in their own time, though much of this
was not done on a regular basis. In all, just under 40 % of the working
respondents reported extra earnings from these sources. Involvement
in the second economy was not confined to any occupational sub-group
in the sample, presumably because it could take so many forms.

The financial benefits were quite considerable, averaging 29 roubles
for a month's work. But when averaged across all employed respondents, on an annual basis, such earnings fell to about 12 % of total
income, and raised some 17% of the sample families above the
70-rouble poverty threshold. How low earners fared across the
country must remain a matter of conjecture, but we would take these
findings (despite the specificity of the sample) as generally indicative.

For the majority of those involved, secondary earnings could have offered no real solution to overriding material difficulties.

Finally, mention must be made of contractual work at home, or *nadomnichestvo*, usually in the form of garment-making or traditional crafts. In recent years the authorities have encouraged this practice, indeed, enterprises which employ no other labour have been established in some republics. However, by 1980, the number of people involved on a permanent basis apparently amounted to only 140,000. The breakdown by occupational status was, according to one Soviet source: pensioners and invalids – 43 %; women with small children – 35 %; pupils involved in full-time study – 18 %.[11] The link between activity of this kind and a poverty status is clear from a few available income figures: about 80 % of the pensioners, invalids and housewives, and 100 % of the pupils, had a per capita family income of under 70 roubles a month, including part-time earnings. The incidence of short-term, as opposed to long-term, *nadomnichestvo* is hard to gauge.

THE PEASANTS

The term 'peasant' is rather vague, but is usually taken to mean the field and manual workers in the collective, as distinct from the state, farm. The Russian equivalent, *krestyanin*, is still in common use, though *kolkhoznik* – any member of a collective farm – usually replaces it in official pronouncements. In 1981 the farms' public sector had a registered labour force of 13.2 million, though the total number of toilers, including family members engaged in the private sector and supportive activities, was much larger. A 1978 estimate of the main occupation groups is shown in Table 2.7.

The peasantry as a whole has undoubtedly benefited less than any other major group from Soviet power. Herded into collective farms in the early thirties, it became a kind of second-class citizenry, to be used or exploited for purposes of industrial growth. The closest modern representatives of the traditional peasant are the field workers, termed, even in the early seventies, 'horse and manual personnel'. Their simple physical skills are rarely analysed in detail, like those of farm members engaged in animal husbandry (which tends to be better paid, more mechanised and less seasonal). They are now the most elderly and least educated group in the village.

A peasantry as such can have no long-term place in an avowedly Marxist society, and is ultimately destined to disappear. Between the

Table 2.7. *Collective farm occupation structure, 1978*

	Millions	%
Specialists and office staff	2.3	10.3
Mechanisors (machine handlers, including drivers)	4.0	17.6
Animal husbandry workers	5.5	24.4
Manual labourers and field workers	10.8	47.7
	22.6	100.0

Source: V. M. Popov, M. I. Sidorova, p. 93.

population censuses of 1970 and 1979 it shrank, as a social group, from around 50 million to 39 million souls. Officially, the aim is to replace field workers by skilled mechanisors, as the mechanisation of field jobs increases. More collective farms will be turned into state farms manned by agricultural 'workers'. The number of peasants may also continue to decline as a consequence of low birth rates and the departure of young people for the towns. (The days when the authorities actually drafted peasants into industry are past, as the under-capitalisation of agriculture makes it desirable, in the medium term, to keep as many hands as possible on the land.)

Both Khrushchev and Brezhnev went to some length to lessen distinctions between the peasantry and other groups in society. As a result of benign government policies, the gap between peasant and other earnings was narrowed considerably. Pressure on the private plot (long regarded as a hindrance to stratified agriculture) was eased. The legal status of the peasant was also improved, in so far as he and his family gradually acquired the right to state pensions, trade union membership, and internal passports, with the extra freedom of movement which this entailed. (For further discussion, see chapters 5 and 6 below.) The fact that such policies were in large part forced on the leaderships by the peasants' sullen response to decades of deprivation did not lessen their impact.

Estimating the extent of poverty in the peasantry, as it obtained in the late seventies, presents particular difficulties. It would appear that no 'minimum budget' has been published for them; their income is subject to wide and uncharted variations, by geographical location, farm and year; and there is the additional mystery of the private plot, which was thought, by the beginning of this decade, to provide a quarter of their sustenance. The produce of the plot may be consumed directly by the family; sold through a number of channels, including

Table 2.8. *Average monthly pay by occupation group*
(*Novosibirsk oblast, 1977*)

	Wage	% of all labour
Management (high and middle grade)	153	8.0
Production specialists	142	4.6
Other specialists	117	5.2
Low-grade employees	105	8.8
Workers by qualification:		
Highly skilled	180	11.3
Medium skilled	140	18.6
Unskilled (agricultural)	100	13.2
Unskilled (non-agricultural)	90	17.6
Others (not stipulated)		12.7

Source: A. N. Shaposhnikov, in V. A. Artemov, p. 142.

the collective farm market; or sent to hard-pressed dependents in the towns. But that poverty among the peasantry was still acute, there is no doubt.

We may for present purposes distinguish two common types of hardship in collective farm society. The first obtains when the farm itself is poor, and most (if not all) of the people who work in it earn little. The neglected state of Soviet agriculture has always meant that a large proportion of collective farms found themselves in this situation. In 1976, for example, 30% of them were said to pay an average wage which equalled, or was lower than, the *minimum* for state enterprises. The areas 'below average' were White Russia, the Ukraine, Kirghizia, Moldavia and the majority (!) of economic regions of the RSFSR.[12] Of 166 farms in the relatively poor Vinnitsa oblast in 1978, 41 paid an average wage of only 72 roubles; 84 paid 82 roubles, while the remainder paid 101 roubles.[13]

Even successful farms, however, may have their poor members (this being the second situation we have in mind). Though we have found no recent figures for the collective farm labour force nationally, data on all rural labour in the Novosibirsk oblast in 1977 show which occupation groups were most likely to suffer (Table 2.8). It will come as no surprise to find that the worst-paid toilers were (going down the scale) specialists not involved in the production process; white-collar non-specialist employees (i.e., service personnel); unskilled agricultural and non-agricultural manuals. The same source showed that the average wage of collective farmers, including an allowance for the private plot, was some 9% below that of non-agricultural workers, and 17% below that of state farm workers. Rural Novosibirsk was, as we have noted, held to be typical of West Siberia. The authors of this study, incidentally, noted increasing differentiation of collective farm incomes as a result of the faster growth of higher wages.

No consideration of peasant earnings would, however, be complete without reference to the nature of agricultural labour. Work on the collective farm in particular carries two major disadvantages which need brief emphasis. The first lies in the physical demands of the private plot, output from which is often used to boost earnings statistics. The Novosibirsk studies show that 82% of the respondents worked on such plots, and nearly half of them devoted three hours or more to the task daily. Mechanisation is, of course, minimal. The second disadvantage, affecting most agricultural jobs, is the lack of limitation on working hours. Data from the same study showed that 40–45% of the labour force in collective and state farms worked '9–11 hours or more' a day in summer, and 25–30% did as much in winter. Free days can be difficult to obtain and annual holidays may be impracticable. This is one of the reasons why labour turnover, particularly among mechanisors, is nationally very high.[14]

PROBLEMS OF OCCUPATIONAL PRESTIGE

Low-paid jobs raise an ideological problem to which, as far as we are aware, the authorities have so far found no satisfactory answer. In a socialist society labour is supposed to be free from exploitation and directed to the common good. In such circumstance all jobs should enjoy an equal measure of prestige; if there *is* a variation, it should be related only to their social usefulness. Nevertheless, Soviet occupations may be hierarchically arranged by prestige; and the lowest-paid jobs tend to be the least popular, regardless of their usefulness to the cause of socialism.

A good deal of academic research was done on the prestige ratings of jobs in the mid-sixties and early seventies.[15] Since then, perhaps because the Soviet pattern is disconcertingly similar to that of bourgeois lands, or because the problem has failed to recede, investigation of it seems to have been discouraged. We commented upon it in another context some years ago, but the poverty aspects deserve further elaboration here. Table 2.9 lists the lowest-scoring jobs from a well-known 1964–6 study from Leningrad, juxtaposed with those

Table 2.9. *Occupations with low prestige ratings*[a]

	Leningrad school-leavers, 1964–66 (1)	Novosibirsk school children, 1970 (2)
Skilled manuals, various metal workers, carpenter, electrician	3.8–4.0	2.46–4.58
Textile workers		
Seamstress, tailor	4.0	4.02
Loom operator, spinner	3.9	4.36
Shoemaker	4.8	
Food processing, catering, trade		
Cook, waiter	3.6	
Shop assistant	3.2	2.75
Local services worker	2.6	2.27
Agricultural workers		
Tractor driver	3.9	4.02
Animal husband	3.7	
Field worker	3.4	
Forestry worker	2.9	
Low-skilled manuals, various		
Painter	3.2	
Stonemason, Plasterer	3.1	3.57
Office staff		
Cashier	3.2	2.50
Clerk (accounts)	3.2	
Clerk (general)	2.8	1.96

[a] Below 5 on a 10-point scale.
Sources: (1) V. V. Vodzinskaya, in G. V. Osipov and Jan Szczepański, p. 39. (2) V. N. Shubkin, in A. Z. Rubinov, p. 23.

from a 1970 study done in Novosibirsk. As may be observed, the two sets correspond quite closely, suggesting some degree of generality. It is significant that intellectual occupations (those of scientist, scholar, pilot, engineer, writer, doctor, etc.) gained ratings of 7.2 to 9.2 on the same 10-point scales.

Any detailed pattern of occupational prestige must be exceedingly complex, varying by social group, location and time, as popular perceptions, fashions and wage rates change. Both listings in the table represent only the views of young people about to leave school; but it can be argued that school-leavers, having little experience of their own, have already absorbed common attitudes, and express them in their choices. Some of the 'least unprestigious' jobs in the list (those of seamstress, tailor, carpenter and electrician, for example) owe a relative popularity to the opportunities they offer for secondary earnings. Tractor drivers in the agricultural sector not only earn most money, but also find it easiest to obtain jobs in the towns (urban drivers scored 5.2). Animal husbandry has advantages over field work, in that it may be partly indoor, is less seasonal, and better-paid. Altogether absent form the listings, as published, were unskilled manual and low-grade service jobs, primarily, we believe, because they would have earned shamefully low scores.[16]

Some Soviet scholars have suggested, by way of justification for this gradation, that prestige ratings in Soviet society are less differentiated than those in bourgeois societies. But that must be a matter of much substantive argument.

FAMILY POVERTY

Low earnings are only one side of the poverty equation. The other is the presence of dependents who, in certain circumstances, may reduce per capita family income to poverty levels. The probability of financial difficulty in large families was recognised by the Soviet authorities in the law of November 1947, which provided for payments of from 5 to 15 roubles a month for each child after the fourth, up to five years of age.*

There is no data which allows us to correlate family size by number of working members and income. It is in this sense fortunate that the average Soviet family should be small, numbering only 3.5 members, with 1.8 earners at the time of the 1979 Population Census.[17] However, large families there were as well, and the Census figures showed that throughout the USSR about 6 million families, or 9% of the total, contained six members or more. They were most likely to be of Islamic culture, which is still widespread among the Turkic and Iranian peoples. Figures for family size by ethnic group have not been made available for many years, but republican data showed Tadzhikistan, Turkmenistan, Uzbekistan and Azerbaidzhan to be top, with families averaging between 5.7 and 5.1 members. The two 'Christian' Caucasian republics, Armenia and Georgia, came next with averages of

* This and other regulations are assessed in our review of the social security system in Chapter Five.

Table 2.10. *Child support payments*

	1975	1976	1977	1978	1979	1980
Total of all possible 'child months' (millions)	400.7	405.7	412.0	423.6	431.3	439.1
Number of all 'child months' paid (millions)	43.4	75.4	73.1	70.1	67.6	65.3
% of children supported	10.8	18.6	17.7	16.5	15.7	14.9

Sources: Nar. khoz. SSSR v 1979, p. 557; 1980, p. 527. Estimates and Projections of the Population of the USSR, Table 6.

4.7 and 4.0 respectively. Of religious groups, the Mennonite Germans and Seventh Day Adventists are known to be most fertile. At the same time, family poverty must not be assumed from numbers alone, as rural and religious traditions may encourage sharing and alleviate hardship.

Strange though it may seem, the best indication of the extent of poverty in families with dependent members may be derived from official statistics on certain social security benefits. Since the end of 1974 families with a per capita income of less than 50 roubles have been entitled to monthly payments of 12 roubles for each child aged between one and eight. These benefits are paid for a year at a time, at the full rate per child, and must be applied for anew annually. The figure published for payments in any given year may therefore be regarded as the sums of 'child-months' covered. If this is set against American estimates (the only ones available) of the *total* number of children aged one to eight in the same year, and multiplied by twelve, then the nominal proportion of children subsidised may be calculated. As may be seen from Table 2.10 by 1980 more than one child in seven was in this situation. Since most families entitled to the benefit in all probability received it, these figures represent a fairly firm arithmetical contingent. Many children, of course, would have moved into, or out of, poverty in any calendar year, but these movements would presumably tend to cancel one another out. If the 70-rouble poverty threshold, rather than a 50-rouble income, were used to establish eligibility, the number of beneficiaries would obviously have been considerably greater. The slow fall registered between 1976 and 1980 would be consistent with the wage increases already discussed.

Broken marriages and illegitimacy can be direct causes of poverty if children have to be maintained on one adult income. At the time of the 1979 Census divorces were running at about 945,000 per annum (or 33% of new marriages) and some 500,000 children were born out of wedlock annually, of whom 180,000 do not seem to have been acknowledged or supported by their fathers. The number of one-parent families, with or without support was returned as 7.9 million.[18] Broken families would seem to be most frequent among the Slavs and Baltic peoples living in large towns, and rarest amongst the Islamic, primarily rural minorities.

The measures introduced to ease these problems include alimony deducted from an absent parent's wages; state payments for any number of children of an unmarried mother up to the age of twelve; and easier access to childrens' homes. These provisions will be considered in more detail in Chapter Five. The point we wish to make here is that in the late seventies such assistance, except in the case of very high alimony, was far below the per capita poverty threshold. In any case, most maintenance payments terminated at early ages, when the child's needs were still increasing.

OLD-AGE PENSIONERS AS A POVERTY GROUP

The Soviet Union had, in 1980, some 33 million old-age pensioners. The reasons for so large a number lay not only in the ageing population structure, but also in the relatively low age at which such pension provision starts – fifty-five for women, and sixty for men. Pensioners present an economic problem in most societies, insofar as they cease to be productive. Their personal needs may diminish, their family responsibilities lessen, and they may have the acquisitions of a life-time to fall back on. Nevertheless, transfer to pensioned status greatly increases the likelihood of poverty. This holds true for Soviet society as well.

The details of the system by which Soviet pensioners are paid are a topic in their own right, and will also be dealt with later. Suffice it to say here that a person retiring with a full entitlement of twenty-five years of state service would expect to get the equivalent of between 50% and 100% of his best earnings. Although these rates are remarkably good by most 'capitalist' standards, they yield but modest incomes in the Soviet context. The stipulated minima are also low: in the late seventies the minimum full pension for workers and employees was 45 roubles, while peasants got only 29 roubles (against a maximum, for most categories, of 120 roubles).

The system, itself, moreover, contains a number of poverty-generating factors. Firstly, there is no mechanism for automatic up-grading of pensions as the years go by, provided that these pensions are above the minimum rate. As they get older, therefore, pensioners tend to fall further behind individuals who did the same job, but retired after them at a higher rate of pay. Secondly, there is no supplementation of income for persons unable to qualify for a full pension if they have not worked long enough in state jobs, or for other reasons. The practice here is to estimate a pension only on the basis of earnings registered, the state minimum being inapplicable. (It was for these reasons that of 127 grandparents in our survey, 35 had partial pensions averaging 35 roubles, and 18 declared no pension at all.) Thirdly, a pension system based on a service record, rather than on current *need*, places pensioners with several dependents in a particularly difficult position. Finally, pension rates take no account of inflation or illegal price mechanisms. The few indirect financial benefits granted to pensioners (principally guaranteed housing on cessation of employment, at a normal rent; continued use of any existing private plot; freedom from income tax; plus any marginal benefits emanating from local organisations or former employers) would not have done much to counterbalance these shortcomings.

No national figures seem to be published for the distribution of pensioners by income; total officially declared payments in 1980, including partial pensions, averaged just over 64 roubles a month per recipient.[19] Pensioners above the minimum in our survey averaged 57 roubles. It is significant that the achievement of a pension of 70 roubles, needed to surpass the family threshold, required the individual to earn an average wage, over five years, of 140 roubles a month, while the published national average for the years 1975–9 rose from only 145.8 roubles to 163.3 roubles. A limited study of old-age pensioners in the Moscow Cheremushki District conducted in the mid or late seventies revealed that around 30% of them received less than 60 roubles a month.[20] Clearly, pension rates of this order meant penury for pensioners living alone, and an extra burden for their families if they lived together.

An obvious response for pensioners is to continue working, either on a full or part-time basis. The Khrushchev leadership at first discouraged this practice, but reversed its policy after a few years, no

Table 2.11. *Working old-age pensioners (workers and employees only)*

	Old-age pensioners (millions)	No. still at work (millions)	% still at work
1956	1.9	1.1	59.0
1960	4.5	0.5	11.7
1965	8.2	1.0	12.5
1970	13.2	2.5	19.0
1975	18.2	4.4	24.2
1979	22.0	6.1	27.8

Source: A. G. Novitski and G. V. Mil', p. 37. Adapted.

doubt to counter increasing deprivation. As a result of various changes in the law since, working pensioners have been allowed to receive 50% to 100% of the pension due on retirement, according to the nature of work undertaken.[21] The number taking advantage of these provisions, itself as much an indication of need as of enthusiasm, has grown steadily, and by 1979 surpassed 6 million (Table 2.11). In addition, a large proportion of the 10 million or so collective farm pensioners must have continued to work, in so far as they laboured on their private plots. A survey of 8,000 working pensioners in Leningrad apparently showed that two-thirds of them kept their old jobs, especially if these were of a low-skilled type. The movements effected by the other third was generally into low-grade service jobs, or jobs that required less physical exertion. Most of the pensioners concerned tried to continue working without a break, and the majority did so for at least five years.[22]

The degree to which this arrangement alleviates poverty amongst the aged can, in the absence of proper data, only be a matter of conjecture. According to other surveys done in the late seventies, between a quarter and a third of all non-working pensioners would have taken jobs, had circumstances permitted.[23] Such work at least offers a chance of enhanced income, and a reduction of the number of years to be faced on a pension alone.

Finally, a word must be said about those old people who received no pension at all. The number can be roughly estimated by comparing the official Soviet figure for recipients with American projections of the pensionable age-groups (no Soviet figures being published for the latter). Here we may detect a success story, in so far as the contingent fell from abut 2 million in 1970 to some thousands in 1980. The reduction cannot be measured exactly, because the American figures must contain a margin of error, while the Soviet pensionable ages vary by category of worker. Yet it was probably substantial, reflecting, one would think, not only improved conditions of eligibility (particularly amongst the peasants) but also the death of older folk who had earlier not worked in the communal sector of agriculture, or in pensionable state employment.

INCAPACITATED AND DEPENDENT PERSONS

Persons suffering from long-term disabilities, and those who have no working adult to support them, are obviously vulnerable to hardship. The overall number of people receiving pensions for these reasons in 1979 was 15.7 million, of whom 1.5 million were in collective farms. The relatively high figures may be attributed to such factors as heavy casualty rates during the Second World War; poor health patterns; dubious working conditions and industrial accidents; and the break-up of families through divorce.

No consistent data are published on individual payments, or income from other sources. Nevertheless, the low levels of maintenance revealed in the relevant legislation mean that many incapacitated or dependent persons must live in a state of poverty. The difficulties faced by some were vividly demonstrated to the writer while sitting in a crowded local train at a Moscow station in 1978. A man in his thirties suddenly appeared in the central gangway, and addressing all the passengers, said he found it impossible to live on his 25-rouble state pension. He could not keep a job, as he was subject to epileptic fits, and employers dismissed him quickly. He asked the passengers for any help they could give and then proceeded to collect money. Nobody in the carriage evinced any surprise, and several people gave him some. Soon afterwards, on the same train, a fat gypsy woman went around demanding 'gifts'.

A little official information is available on two categories of institutionalised persons – the denizens of homes for old or disabled people and homeless orphans. Old or incapacitated adults who have no family to support them, or who cannot live alone, may be placed in institutions which are supposed to provide both medical care and work facilities. In 1979 there were said to be about 1,500 institutions with 360,000 inmates, which represented about half of the need. The mentally infirm are maintained separately. Persons in care receive their state pensions in the usual way, but have been required, under regulations of August 1956, to surrender 90% for their upkeep, providing that not less than 5 roubles (in post-1961 currency) are left for their own use.[24] Occasional reports on these institutions suggest that poor amenities and low standards of living are common. Residents have therefore had every incentive to work in the workshops or garden plots attached to them, even though (to quote the April 1985 rules for the RSFSR) they only received 50% of such earnings, the remainder being deducted to finance their 'cultural and daily needs'. A survey of 1,037 pensioners conducted in the town of Sverdlovsk, presumably in the mid-seventies, revealed that only 1.4% would choose to live in an institution rather than alone, or with their children. As may be seen from the relevant documents in Appendix 1, dissident invalids have been quite vociferous in their criticism of living conditions in state institutions.

In 1976 some 105,000 children, presumably 'total' orphans, lacking both father and mother, were said to be housed in 914 orphanages.[25] In addition, around half a million children lived in boarding schools whose admission rules give preference to applicants with unsatisfactory family backgrounds. We know of few published investigations of orphans' well-being, but the reputation of the homes does not suggest great comfort. In any case, occasional reports of malfunction continue to appear in official legislation.[26] Some institutionalised children benefit from the benign interest of local organisations or enterprises, which arrange treats and holiday outings for them. The Soviet authorities take pride in the fact that the number of orphans showed a big fall in the late seventies, but the high divorce and illegitimacy rates augur ill for the future.

OTHER POVERTY GROUPS

Unemployment ceased to be recognised in the USSR as long ago as 1930, when Stalin's plans for accelerated industrial expansion were causing severe labour shortages. In that year unemployment benefit was stopped, and two years later the employment exchanges were closed. Although modern equivalents of these establishments were reopened in 1966, the official stance on the issue has not changed. 'No unemployment' appears with reassuring regularity in all state plan fulfilment reports, and unemployment amongst the able-bodied is not recognised as a continuing state. Consequently, there is no such thing as unemployment benefit, and people who are in fact unemployed for any length of time may experience considerable hardship.

Admittedly, there is much evidence of labour shortage. On the 1st January 1980, for example, 1,200,000 job vacancies were reported in the RSFSR alone.[27] Soviet economists (who count many honest men in their ranks) frequently discuss the nature of the shortage, and its implications; visitors to Russia report numerous advertisements for unfilled posts; and the under-capitalised state of the economy implies a need for working hands. The falling number of youngsters entering the labour market is also a source of concern. At the same time, significant unemployment undoubtedly exists; and if data were available, we might expect to find it running, given the imperfections of the Soviet labour market, at several percent. Anyway, it may be argued that the above-mentioned fund of vacancies equalled only 1.8% of all jobs, which is not, in itself, a startlingly high figure.[28]

The most likely types of unemployment may be easily identified, if not measured. Job-changing (classified as *frictional* unemployment in other lands) is widespread, especially in the non-European areas of the country. Sociological studies have shown that the gap between occupations is normally one of several weeks. *Seasonal* unemployment cannot but exist in some forms, given the severity of the Russian climate. Pockets of long-term unemployment, in underdeveloped small towns, and in the Islamic republics, are covertly admitted. An economy as inefficient as that of the USSR cannot lack hidden reserves of manpower, maintained by managers for times of stress. Failures of graduate placement are another long-standing problem, especially as the Soviet Union now claims to be producing about 95% of all the graduates needed. Finally, the reluctance of school-leavers to take manual jobs has given rise to youth unemployment of various hues and has profoundly affected the government's policy towards education.[29]

No comment on unemployment in the USSR would be complete without a few words on begging. This practice, shameful in an avowedly socialist state, has been virtually ignored by sociologists at home and abroad. Some 44% of the respondents in our emigre survey, however, admitted seeing beggars, with some predominance of men. The number of sightings averaged abut nine a year, the most common locations being churches, streets, suburban trains, and cemeteries. Most beggars were thought to be poorly educated, unqualified workers, or elderly people with little or no pension. The usual income (when there was one) was thought to be in the range of 20–40 roubles a month. By far the most common causes of this form of destitution were held to be low wages, physical incapacity, and drunkenness; but interestingly enough, a few respondents also entered drug addiction. Beggars' clothing was assessed by all who completed the entry as badly worn or ragged. Begging finds no recognition in Soviet social security provisions; vagrancy, ill-defined and often associated with small gypsy communities, is prosecuted with vigour.

We have excluded from review in this chapter pupils, students and learners who have not started earning and are being trained at state expense anyway. But the parlous condition of these (mainly youthful) citizens deserves a concluding comment. According to the 1979 Census, there were 6.6 million people on maintenance grants of various kinds. Of these about 2 million were full-time students in higher education 2 million were in secondary special educational establishments, while most of the remainder must have been post-graduates, military trainees, and learners in manual trade schools. The principle of state maintenance (enjoyed by about three-quarters of all full-time students, on a means-test basis) is wholly admirable, as is the provision of free education, subsidised meals and accommodation. In the late seventies, however, students in higher education were entitled to basic rates of only 40–60 roubles a month, with small supplements for prowess, while students in secondary special institutions got 35–40 roubles. Only certain mature students, including those seconded for further training in Party schools, are known to have received sums approaching their regular salary.[30]

The deleterious effects of low grants, as described by Soviet sociologists, include employment in part or full-time jobs which adversely affect both progress and health. Married students with children are particularly vulnerable, as was shown by an investigation of 1,356 student families recently conducted in Latvia.[31] There the average family income, when both parents were studying, worked out at 124 roubles, excluding help from the older generation. In a fifth of the cases at least one parent was obliged to take on outside work, while nearly half of the older generation provided substantial financial help, usually as much as 50 roubles a month. The researchers found that although 94% of the student families contained one child, only 16% had a separate flat or room. Half of the young families lived with parents, and 10% actually shared the same room. It is not surprising that VUZy are allowed to establish small funds to help virtually destitute students.

3

POVERTY LIFE-STYLES:
FOOD, CLOTHING, SHELTER

———————— ∽ ————————

Our study so far has centred on the problem of subsistence incomes in the Soviet context, and on naming groups of people who for one reason or another may fail to achieve them. We now turn to the question of what Soviet poverty means in terms of day-to-day living. Obviously, food, clothing and housing must be our principle objects of attention. Although a certain amount of relevant data on them may be obtained from published Soviet sources, the narrower topic of poor people's consumption patterns has been sadly neglected. For information on the matters which such sources omit we shall draw on the returns from our emigre sample. Poverty in the Soviet Union is greatly exacerbated by alcoholism and shortages of consumer durables, so these, too will require consideration.

PATTERNS OF FOOD CONSUMPTION

The food basket proposed by Sarkisyan and Kuznetsova for the mid-sixties, as part of their budget studies, was supposed to be ideal for the circumstances and may serve as a reasonable starting point for analysis here. The basket represented the annual per capita requirement of an urban family of four, comprising an industrial worker, a working wife and two children aged eight and thirteen.[1] Its contents, recalculated on a per capita basis, are listed in Table 3.1, column 1. The breakdown is less detailed than is usual in Western sources, but will bear some generalisation. The daily individual calory intake varied from 2,290 to 3,500 units according to family member;

55

Table 3.1. *Food consumption patterns* (*Kilos, per capita, per annum*)

Foods, (Soviet categorisation)	1 Current minimum diet, 1965	2 Average Soviet diet, 1965	3 Average Soviet diet, 1979	4 Average US diet, 1979	5 Prospective minimum diet	6 Emigre sample diet[a]	7 USDA 'Thrifty Food Plan', 1974[b]
Meat, meat products animal fat, conserves	44.0	41.0	58.0	120.4	75.0	38.4	50.5
Fish and fish products	23.0	12.6	16.3	6.1	19.8	8.8	
Milk and milk products	146.0	251.0	319.0	151.2	184.0	289.5	171.4
Eggs (units)	124.0	124.0	235.0	283.0	153.0	130.4	192.0
Sugar	30.0	34.2	42.8	41.4	40.44	12.0	17.9
Vegetable oil	16.0	7.0	8.4	12.2	10.0	5.4	14.9
Potatoes	137.0	142.0	115.0	66.6	126.4	59.8	35.9
Vegetables	121.0	72.0	98.0	89.2	164.0	60.0	136.9
Fruit and berries	28.6	28.0	38.0	62.2	81.0	31.8	
Bread, macaroni, flour	145.0	165.0	139.0	89.9	174.0	90.0	100.7

[a] The returns from the emigre sample, relating mainly to the years 1977–9, are medians and should be regarded as indicative only.
[b] The 'Thrifty Food Plan' of the US Department of Agriculture has been converted into kilos per annum (milk products included), and rearranged as well as the categories permitted. It included 24.8 kilos of 'accessories', omitted here.
Sources: Sarkisyan and Kuznetsova, pp. 58, 105ff, 139ff (Columns 1, 5), *Nar. khoz.*, 1979, p. 432; 1980, p. 405 (Column 4), *SAUS*, 1981, p. 126 (Columns 2, 3). B. Peterkin, p. 125 (Column 7).

the selection of foods was clearly urban in character and adequate for healthy living.

The basket, however, raises a number of awkward questions, beginning with household economics. Sarkisyan and Kuznetsova set the cost, at state prices, at about 29 roubles a month for each member of the family, or 56% of the 51.4-rouble budget. This proportion, ironically, accorded with levels common in the poorer capitalist societies. Beyond that, the estimate depended not only on the foodstuffs being in the shops, but also on acceptable quality and sale at state prices. Unfortunately, many items are known to have been in short supply, or to have reached the consumer in bad condition. Those bought by necessity on the collective farm, or black market, would have cost at least twice as much as in state shops. Relatively few workers could obtain food from garden plots, or had the time to work them. The sum entered for food in the poverty budgets was therefore, in all probability, too low, and would have sufficed only in unusually favourable circumstances.

Another difficult matter was the relationship between the 'poverty' food basket and the national per capita consumption rates. The two sets of figures, it is true, defy proper comparison on account of their differing statistical bases.[2] Yet it seems clear, even allowing for some discrepancy, that the poverty diet proposed for the mid-sixties, recalculated on an annual basis, was actually superior to the national consumption norms. It evidently required *more* meat and meat products (by 7%), more vegetables (by 68%), fish (by 86%) and vegetable oil (by 129%) than were registered in the national average at the time (column 2). The poverty diet was *below* the average only in milk products, sugar, and bread (including flour products). It was thus unrealisable even for the average citizen.

Over the next fifteen years or so the national rates showed a clear improvement (column 3). Most of the 1965 poverty norms in the more nutritious foods were surpassed, while the consumption of starchy items fell. The improvement must, however, be kept in perspective: even ignoring the possibility of inflated official figures, and the problem of national idiosyncrasies, Soviet consumption rates still lagged well behind those of the United States (column 4). The average Soviet citizen consumed far less meat, fruit and vegetable oil than his American counterpart, but vastly more bread, potatoes, milk and fish (presumably tinned). Both supply and quality were undoubtedly superior in the USA.

The long-term or 'prospective' Soviet poverty diet devised by Kuznetsova and Sarkisyan for the mid or late seventies (column 5) presented further problems. It envisaged a higher consumption of meat, fruit and vegetables, and was to cost 33–35 roubles at the same prices, taking up 51% of family outgoings. But by 1979 it would have cost significantly more than its compilers anticipated, even in terms of official prices, for there had been a number of increases, both admitted and covert.[3] Prices collected unofficially in Moscow at the time in fact suggest that it would have required around 40 roubles, i.e., some 60% of the relevant income. Clearly, this would have had serious implications for persons on or below the poverty line. Secondly, the prospective diet stipulated some quantities which were still well beyond the 1979 national averages, particularly with regard to meat, fish, potatoes, vegetables, fruit and flour products.

The question of how well the Soviet poor were in fact eating by the end of the decade cannot be deduced from Soviet sources, but the returns of our emigre sample provide some clues (column 6). The average cost of all food consumed, by the families covered, including an allowance of about 15% for meals taken outside the home, was around 39 roubles per head, or 64% of total family income. The sum appeared to rise steadily with family income, implying insufficiency at the lower end of the scale. A heavy expenditure on food would therefore seem to have remained a dominant, rather than a diminishing, characteristic of the Soviet poverty state. In general, the sample food basket resembled quite closely the national averages a decade and a half earlier, and still betokened a relatively meagre level of sufficiency.[4] It lagged markedly behind the declared national averages for 1980, and behind the minimum built into the prospective budget. Finally, the reader may care to peruse, for purposes of further comparison, a metric conversion of the US Department of Agriculture 'Thrifty Food Plan' (column 7), which resembled the actual diets of an earlier sample of poor New York families. Again there is no doubt about the lower quality of the Soviet poverty food basket, as reported by the emigres. In particular, it contained less meat and fish, sugar, fruit and vegetables.[5]

Other replies to the questionnaire reveal a rather specific pattern of purchase. Respondents bought very few vegetables over and above the most common varieties (potatoes, cabbage, onion and to some extent carrots). Few others were available in the shops anyway. Through the winter months, some 52% of the respondents bought no fruit, and 15% bought no salad. In nearly all cases, the quantities returned were tiny, and averaged less than a kilo per head monthly. Our attempt to categorise meat purchases by quality revealed that 76% comprised average to poor cuts and salami. Forty-seven percent of the families evidently bought no good meat at all. Conserved foods, citrus fruit, bananas, cakes and confectionary seem to have been foregone by about a third of the sample, and the average amounts, when purchased, were again minimal. On the other hand, berries (normally for jam or compote) were very popular during their short season, and only 5% of the families bought no tea. The reasons for failure to purchase food were given as lack of money (8%), absence of goods (33%) or a combination of the two (59%).

Selective, but frequent use was made of the collective farm markets. It would seem that this was done reluctantly, to make up for shortages or poor quality in state shops, as prices in the markets may be two and a half times higher. Individual purchases could not be assessed by location, but the markets were most important for fresh fruit and vegetables (in the summer, when prices were lower) and good quality meat. In fact, between 40% and 75% of the respondents relied on them to some extent for these comestibles. The market prices, we believe, contributed 2 or 3 roubles per head to the overall cost of the poverty food basket.

The respondents' attitudes to their diets were of interest, given the many constraints on procurement: 28% found it satisfactory, and another 10% had no particular opinion (which amounted to the same thing). These responses reflected, perhaps, successful shopping, ignorance of what might be bought in conditions of plenty, or long-term mental conditioning. On the other hand, 49% expressed themselves 'rather' dissatisfied, and 12% were 'very' dissatisfied. It would seem likely that the poorest families in the USSR, who were hardly represented in our sample, ate worse than those who were; but the absence of information on them leaves that question in the realm of conjecture.

THE FOOD IN THE SHOPS

Estimates of food consumption are interesting as far as they go, but they must, as we have noted, be considered in the context of massive supply failures and poor quality. Such shortcomings are not reflected in official statistics or in sociological surveys, so a few observations which we made personally on a visit to Russia in the summer of 1978, and data collected by other means, may serve as a basis for generalisation. Our own comments mostly concern the centre of Moscow, where distribution is said to be best organised. Our observations were random, and designed to test shopping conditions rather than locate deficiency.

As far as availability was concerned, some foodstuffs, including bread, certain milk products, cheese and butter, appeared to raise no problems. Eggs, sugar, biscuits and tea were reasonably plentiful, while tinned fish and vegetables, though expensive, were not hard to find.

The purchase of anything over and above such staples, however, presented great difficulty. Fresh milk, even when bought early in the day, could be sour. Supplies of meat, even in the form of cheap boiled sausage, meat loaf and chicken, were uncertain. Meat of good or average quality, when available, was usually sold in small hunks, with little regard to customers' personal requirements. Pieces of pork fat sold as 'meat' in a collective farm market at 4 roubles a kilo, approximately twice the state price.

The only vegetable which seemed to be in steady supply in the state shops was cabbage. Potatoes and carrots were not always on sale, and often reached the shelves in a half-rotten state. (Supply difficulties obviously affect perishable foods most, and reduce usable quantities.) Onions, when they appeared, were like the small, pickling variety, and tomatoes were only located once outside the collective farm market. Even in August, the only fruit on sale in the shops were little green apples which would certainly have gone for animal fodder in West Europe. The average greengrocer's shop displayed a battery of empty, or almost empty, shelves, with jars of pickled gherkins set out to relieve the monotony. Built-in mirrors sometimes intensified the visual aspect of the goods in stock. Fruit and vegetables could be purchased without difficulty in the collective farm markets, but the range was narrow, and the usual high prices prevailed.

Shortages of products, poor service in the shops, and a huge demand after every delivery made queueing a frequent occurrence. On many occasions we observed lines of would-be customers (forty seemed to be a critical number) waiting to be served by a single sales assistant. In such circumstances an hour's wait was by no means unusual. The situation in the provinces was undoubtedly worse; many people travelled to Moscow precisely to purchase food. A worker of our acquaintance, when discussing the absence of meat in Kuibyshev for

Table 3.2. *Availability of selected foodstuffs (Reported April, 1982: percentages of replies)*

	General sample – State shops only			Small town sample[a]	
	Usually available	Irregular or unavailable	Rationed	State shops	Collective Farm markets
Meat:					
Pork } Beef }	9	79	12	1	35
Chicken } Sausage }	13	79	8	2	50
Fish	69	30	2	60	
Milk	24	75	1	7	70
Butter } Cheese }	23	73	4	4	64
Eggs	39	59	1	19	69
Sugar	83	17		62	
Vegetables (beet and cabbage)	46	55	1	36	76
Fruit	22	78		17	82
Potatoes	30	69	1	28	82
Bread	89	11		65	
Flour	46	48	6	16	
Vegetable oil	74	25		58	
Vodka	93	7		95	

[a] Partial sample, 42 respondents.
Source: RFE-RL Soviet Area Audience and Opinion Research (Cyclostyled Bulletin), April 1982, pp. 5, 8, modified.

months on end, seriously suggested that the situation wasn't *that* bad, because the shopper only had to make a forty-minute train journey to a neighbouring town, where it could probably be procured.

Public catering facilities, incidentally, offered little by way of relief. The official handbooks show that they provided the equivalent of about 200 meals per head of the population aged five or over, annually.[6] Some of these offerings must have been in the luxury class, but the vast majority were cheap school and factory repasts. Our own visits to a few popular dining halls revealed a limited choice of exceptionally poor quality. Thus public catering reflected, rather than relieved, the inadequacies of supply: its main saving grace lay in the low cost of the food served.

These personal observations largely accord with data collected by the Radio Free Europe/Radio Liberty audience research office. Results from questionnaires completed by 782 Soviet respondents in 1982 are shown in Table 3.2. As may be seen, meat was by far the scarcest product, and most frequently rationed. Supplies of dairy produce and fruit were grossly inadequate; difficulties were often reported with regard to potatoes and eggs. Bread, sugar, vegetable oil and fish, on the other hand, were nearly always available, and the supply of vodka was exemplary. Meat, fruit, vegetables and dairy products were said to be much easier to get in the collective farm markets. Virtually all commodities, with the sole exception of vodka, were scarcer in small towns. Geographical location did not, however, seem to make much difference, except that fruit was perhaps more readily available in the south.

There is no doubt that supply failures bear heavily on the poor. Some 90% of the respondents to our survey stated that there were occasions every month when they were unable to buy essential food, the number varying between three and twenty. People with little money in their pockets tend to buy cheaper products which are sold out first. Poor customers must either start queueing earlier, so as to get what is available, or buy smaller quantities of the more expensive items left over. Such people find it harder to make sporadic purchases of large quantities, or meet illegally inflated prices. The families most sheltered from these rigours would be those whose members worked in enterprises where pilferage or under-the-counter purchases were possible. The few having garden plots could supply some personal needs for part of the year.

THE PROBLEM OF ALCOHOLISM

No consideration of the poverty food basket would be complete without reference to alcoholic beverages. Though expensive, they may absorb a significant part of family income, and raise many familiar problems.

The Russian people have a long-standing reputation for heavy drinking, popularly ascribed to climate, boredom and a kind of melancholic hopelessness. In the relatively calm years of the mid-twenties the Bolshevik leadership showed a keen awareness of the problem, and enacted many measures to control sales of alcohol and castigate drunken behaviour. Under Stalin, drunkenness was either ignored or tolerated as a concomitant of social change; indeed, workers in vodka factories were sometimes paid in kind. Destalinisation, however, brought a return to more responsible official attitudes and, as time went by, new laws were introduced to contain the problem. Although the detail lies rather beyond the scope of our discussion, we may note that a major decree passed in May 1972 placed extra restrictions on the alcohol content of the spirits on sale; limited the number of establishments selling them; narrowed the hours of sale to between 11 a.m. and 7 p.m.; and withdrew certain sickness benefits from persons whose incapacity was due to over-indulgence.[7] There was a marked intensification of anti-alcoholic propaganda, and a stream of somewhat conflicting explanations of why this evil should still exist in Soviet society six decades after the Revolution.[8]

Even so, the state has found no effective forms of protection against it; episodic comment in the press indicates a close association, if not with poverty, then with delinquency, ill-health and marriage failure. An outstanding feature of alcoholism in the USSR, it would seem, is drinking in the street, or at home, due to a lack of public bars and beer halls. There has also been a great deal of official intervention of a specifically socialist character. Most towns have 'Boards of Shame', on which drunkards may be publically castigated. Sobering-up centres, run by the militia, not only impose fines, but also inform managements about their employees' misdemeanours, thus raising the possibility of pungent criticism at the work place.

It is ironic, in the light of this campaign, that the authorities should not only have maintained good supplies of vodka, but also have allowed the volume of sales to *rise* by no less than 77 % between 1970 and 1980.[9] Policy conflicts between ideologists and trade officials, a desire to appease public dissatisfaction with social conditions, or lax observance of anti-drunk laws may explain the evident contradiction.

The level of alcohol consumption in the late seventies is not easy to determine, since the publication of the relevant statistics is expressly forbidden.[10] Professor V. Treml of Duke University has, however, succeeded in producing some reasonable estimates based on crude alcohol production, retail sales and certain other data. His tentative conclusion was that in 1979 pure alcohol consumption, from all sources, amongst persons aged fifteen years and older, was about seventeen litres per capita.[11] Translated into vodka alone (which is adequate for an assessment here) this gives an annual total of about 44 litres. Quantities of this order imply that the Soviet Union had one of the highest drinking rates among advanced nations.

Although the consumption rates of the families in the emigre survey were very low and not, we believe, useful as an indicator, the respondents' opinions regarding drinking amongst the public at large were of some value.[12] Nearly 95% of them thought the 'ordinary worker's' consumption of vodka and other spirits, without wine or beer, was between 1 and 3 litres a week, with a median of 1.5 litres. This equals 78 litres a year, and, given Professor Treml's (cautions) estimate, seems rather high. It need not, however, be as discordant as might at first appear, since any regular drinker has to make up for the non or light drinkers who depress the average (to some extent women, the Muslim peoples, younger teenagers and the elderly). Everyone knows that when the hour for imbibation arrives (and the day may contain several) Russian workers commonly share a half-litre of vodka between three, and drink a half a tumbler each at one gulp.

The financial implications of high consumption rates, whatever the actual level, are lamentable. In the late seventies, vodka averaged 7.5 roubles a bottle (wine – 2.6 roubles, beer – 50 kopecks). Drinking 1.5 litres of vodka a week would have cost about 48 roubles in a calendar month. The sum might be reduced by the use of home-brewed spirit, or *samogon*, but this is, of course, illegal, messy to produce and potentially dangerous. The incorporation of outgoings of this order into a family budget could spell disaster, and easily reduce an average family to poverty status. On the other hand, there is no hard evidence that poor people drink less than others. Cost may indeed force some abstention, but material hardship may increase the propensity to consume. It is noteworthy that no less than 97% of the respondents in the emigre sample considered drinking to be a 'very important' or 'important' cause of poverty in the USSR.

CLOTHES FOR THE POOR

The assessment of a 'poverty wardrobe' in the USSR presents about as much difficulty as the food basket, not least on account of the number of variables involved. Apart from the matter of personal interest, economic and cultural factors, age, sex, work and fashion, may affect the issue. Climatic conditions are particularly difficult to allow for, as exceptionally heavy garments are needed in winter, and light ones are desirable for the short, hot summer. Long-standing tradition suggests fur headgear, collars and linings, especially for children, though such items are fearfully expensive. The purchase of dress, unlike food, is usually a capital outlay, and relatively infrequent, so monthly outgoings must be estimated by notionally spreading the purchase price over the life-span of the garment. Yet clothes are such an important element in the Soviet life-style that they cannot be passed over in silence.

The poverty wardrobe as formulated by Kuznetsova and Sarkisyan was supposed to suit a poor urban family which faced the rigours of an East European climate, and which evinced no more than a moderate interest in fashion. (In other words, members were willing to don what their budget would bear, rather than forego other purchases to dress better.) But it included, for unexplained reasons, a fairly lavish assortment of secondary garments, bedclothes, household linens, and soft furnishings. Translated into cloth lengths (!) it was costed for the whole family at about 43 roubles a month in the 'current' minimum budget, and 54 roubles in the 'prospective' version, this being just over 20 % of all outgoings in each case.

In terms of purchase costs at 'new' prices, the selection was quite unrealistic. Clothes in the Soviet Union have always been expensive, mostly on account of high state mark-ups: some prices current in the late seventies are shown in Table 3.3. If approximate prices are entered for new garments, like those proposed for the husband alone, the total outlay would have been in the region of 1,100 roubles; and if this sum is spread over reasonable periods of wear, we end up with a monthly outgoing of between 20 to 30 roubles for one person. The modest figures proposed by Sarkisyan and Kuznetsova for a family of four could thus have been achieved only by greatly reducing the size of the wardrobe, extending the length of use, or avoiding the purchase of new items. The authors were doubtless cognisant of these possibilities, and allowed for them without admitting it.

As for availability, matters have been improving. Official figures showed that by the late seventies the supply of clothing, which had been grossly inadequate, increased by more than two and a half times over the mid-sixties. State prices fell by a percentage point or two, which presumably meant less illegal price inflation and easier second-hand purchase. The rise in the average wage must have further facilitated the purchase of clothing for the average family.[13]

Yet such evidence as we have from the emigre sample indicates that

Table 3.3. *Clothes prices in state shops (circa 1979)*

Item	Cost Range[a] (roubles)
Winter coat	120–200
Fur hat	30–100
Raincoat	50–80
Light suit	80–140
Dress (not summer)	25–50
Sweater	25–40
Trousers	15–30
Shirt, blouse	8–12
Shoes, outdoor	20–40

[a] The items listed are presumed to be of *average* quality, mixed fibres. Pricing in state shops is rigidly controlled and very complex (N. T. Glushkov, p. 295ff). Price lists as such are not published, and given the variables involved, exact prices are hardly meaningful for purposes of generalisation. The ranges shown here, however, are fairly stable. As noted on p. 26, they must be set against a monthly average gross wage of 163.3 roubles.
Sources: These prices have been estimated by comparing returns from our emigre survey, a few lists compiled for us by acquaintances then resident in the USSR, and data collected by Mr K. Bush in L. Schapiro and J. Godson, p. 265.

clothes were still a headache for the poor. Taking the adult males, mostly with only a moderate interest in dress, as the most manageable group, we found that 67% considered clothes to be an 'acute problem', while another 30% thought they were a 'problem'. As far as we could determine, there was a distinct shortage of heavier garments. Thus 22% of these respondents managed without a winter coat and 25% had no fur hat. Some 80%–90% had light overcoats or mackintoshes, which they presumably wore in lieu of something warmer; 10% declared they had only one pair, and 40% – two pairs of outside shoes. Only 2% said their overcoats were 'new' or 'as new': generally, less than 16% of all items were so categorised.

Although holdings of secondary items (linen, sweaters, socks, etc.) matched the Sarkisyan–Kuznetsova standards, such responses indicated considerable malaise. The problems of dress were presumably worst among poorer groups in the community who did not figure in our sample, and more stressfull for young women than young men.

THE HOUSING SITUATION IN GENERAL

In Western countries housing is by and large subject to economic laws, which leads to greatly differentiated housing costs. State intervention of one kind or another may be considerable, but it is usually insufficient, or not designed, to ensure anything like equality of access. Low income groups thus tend to find themselves inhabiting meagre or sub-standard accommodation in unattractive urban districts, or primitive houses in the countryside.

The situation in the Soviet Union has always been somewhat different. The Bolshevik government set rigid egalitarian-type controls on most aspects of housing soon after the Revolution, and most of these controls have been retained up to the present. By 1980 about 77 % of all housing space in the towns, and a smaller, but unspecified proportion of dwellings in the country, belonged to state organisations, enterprises and local soviets. Space in the public sector is allotted at so many square metres per head; quotas are fixed locally and, in the late seventies, varied mostly between six and nine metres, with a normal maximum of sixty per dwelling. This entitlement was based on habitable rooms, or 'living space' proper, exclusive of kitchen, bathroom, corridors, etc.[14] Rents, which are supposed to cover capital maintenance as well, varied from about 3 to 5 *kopecks* a square metre a month, according to the location and quality of the dwelling. A large flat, therefore, should not have cost more than 3 roubles, though modest heating, electricity and gas charges would have raised the figure somewhat. The 'apartment payments' (the term 'rent' is avoided in the public sector) were fixed as long ago as 1934, and the authorities make much of the fact that no increase has been made since. Rebates are available for some citizens who need extra help. Not surprisingly, the minimum budgets compiled by Sarkisyan and Kuznetsova lumped state housing together with communal amenities, and costed them at only 5 % or so of all outgoings.

The private sector comprises, by and large, cooperatively built flats in urban areas; individual (and often sub-standard) dwellings in the countryside; and a small number of good quality villas owned by persons of elite status. Space norms are usually decided by the cooperative, or individual builder, and are less restrictive than in the state sector. However, no one is allowed to own more than one dwelling, and even country dachas are limited to summer occupation (a rule enforced by flimsy construction, or a ban on stoves). Although state mortgages are available at nominal rates of interest, the opportunities for the acquisition of private living space have varied much with time and circumstance. Purchase prices are high, but strict controls on resale values prevent profit-taking.[15]

A system such as this, oriented towards the provision of standard amounts of housing for all, with strict financial restraints, might be regarded as protective of poor people's interests. One might further imagine that the relationship between poverty and slum-dwelling, so characteristic of 'capitalist' lands, would be weakened.

This has not happened for several cogent reasons. Firstly, Soviet towns have always been characterised by acute housing shortages from which most people suffer. Secondly, the provision of superior accommodation has long been used as a reward for service to the state, or as an incentive to work harder. The sharp fall in the per capita provision of urban housing during the first Five Year Plans, for example, necessitated special provision for managers and outstanding workers. The destruction wrought by the Second World War, and the neglect of the sector in the post-war decade, had the same effect. The Khrushchev leadership endeavoured to increase housing stocks, but it still had to urbanise rapidly in the interests of economic growth, and most housing privileges were retained. When the rate of urbanisation began to slow in the mid-sixties, the housing sector, though lacking the variety found in capitalist society, was still characterised by a good deal of differentiation. The Brezhnev leadership adopted a highly protective attitude to most forms of privilege, and maintained the existing accommodation benefits.[16]

Thirdly, the allocation system has over time developed subtle informal mechanisms which work to the detriment of the less privileged citizens. The poor, for instance, have fewer chances of acquiring the better-quality accommodation erected by powerful organisations or enterprises, and are more likely to end up in meaner flats belonging to local soviets. Poor people cannot usually buy living space in cooperative housing projects because, compared with the nominal rents in the state sector, such housing is extremely expensive. If they do so, the space they acquire is (to judge from our sample returns) close to the minimum, and mortgage repayments greatly exacerbate their financial difficulties. The poor have less of the political influence needed to speed progress through the local waiting lists (see Chapter Six).

Table 3.4. *Distribution of Novosibirsk workers by amount of living space (1966)*

Amount (square metres)	Men	%	Women	%	Both sexes	%
1–3	155	12.7	70	15.5	225	13.5
4–6	440	36.0	178	39.5	618	36.9
7–9	265	21.6	67	14.8	332	19.8
over 9	106	8.7	40	8.9	146	8.7
No accommodation, or no details	257	21.0	96	21.3	353	21.1

Source: E. G. Antosenkova and V. A. Kalmyk, *Prilozhenie* 15, p. 26, Total number in sample – 1,674.

The problem of Soviet slums has, of course, always been veiled in secrecy. The term, like 'poverty' still cannot be officially ascribed to any Soviet dwelling. But such dwellings continue to exist and are likely to house the poorest members of society. We shall now consider a few statistics available on the problem as it developed through the Brezhnev years.

OVERCROWDING, COSTS AND AMENITIES

The average per capita provision of living space in Soviet towns by the mid-sixties may be estimated as 6.1 square metres. This was well below the declared 'sanitary minimum' of 9 square metres; given the inevitable vagaries of family size and circumstance, it indicated extreme overcrowding for the great majority of townsfolk. The most revealing data to come to our notice on slum conditions at that time were provided by a study of 1,673 men and women workers, in five Novosibirsk factories in 1966. Published in cyclo-styled format only, it was clearly not intended for widespread circulation.

The distribution of space occupied by the respondents, shown in Table 3.4, cannot be described other than as appalling. Some 13.5 % had less than four square metres a head, while only 8.7 % enjoyed the sanitary minimum. It is difficult to imagine how people managed with so little, even in dormitory conditions. In general, the women were worse off than the men. It will be noted, incidentally, that 21 % of the respondents did not answer the question at all. Some of these may

Table 3.5. *Living space in selected large towns*

	(Square metres, per capita)	
	1965	1980
Moscow	7.9	10.8
Tallin	7.8	10.7
Leningrad	6.6	9.4
Khar'kov	6.1	9.6
Novosibirsk	6.1	8.6
Kishinev	6.6	8.5
Perm'	5.7	7.9
Tashkent	5.3	6.6

Sources: Nar. khoz. SSR, 1965; 1979; 1980; tables bearing on urban population and housing stocks. See note 14 for details of assessment.

have been unwilling to admit that they had such cramped quarters, or were trying to conceal living space that they were not entitled to. Others may not have been properly registered, and feared eviction.

The sociologists who did this study were interested in its representativeness. The enterprises chosen for investigation were in most respects average, and the published occupancy rate for Novosibirsk, at 5.7 square metres per capita, was but little less than the national figure. The average *wage* of the sample was, however, only some 65 roubles, as against 101 roubles for industrial workers throughout the country. From this we would conclude that the conditions revealed by the report were typical for low-paid workers in many areas.

In the course of the next decade and a half urban housing stocks increased considerably and, by 1980, were said to provide about 8.6 square metres of living space per dweller. Table 3.5 illustrates the variation between selected towns, as revealed by official statistics in 1965 and 1980. Tallin and the larger 'show' cities of the European plain tended to be most favoured; fast-growing, industrial towns, and those inhabited by Islamic minorities, were most likely to have overcrowding problems. The smaller towns and settlements not normally included in national statistical compendia were evidently less pressed for space, but had less to offer in terms of communal amenities.[17]

The increase in housing stocks has often been flaunted as proof of the government's concern for popular well-being. A simple calculation shows, however, that the improvement averaged only 0.15 metres per capita annually, and still left most rooms in multiple occupation. (The median occupancy rate for the USA in 1979 was, by contrast, about two rooms per person.)[18] Although Soviet sources lack detailed data on overcrowding, occasional pointers abound. G. S. Sarkisyan stated recently that by 1980 no less than 20% of all urban families still awaited accommodation in a separate unit, while the occupancy rate in Leningrad in 1978 was said to be 1.9 persons a room.[19] The median amount of living space held by respondents in the emigre survey was 8.2 square metres, but some 10 % of them had less than five. Although the median family size was 3.9, 28% of the families lived in one room, and none had more than three. Some 19% had space in multi-occupational (or 'communal') flats, and five families (1.4%) actually lived in hostels. We found that most local authorities accepted applications for re-housing only from persons who had less than 5 square metres of living space, and some authorities did not guarantee the sanitary norm of nine metres on resettlement, either.

The minimum budgets illustrated in Chapter One allowed for housing costs of a mere 5 % or so of outgoings. The results of the emigre survey suggested that the poor in practice had to spend far more. The median per capita outgoing on rent, electricity, gas, telephone, heating, and cleaning, without repairs, ran at 5.1 roubles per capita, or 9.4% of net official income. In addition, the great majority of families had to do their own repairs, or hire labour for them at their own expense. Interestingly enough, only 6% recorded instances of failure to pay housing bills, and the derelictions resulted in nothing more than official warnings or small fines. Soviet citizens have a fair degree of security of tenure, and eviction normally requires a court order.[20] As for popular reaction to these problems, years of over-crowding, sub-standard accommodation, and ignorance of conditions elsewhere have evidently engendered modest expectations.

No less than 40% of the respondents thought they had enough, or more than enough, space at their disposal, 35% thought their space 'rather' inadequate, and 25% thought it 'grossly' inadequate. Dissatisfaction was naturally highest in the most crowded households.

The quality of accommodation is hardly less important than quantity, though this, again, is a matter on which statistics are scarce. The largest Soviet cities would seem to have adequate running water and sanitation, a gas supply and some kind of central heating. Virtually all settlements have been at least partially electrified. However, the provinces still lag well behind in many important

Table 3.6. *Living space equipped with domestic amenities (percentages)*

Size of settlement	White Russia, 1975			
	Sanitation	Cold water supply	Hot water supply	Central heating
Up to 5,000	12.8	10.3	1.8	14.6
5,000–10,000	13.7	15.7	5.4	15.0
50,000–100,000	55.2	56.0	37.0	52.3
Over 500,000	86.9	87.6	67.5	91.6
Average, all settlements	62.1	63.9	45.5	58.3

	Stavropol' Krai		Kalmyk ASSR	
	1970	1980	1970	1980
Sanitation	62	82	20	84
Water	64	85	20	84
Central heating	57	78	22	86
Bath or shower	50	76	19	84
Gas	87	93	26	94

Sources: White Russia: L. V. Kozlovskaya, p. 161. *Stavropol' Krai*: N. V. Tsogoev (ed.) p. 159. *Kalmyk ASSR*: Sh. M. Nalaev (ed.) p. 139.

respects. Figures available for White Russia in the mid-seventies (Table 3.6) revealed an immense divergence in the provision of the services by size of settlement, but even in the largest cities, some 13% of the inhabitants still lacked sanitation and cold water supply. The data available for urban districts in two more distant corners of the land – Stavropol' Krai and the Kalmyk Autonomous Republic – showed that although the authorities made considerable efforts at modernisation, by 1980, 15–18% of housing stocks were still without sanitation and water.

How far the urban poor conglomerate in less attractive, or underdeveloped districts has been virtually ignored by Soviet scholarship, so opinions expressed by respondents in our survey may again be used as a touchstone. Of the sample, 11% replied (regardless of where they themselves lived) that such differentiation was clear, and another 57% said that it was at least discernible. There was much diversity of opinion on what characterised a 'poor district', but the features judged to be most unsatisfactory were, in descending order of frequency, housing (65.9%), communal services (61.0%), physical safety (51.0%), shopping facilities (45.1%), the condition of the streets (39.0%), transport (31.3%), and the atmosphere (23.6%). No less than 60.8% of the respondents located the district they had in mind within two kilometres of dirty or unhealthy production enterprises. Respondents were asked to say when they thought construction of the given district was started. Of the 205 who replied, 33% entered 1940 to 1959, and 36.6% 1960 to 1980, suggesting that local authorities have not been able to mould the character of local communities merely by new building. In other words, poor districts are not necessarily old districts, and may continue to form as new buildings go up, like unsuccessful housing estates in western countries.

As for apartment blocks, most respondents considered them to be socially mixed, regardless of location. But the Soviet elite (defined at this point as 'specialists and highly-paid personnel') were thought likely to enjoy more exclusive housing. Just over 50% of the respondents believed they predominated in houses belonging to (large) ministries and organisations; some 30% – in cooperative blocks; and only four respondents (0.9%) thought they would be numerous in accommodation belonging to local soviets.

A moment's thought will show that the respondents' hesitations about residential distinctions are justified. In capitalist countries such distinctions tend to be clear. Local communities have much influence (destructive as well as constructive) over their immediate environment: a good deal of property is privately owned; and the quality of the services provided by various entrepreneurs will tend to match local needs. Conglomerations of the poor may be encouraged by the reluctance of richer people to live in unattractive spots, or in those which have acquired a poverty image. In the Soviet Union, on the other hand, the standardisation of urban development, ubiquitous housing shortages, nominal rents, and the absence of private commerce, have tended to suppress locational distinctions and mask, rather than reflect the social characteristics of the inhabitants.

Rural housing presents, of course, its own problems. An illustration of the quality of accommodation in the Novosibirsk oblast is given in Table 3.7a. There, even by 1977, 14.2% of the dwelling houses were declared to be dilapidated, and 15.7% made of clay, reed or similar material. Many of the wooden houses would, of course, also have been rough-hewn and primitive. The availability of services, with an urban comparison, is shown in Table 3.7b. The figures speak for themselves; the compilers categorised the lag of the village behind the town as one of 'several decades'. Some rare, but older, data correlating the amount

Table 3.7. *Housing conditions, Novosibirsk oblast*

a Distribution of housing by quality, rural areas, 1977 (percentages)

	Wooden	Clay and lath mixtures	Brick, block or panel	Total
Dilapidated	7.0	6.0	1.2	14.2
Average	16.3	3.6	1.9	21.8
Sound	21.3	1.9	7.5	30.7
New	10.1	1.4	12.3	23.8
Unknown	5.3	2.8	0.5	9.5[a]
Total	60.0	15.7	23.4	100.0

b Domestic amenities (percentages)

	Towns and workers' settlements (1975)	Rural areas (1977)
Sanitation	65	17
Cold water supply	70	29
Hot water supply	59	8
Bath, shower	59	13
Central heating	72	22

c Distribution of living space by income group, 1972 (3,072 families)

Income[b] group	%	Per capita living space	Persons per room
1	4.4	6.7	1.7
2	18.0	7.2	1.8
3	27.6	8.0	1.6
4	28.9	10.0	1.3
5	16.4	12.0	1.1
6	3.8	15.0	0.8
Averages	(100.0)	8.9	1.5

[a] To include 0.9% for unspecified types of construction.
[b] The income groups are unspecified, but evidently rise from lower to higher.
Sources: 3.7a, 3.7b Ts. B. Budaeva, in V. A. Artemov, pp. 202, 204. 3.7c, T. I. Zaslavskaya, V. A. Kalmyk, Chast' I, pp. 158, 163, 164.

of living space with income group are set out in Table 3.7c. There is clear differentiation to the disadvantage of the poor.

All of the data in Table 3.7 are taken from major studies of villages in the Novosibirsk oblast. We have already had occasion to mention the researchers' claim that the oblast was typical of West Siberia as a whole. One is reluctant to describe the Russian village, with all its natural charm and beauty, as a focus of slum living, but figures like these indicate that even in the late seventies, such must often have been the case.

We may note, in conclusion, that the immediate outlook is far from rosy. The eleventh Five Year Plan, covering the years 1981–5, envisaged the same rates of house construction as its predecessor. If these are maintained in the twelfth, the sanitary norm of living space will not be reached, as an urban per capita average, until the end of the decade. The 'rational norms', varying from 15 to 18 metres, and the so-called 'social ideal' of 22 square metres, as discussed in various Soviet sources, are way beyond the horizon.[21]

FURNITURE AND HOUSEHOLD DURABLES

Soviet society long since reached the stage at which families in all but the most backward areas seek to equip their homes with the accoutrements of modern living – comfortable furniture, kitchen and household gadgets. Poverty normally places its own limits on the acquisition of such goods. Given the sparcity of information about such matters, we must limit ourselves to a few general comments.

The minimum needs of a family living in a two-roomed flat were assessed by the USSR Housing Institute as: a dinner table, a kitchen table, a divan and three beds, eight chairs, a sideboard, three cupboards (for clothes, books and crockery); curtains for three windows, four kitchen stools and a few smaller objects; two services of crockery and some kitchen utensils. Apart from furniture, poor families were expected to possess a fair range of 'cultural' goods – radio, television, refrigerator, bicycle, camera, watches and sports items.[22] This selection was built into Sarkisyan and Kuznetsova's prospective budget with a proposed annual outlay of 178 roubles.

It is, however, difficult to see how any relatively poor family could have aspired to it. We estimate that by 1979, allowing for some fall in prices, the furniture alone would have cost in the region of 1,000 roubles (presuming it to be new, but of average quality). The cultural goods were worth 400 roubles or more, making a nominal outlay of at least 1,400 roubles. Costs of this order would have meant an acquisition period of nearly eight years, ignoring wear, tear and breakages.

It is relevant to note, moreover, that the possibilities of borrowing money for capital purchases are very restricted. The USSR State Bank does not offer borrowing facilities to private persons, and no other substantive lending agency exists. Hire-purchase is sometimes possible, but must be effected through deductions at source from a regular wage, and cannot exceed 20% of it. Some trade union organisations run 'Mutual Help Funds' (*kassy vzaimopomoshchi*) from membership contributions, but loans of this kind, though interest-free, are usually short-term and limited to 30 roubles or less.[23]

The second problem lies in finding household goods in the shops. State sales of furniture, it is true, almost trebled between 1965 and 1980, rising from 1,986 to 5,976 million roubles nationally.[24] But this growth is less impressive when viewed in the context of long-standing shortages and pent-up demand. And if sales are recalculated on a per capita basis, we find that they rose over the same period only from 8.6 to 22.5 roubles a year. Furthermore, marketing is poorly organised. In 1977, Moscow, a town of nearly 8 million inhabitants, boasted only sixty-six furniture stores, or one for every 121,000 people. The few furniture departments in multiple stores would have eased pressures but slightly. Second-hand furniture shops deal mainly in expensive antiques; ordinary second-hand furniture in good condition is hard to come by, and 'do-it-yourself' supplies are virtually non-existent.

Household appliances also became less scarce between 1965 and 1980, and here some figures for personal possession are available. By the latter year most Soviet urban households had a radio, a television set, and a refrigerator.[25] If allowance is made for families which did not wish to acquire these and other things, then the levels appear to have been adequate. At the same time, no indication of the state of repair, or indeed quality, is available, and many families living in multiple occupation undoubtedly shared certain articles. The data also showed that villagers were generally less well provided for than townsfolk.

No study specifically concerned with poor people's holdings of furniture or 'cultural' goods has ever, to our knowledge, been published. Turning again to the results of our emigre survey, we find a reasonably satisfactory picture (though one well below the minimum levels proposed by the Housing Institute). Of the seven items of furniture named in the questionnaire, four – a table, upright chairs, beds and clothes-cupboards were owned by virtually all families, apparently in adequate quantities. Most pieces were, however, rather old, and had been in the household for five years or more. At least two thirds were bought new, in state shops; of the remainder about half were second-hand, and half obtained as gifts or legacies.

Fewer families had the three other named items of furniture; thus, only 51% possessed armchairs, 63% had a carpet, and 83% a sideboard. The reasons for the absence of an armchair (!) were given as: lack of desire to have one (31%), no money to buy it (33%), and nowhere to put it (35%). The shortage of living space, and presence, on average, of 2.6 beds per family, lends credence to this response. Carpets, which present no such problem and are a traditional sign of well-being, were 'not wanted' by only 6% of the families which did not have them. Most respondents gave lack of funds as the main reason for a bare floor (or wall). Nearly everyone without a sideboard wanted one: 35% of the non-owners blamed lack of money, and 50% – lack of space. Again, 30%–70% of these items had been obtained outside the state network.

Holdings of other cultural goods (radio, television, refrigerator, vacuum cleaner, washing machine, and sewing machine) more or less matched the national urban figures. Their absence was explained, more frequently than in the case of furniture, by the fact that they were not wanted. As with furniture, many items were old; generally between a quarter and a half were bought second-hand, or procured without repayment.

If the presence of a fair range of household goods is characteristic of some types of urban poverty in the USSR, several explanations may be proposed. The official ethic vaunts a high, 'European' standard of living (even if it does not ensure one). Long-term deficits of goods have no doubt engendered acquisitive responses, encouraging purchase as an opportunity 'not to be missed', and the longer use of personal property. Furniture and other substantial goods may be bought with help from family or friends, after years of saving, or through the sale of some other capital good (like a valuable item of clothing). The small size of (Slav and Baltic) families may help, in that it implies lower current outgoings and less sharing of inheritances. Ironically, the housing shortage itself also reduces the problem, in that there is less space to furnish. Young couples obliged to start their married life with parents involuntarily share their elders' chattels.

The development of heavy industry is not unconducive to the production of 'heavy' household goods. As for the radio and television sets, the authorities have always evinced the strongest possible interest in encouraging their use for propaganda purposes. The high incidence of refrigerators reflects the need to preserve scarce foodstuffs, while the possession of sewing machines has been encouraged by clothing shortages. Thus do the exigencies of Soviet reality impose themselves on the life-styles of the least fortunate members of society.

PART II

4

POVERTY LIFE-STYLES:
OTHER ASPECTS

———————— ·◌· ————————

Food, clothing and shelter are central elements in a life-style, but there are many others. Everybody has a wide variety of needs which, though less immediate, may be of considerable social importance. The nature of these needs depends on the individual's proclivities and the constraints which his various social roles impose on him. Participation in the educational process, access to medical and legal services, and certain time uses are what we have chosen for analysis here.

Once again we find great difficulty in mapping salient patterns. Most of the information available is even less specific than that considered in Chapter Three, so we must adjust our treatment accordingly. The educational and medical services provided by the state will be analysed in terms of their general accessibility to poor people and what, if anything, inhibits use. Some common activities may be best measured by the hours and minutes they require, so here we ask how poverty is likely to affect time inputs. In a few instances, when material is unavailable from official sources, we shall adduce relevant results from our emigre survey.

A 'POVERTY-ORIENTATED' SCHOOL?

The Soviet authorities have always attached considerable importance to education, and have constructed one of the most comprehensive educational systems in the world. Poverty in most capitalist states is usually coupled with an inability to take advantage of educational opportunity, even when it is offered. The more favoured social groups tend to procure the best facilities for themselves and their children, to the detriment of the underprivileged. Here we need to consider how successful the Soviet authorities have been in countering such propensities. But let us begin with the specific *advantages* which the Soviet educational system offers children from relatively deprived families.*

There is no doubt that early Soviet educational policy was aimed primarily at satisfying the needs of poor workers and peasants. The Bolsheviks attached great importance to establishing a general school which was both obligatory and free of cost, and to ending the predominance of 'bourgeois' children at higher levels of training. The first constitution of the RSFSR, promulgated in July 1918, stated specifically that 'workers and the poorest peasants' should be provided with a 'complete, all-round and free' education. To ensure centralised control, the administration and financing of virtually all existing pedagogical institutions were handed over to the People's Commissariat for Enlightenment. The egalitarian principle, with the ensuing suppression of private and religious schooling, has been retained to the present. Provision of a full ten years' general education for every child (up to seventeen plus) was proclaimed as a national goal at the 18th Party Congress, in March 1939. Although there was some temporary abandonment of it during the Second World War, and again under Khrushchev, it was enshrined in the 1973 Fundamental Law on Education, which is still operative.

Institutions and coverage

Free and obligatory education is, of course, a great benefit for poor children, in so far as their parents might otherwise neglect or curtail their school-going. Under the rules current in the early eighties children had to be registered with the local authorities at six, and start school at seven: parents who failed to ensure attendance were liable to prosecution.

By 1980 virtually all Soviet children were getting eight years of education in the so-called general school, and about two-thirds were completing the ten-year course on a full-time basis. Without releasing detailed data, the authorities claimed that over 90% of all youngsters were by then completing the tenth class on full-time and part-time courses together. Some 1.5 million children who lived in settlements

* Many of the points made in this section are discussed at greater length in our study *Education in the Soviet Union*, London, 1982, as referred to below.

too small to support a school, who were orphaned, or came from single-parent and 'problem' families, were maintained in a network of boarding schools.

The general school system is backed by a well-developed system of pre-school facilities. By 1980, 14.3 million children, or about 60% of the 1–6 age group, were registered in nurseries and kindergartens. Though not, of course, obligatory, these were of considerable help for working mothers (who made up 51% of the non-peasant labour force). Beyond the general school, the provision of secondary special and higher education is also extremely good. By 1980 the annual intakes onto full and part-time courses were just under 1.5 and 1.1 million respectively, against annual age cohorts of around 4 million. With approximately 196 persons per 10,000 of the population in higher education, the USSR claimed a leading place in the world league, the corresponding figures for Great Britain and the USA being given as 98 and 261.[1]

The large part-time sector at all levels above the eighth class of the general school has proved particularly helpful to people who were unable to finish general school full-time, or could not manage without a full-time job. Despite some lapses under Brezhnev, this sector has tended to become ever more important. By 1980 some 10% of all places in the senior classes of the general school, and around 40% of all places in secondary special and higher education institutions, involved evening or correspondence instruction. Such information as is available confirms that a relatively high proportion of part-time students came from the families of workers, peasants, and low-grade white-collar workers.

In addition to a good overall coverage, well developed pre-school and part-time facilities, a number of administrative practices help pupils from less privileged homes. Pupils cannot be selected, (except for 'special' and language schools) and Soviet towns for the most part lack clear-cut residential distinctions. Individual schools do not normally acquire specific social profiles. Poor children have less chance, therefore, of being isolated from their more fortunate peers. Detailed control and standardisation of the general school curriculum militate against differentiation, and the 'streaming' of children by ability is forbidden. Schools in remote areas benefit from the high degree of centralised control, in so far as staff are directed to them, and they must conform to national norms. Admission to higher levels of study depends very largely on ability and enthusiasm.

Educational costs and child maintenance

Educational services in the Soviet Union are in principle 'free' (in other words, funded from the state budget). As in so many other countries, this is of central importance to people on low incomes. The phrase 'in principle' is, however, significant, for certain facilities may have to be paid for. The strange duality of government policy in this sphere deserves a short digression.

Contrary to the overriding constitutional guarantees, payments have long been required for nursery and kindergarten attendance, and for maintenance at boarding schools. Attendance at the general school, and at full-time secondary special and higher educational institutions was subject to fees between 1940 and 1954. Government policy has, however, been partially protective of those most in need, and the fees charged have tended to assume token values as average incomes have risen.

As for pre-school institutions, the fees set in August, 1948 amounted to between 3 and 18 roubles per child, monthly, according to frequency of usage, type, and parental income. The average national wage was then only 44 roubles, so the charges were by no means nominal. But since poor parents, large families, widows who had lost their husbands in military action, and single mothers were entitled to reductions of up to half, the minimum rate could go down to as little as 1 rouble 50 kopecks. No change had been made in these rates up to 1982.[2]

Boarding schools were authorised to set fees which by the late fifties could reach a maximum of 54 roubles a month. The principle of payment in this case was particularly puzzling, in so far as the schools were required by law to give preference to orphans and children with difficult family circumstances. Perhaps the unannounced aim was to deter less responsible, or over-burdened parents from ridding themselves of tiresome progeny: the schools on the whole never had an attractive, 'upper-class' image. In this case, regulations approved in April 1957, and still apparently valid in the late seventies, allowed local authorities to admit up to a quarter of all pupils free, or at a reduction of 50%.[3]

The system of fees for instruction at levels above the seventh class of the general school, while it existed, ranged from 150 to 500 roubles a *year* according to the type of institution attended. The object here was more obvious – to generate funds for education at a time of increasing financial stringency, regardless of the social differentiation engendered. The introduction of fees coincided with the establishment of the low-grade vocational schools (the so-called 'State Labour Reserves') for children whose parents could not now afford to keep them in the general school. There were again special dispensations for orphans, needy children and poor students (who were normally entitled to maintenance grants anyway). All of the fee-paying arrangements, therefore, must have involved some degree of financial difficulty for people in the middle income ranges, i.e., those who did not benefit from the authorised reductions, and found the outgoings burdensome. A curious situation indeed, and one which may never be properly explained.

The need to maintain school-children and students at home, as it were, has prompted several kinds of state assistance. A law passed in August 1959 allowed individual schools to allot small sums of money, on an occasional basis, to poor families with children in the first to seventh classes. In June 1972 this practice was extended to cover the senior classes as well. The grants were intended for clothes and other needs, but no figures, as far as we are aware, have ever been published. School uniforms, costing as much as 40 roubles a year, still have to be bought privately. In July 1965 school-children in the RSFSR were released from the obligation to pay for their journeys to and from school, but ordinary fares were nominal anyway. Under the terms of a decree of July 1973, schools were authorised to provide dinners (costing about 35 kopecks each in the late seventies) free of charge, or at a 50% reduction, for an unspecified proportion of the pupils.

In November 1973 the principle of free use of text-books was at last established: before that parents usually had to buy their own. In addition, school-children had always benefited from social security payments to large or poor families and single mothers, as described in Chapter Five. Students of secondary special and higher educational institutions became eligible for state grants as early as 1919, and the system soon developed a 'means test' and 'fair progress' basis. In 1976, just over 70% of these students were assisted at the rates quoted in Chapter Two, while about 40% of all full-timers were resident at nominal charges in hostels.

There is little doubt, however, that state assistance of these types, though useful, leaves a majority of Soviet parents with economic problems all too familiar in the West. Similarly, the circumstances of Soviet reality make the upkeep of children more of a problem for the poor. The standard of living of the average Soviet family is modest: and casual jobs, which young people in the West may find with some ease, are not numerous in the Soviet economy. Small private shops and businesses, delivery and other services which may hire at the manager's discretion, are, of course, lacking. Much of the remaining demand for menial labour, especially baby-sitting, gardening and handiwork, seems to be taken up by pensioners. In any case, students are subject to other pressures. They are often expected to give up spare time for unpaid tasks – tidying up, decorating schools or public places, helping with the harvest, not to mention military service – all arranged by a variety of official organisations. Under the terms of successive polytechnisation drives school authorities may send pupils to local enterprises for 'practice' periods at nominal rates of pay. In this respect society is not especially supportive of young people who wish to earn extra money so as to continue their studies.

OPTIONS FOR YOUNGSTERS AT 15-PLUS

A choice of career becomes possible when youngsters complete eight classes of the general school, though under current provisions most of them are kept on for further courses of one kind or another. Ironically, this involves an extra burden for poor parents, and one which the state has failed to ease in any significant measure. The number who actually start work at fifteen plus is not revealed in the statistical handbooks, but other figures suggest that by 1980 at least one young person in six was doing so.

Most likely to leave school early would be young people from areas with less adequate educational facilities; those who could not cope academically; those who were weakly motivated; and finally, those whose parents simply could not afford to keep them on. Thus it is probable that the early leavers include an inordinately large proportion of poorer children.

Untrained fifteen-year-olds can hardly aspire to attractive employment in any industrialised labour market, and Soviet school-leavers are no exception. They could, firstly, take menial, unprestigious work with little or no prospect of advancement or training. The high proportion of unskilled jobs in the Soviet economy implies a continuing demand for entrants of this type. Secondly, such youngsters could take a job with a promise of 'production' training of a few months' duration directly at the workplace. The problem here is that such training tends to be superficial, and subject to the productive needs of the moment. Indeed, a sporadic debate over its viability has been going on for decades. A third option is to take any job available, but continue general schooling on a part-time basis, with the aim of enrolling in a full-time educational institution later.

Youngsters who stay on in school *after* the eighth class have four main options to choose from. Those who intend to study to degree level stay in the 'ordinary' ten-year schools, or in one of the several thousand 'special' schools which offer extra training in some subject, and better prospects of admission to a university or institute. Children with less academic ambition may switch to a 'secondary special' institution, and train as technicians and middle-grade staff of various kinds. Thirdly, a network of 'professional and technical' colleges (or PTU in the Soviet abbreviation) provides short-term, but structured, courses for school-leavers interested primarily in acquiring *manual* skills. These colleges may be subdivided into those which grant their trainees a school-leaving certificate, (needed for admission to a higher educational institution or VUZ later) and those which offer only certification of manual accomplishment. PTU courses last from one to four years, and trainees are directed into jobs of a manual, or low-grade white-collar variety. The fourth option involves taking a job under much the same conditions as were outlined for the 15-plus age group.

Each of these channels contains a mixture of people from different social strata, according to circumstances and location. But that there is a social 'sieving' effect has been shown by many sociological surveys. On the whole, the simpler or shorter the training, the more likely is it to be undertaken by youngsters from less skilled or less educated families. Moreover, renunciation of full-time education before the age of eighteen entails, for most young men, a period of two to four years' military service in the ranks. Degree students intersperse this training with their courses, and are normally commissioned after graduation.[4]

ACCESS TO HIGHER EDUCATION

Higher education is particularly important for personal advancement in the Soviet Union. The absence of a private sector in the economy, the lack of freedom of emigration, and absence of professional associations offering their own ratings, make the higher education institution (VUZ) almost the sole avenue for upward mobility. At the same time, all higher-grade posts have officially stipulated degree requirements. It is thus all the more regrettable that full-time study at advanced levels should have retained several built-in disadvantages for the poor.

The problem of maintenance, as at the lower levels, has never been adequately solved. Since grants are generally inadequate, full-time students have to rely on parental support, or take on full or part-time jobs, to make ends meet. We have already suggested that married students with children are a poverty group in their own right. Obviously, those whose families are unable to support them are most vulnerable to hardship.

The part-time sector, which tends to attract students from less favoured backgrounds, suffers from well-known short-comings. The quality of courses is often poor, and there is evidence that the qualifications received are rated lower by potential employers. The courses are as onerous as those in full-time establishments, yet extended by only one year. The array of day-release schemes is impressive, but they often entail wage reductions, and many young people prefer to study without taking advantage of them. The burden of work and study together can be almost unbearable, and it is not surprising that those who can possibly join full-time courses do so.[5]

Soviet higher and secondary special educational institutions tend to be stratified, as one would expect, in terms of appeal and quality. The better establishments require not only a good school-leaving certificate, but also higher marks in the competitive entry examinations. Over the years Soviet VUZy, and to some extent the secondary special institutions, have tended to become socially differentiated according to their size, academic status, and subject area. Obviously, candidates who had to contend with material deprivation while at school, or were obliged to study for entrance examinations whilst in full-time employment, stand a better chance of a place in the less demanding establishments. Soviet authorities are reticent about the student fall-out rate, but there is no doubt that it is higher not only amongst the less able students, but also amongst those with financial problems at home.

The authorities have made several attempts to counter disadvantages of this nature, and help working, or possibly older applicants. Protective quotas have been introduced into the VUZ annual intakes, preparatory courses have been set up (reminiscent of the so-called 'workers's faculties' of the 1920s) and enterprises have been allowed

to recommend their own candidates for VUZ places with some degree
of priority.

The measures have unquestionably helped many a young person
who would not otherwise have been able to continue his or her
education. But like so much other supportive legislation, this batch
has been limited in scope and only partially successful. The most
beneficial admission arrangements seem to be made for the less
attractive educational establishments – particularly pedagogical,
agricultural and technical institutes – which train students for lower-
paid jobs. Young workers directed to VUZy by their own enterprises
are expected to return after graduation, but may then be regarded
as second-class graduates, and expect only slow promotion. The so-
called 'worker-specialists' – young graduates who have chosen to
take skilled manual, rather than specialist jobs – are mentioned
with increasing, and in our view, ominous approval. The quota
arrangements are subject to abuse by students from more favoured
backgrounds who wish to improve their chances of admission,
and take short-term jobs merely for this purpose.[6]

It will be apparent from this short exposition that the educational
difficulties encountered by poor or disadvantaged people tend to be
cumulative. The fact that the Soviet education system has features
which favour the less privileged members of society, is in itself no
guarantee of equal educational opportunity as between rich and poor.
A slow start, or missed opportunity in early years may well mean
unattractive options later. Lack of a good school-leaving certificate at
17-plus, for example, significantly reduces the chances of admission
to a good, full-time VUZ, successful completion of the course, and a
more promising career at the end of it. Attempts to rectify such
imbalances have not proved very successful in the past, and it is
unlikely that they will become much more effective in the future.

POVERTY AND HEALTH

All human beings, regardless of their place in society, sometimes find
themselves in need of medical advice or assistance. The need first arises
when the child is still in its mother's womb, and ends with attempts
to prolong the life of the dying. As we well know, countless accidents
or illnesses may require skilled attention in the intervening years.

The more advanced a society in material terms, the better is it able to care for the health of its members. The questions which we shall ask at this point are firstly, how the health of the Soviet people at large compares with that of people in other lands: secondly, whether the poor in the Soviet Union are observably less healthy than other social groups: and lastly, how well the Soviet medical services meet their particular needs. The answers proposed will mostly take the form of careful generalisation, since the dearth of statistics makes it virtually impossible to isolate the health problems of any one social group.[7]

PATTERNS OF ILL-HEALTH

Soviet health standards are still demonstrably lower than those of advanced capitalist lands. The two measures usually taken for purposes of elementary comparison are life expectancy at birth, and infant mortality. In 1980 the US figures, characteristic of countries with a high standard of living, were respectively 74 years (averaged for both sexes) and 12 per thousand of all live births. The Soviet rates, by contrast, were 69 years and 28–30 per thousand. A more realistic Soviet infant mortality rate was in fact calculated at 35.6 per thousand for 1976, and there have been indications of an alarming rise since.[8] The incidence of six of the seven diseases for which the Soviet authorities do provide regular figures was also far higher than in the USA (Table 4.1).

It is probable that many easily-recognised elements in the life-style of the Soviet poor worsen their health indices, as against the national averages. In many parts of the country the deficiencies of fruit, vegetables and meat already described may cause nutritional im-balances and result in an unsatisfactory diet from which the poor are more likely to suffer. Poverty, it is true, may restrict alcohol consumption but the cultural pressures to drink are intense at all levels of society. In any case, the numerous social problems posed by drunkenness have a negative impact on health. Overcrowding and unhygienic housing conditions, especially in communal flats and hostels, must increase the likelihood of disease, pre- and post-natal complications, psychological stress, etc.

Manual, and low-skilled jobs, or employment in the less capitalised branches of the economy, are likely to involve less healthy surround-ings. Female employment, which is encouraged by low income, increases health hazards for both mother and child, and (regardless of state facilities) leaves a long-term problem of child care. The

Table 4.1. *Incidence of selected diseases, USSR and USA (1979) (cases
per 100,000 of the population)*[a]

	USSR	USA
Typhus and typhoid fever	6.0	0.74
Scarlet fever	87.0	206.75
Diphtheria	0.13	0.026
Whooping cough	5.0	0.71
Tetanus	0.11	0.036
Acute poliomyelitis	0.06	0.015
Measles	134.0	6.04

[a] The listing given here is the Soviet one: the US source contains 34 items. The categorisation may not correspond exactly in all cases.
Sources: Nar. khoz. 1980, p. 499; *SAUS*, 1981, pp. 5, 119.

necessity to continue work after reaching pensionable age may have a negative impact on the physical condition of the elderly. Rising, but unfulfilled material expectations, encouraged by wholly optimistic propaganda, may possibly evoke stresses which adversely affect the health of all age groups.

MEDICINE FOR THE PEOPLE

Soviet health care, like the educational system, is at first singularly well adapted to serving the poorer sections of the community. It is in principle free, and equally available to all citizens, regardless of income. This reflects not only the proclaimed humanitarianism of the Soviet system, but also the view that state medicine should promote efficiency at work.

The right to free attention is, indeed, of long-standing. Medical services were completely nationalised in July 1918, when the newly-established Peoples' Commissariat of Health was entrusted with the management and financial control of all medical establishments. Medical training passed to the Peoples' Commissariat of Enlightenment. The old medical 'unions' were abolished, and their personnel became employees of the new Soviet state. Private medicine, though not disallowed, was excluded from state institutions, and practitioners were denied use of state equipment. Their fees, if declared, were subject to heavy taxation. The law on social security of 31 October 1918 provided complete medical cover for those who worked 'without exploiting the labour of others', together with their dependants; the costs were to be borne by the enterprises and organisations where they worked.[9] Under the terms of the 1936 Constitution all citizens, (regardless of status) were guaranteed free medical assistance, and they have retained it ever since.

A second advantage of the system lies in its size. Generally, the smaller a medical system, the more socially exclusive are its services. In terms of medical personnel and hospital beds the USSR had by 1980 achieved very respectable levels. There were said to be 37.4 doctors of all specialities (including dentistry), and 124.9 hospital beds per 10,000 of the population. By contrast the USA, with a partially private, high-cost system, yielded figures of 21 doctors, 5.4 dentists, and 61 hospital beds.[10] In the USSR local town and district soviets, numbering some 5,800 in 1981, typically have their own health departments, concerned with the administration of local hospitals, clinics and public health in general. These facilities are supplemented, in the larger enterprises and organisations, by clinics for prophylactic medicine and the treatment of non-incapacitatory illness. Such clinics are the joint responsibility of the Ministry of Health and the ministry to which the given enterprise belongs.

Thirdly, the poor were likely to benefit, rather than otherwise, from a high degree of centralisation. All developments in the sphere of medical services – including the control and siting of medical centres, research, pharmaceutical supplies, and the provision of public services – have remained within ministerial purview. Doctors, dentists and other medical personnel may be posted to state-approved jobs any-where after they have completed their training. A mechanism therefore exists for the planned use of resources which could be particularly favourable to people in greatest need. Finally, mention needs to be made of the national network of sanitoria and rest-homes. Although all sojourns at these establishments, when not medically prescribed, have to be paid for, trade union organisations frequently subsidise the purchase of vouchers, and this practice may be of great benefit to the poor.

PROBLEMS FOR POOR PATIENTS

Yet despite all its advantages, state medicine is far from providing an ideal service. The first shortcoming lies in the generally inferior quality of treatment. Although Soviet medicine is apparently well advanced in a few respects, it lags far behind the USA and West Europe in the provision of up-to-date equipment and pharmaceuticals. This results in poorer clinical work, and reliance on quaint, antiquated treatments (like herbal medicine, mustard plasters and cupping glasses). The situation is exacerbated by the creaming-off of better facilities for the exclusive use of political and administrative elites. The best institutional clinics, for example, are known to serve prestigious party and state organisations, the security organs and military complex. Furthermore, as though in recognition of a more sophisticated need, the state has established public fee-paying clinics (of which nine were officially listed in Moscow in 1977). Persons who have no access to the privileged health sector must suffer indirectly from the diversion of staff and equipment into it.[11]

A further difficulty lies in unequal regional provision. Centralised though it is, the medical bureaucracy has to allow for some republican autonomy; and the republics are not always successful in serving their more remote or neglected areas. The variation in the supply of doctors, paramedics and hospital beds per 10,000 of the population, as reflected in the best and worst republican averages for 1980, is somewhat illustrative of this:[12]

Doctors	Georgia	46.7	Tadzhikistan	23.4
Paramedics	Latvia	115.9	Tadzhikistan	65.0
Hospital beds	Latvia	136.8	Armenia	83.4

The average figures conceal, of course, further internal differentials. Medical staff in general are notoriously reluctant to reside permanently in distant or uncongenial spots, once their three-year state postings have expired. Medical facilities are likely to be inferior precisely in locations where other factors might be expected to promote a higher incidence of poverty.

Medicines are available free of charge for in-patients, but out-patients must buy them at chemist's shops. Although the simpler ones are relatively cheap and easy to find, newer, or foreign-produced drugs are neither. Two varieties of penicillin on sale in 1983, for example, cost about 2 roubles for packets of 8 and 16 capsules respectively, which represented almost a day's earnings for a worker on a minimum wage. Even so, the drug was said to be virtually unobtainable in Moscow (implying even greater rarity in the provinces). Deficit medicines must be procured through friends, or by making gifts to potential suppliers.

The relatively low pay of medical staff, which we noted in another connection, inevitably has a negative impact on the service provided: even senior surgeons may have a formal salary of as little as 200 roubles a month. Isolation from invigorating advances in medical science abroad, and lack of opportunity for foreign travel, may further dampen professional enthusiasms. Although it would be rash to affirm that Soviet doctors are less moved by humanitarian considerations than their confreres in the West, or that they treat patients more peremptorily, they certainly have fewer material inducements to work well, and less technological back-up to ease their labours.

There is a correspondingly greater incentive to sell advice privately, whenever the constraints on working time permit. The private rates charged by practitioners vary according to their seniority and circumstance, but by 1982 were rarely less than 10 roubles for a consultation (in Moscow). Clearly, such personalised services are usually well beyond the reach of the poor.

Inside the hospital underhanded commercialism, another consequence of low staff salaries, may again place the poorer patient at a disadvantage. There is much evidence that inmates are in fact expected to pay for many nominally free services. Nurses, bed-changers, and cleaners may require tips for their services, and failure to respond may result in long and uncomfortable periods of waiting. Hospital rations are said to be budgeted at only 45 kopecks per patient per day, and the food is proverbially frugal. Patients who cannot rely on comestibles brought in by friends and relatives are at a considerable gastronomic disadvantage. Some major services, like operations, may require substantial gifts to surgeons and theatre staff. Since all of this is a matter of custom, rather than regulation, visibly poor patients may not be approached for payment; but they may also, in consequence, forego the best skills available.[13]

LEGAL AID FOR THE POOR

Involvement with the law is popularly regarded as a tedious matter, regardless of place or circumstance. There is no reason to believe that the Soviet poor think otherwise: yet occasions arise when they need legal advice or assistance, much as anyone else. The question we now address is the extent to which Soviet legal machinery is attuned to their use.

Soviet legal aid may be thought of as falling into three broad categories: advice about the law, representation in a court, or other legal action, and the registration of civil acts. The first two categories are performed by 'advocates', and the last by 'notaries public'. Strange though it may seem, Soviet citizens are expected to pay for many of these services. Costs are, however, moderate and may be waived in certain cases.[14]

Legal advice – explanation of the law, or of an individual's rights and duties before it – is proffered at legal centres in most Soviet towns. Moscow, for example, had over forty in 1977. If the matter is a small one, the citizen may merely call in, and speak to the advocate on duty: if it is more complex, requiring the perusal of documentation, one or more appointments may be necessary. No advocate's fees are payable if the consultation is short; if it concerns child maintenance payments; labour disputes or injuries; pension or similar rights; or a member's claim against a collective farm. Certain invalids and servicemen get free advice on all matters, while the director of the centre may waive payments for citizens in difficult material circumstances.

The cost of advice of this kind is in any case low. A complex consultation carries a standard fee of 1 rouble, while the formulation of statements and legal declarations (to include any preceding discussion), may cost 2 or 3 roubles. Notarial certification of documents relating to criminal offences, child maintenance, guardianship, youth protection, schooling and pensions are likewise free, while the charges for certification of civil contracts, wills and other agreements are nominal. Payments are always made at a cashier's desk, and not directly to the consultants concerned.

More substantial are advocates' charges for the defence of criminal cases or for civil representation in court. Criminal cases heard in the peoples' courts (the first instance), cost up to 25 roubles for one day, 40 roubles for three, and 10 roubles a day thereafter. The ceiling for exceptionally long and complex cases is 250 roubles. Fees in civil cases which do not involve property generally may go up to 15 roubles, while the ceiling for property cases is 30 roubles. The settlement of advocates' fees, when they are in dispute, or when the client is unable to pay, is a matter for the judge. If relatives will not help, payment may be effected by instalments from a civil litigant's wage packet, or a convict's prison earnings. Legal centres retain a proportion of fees paid for advocates' services to cover running costs.

It is evident from these comments that (except in complex court cases) poverty need be no bar to justice in the Soviet Union. The poor benefit from the complete statification of legal services (private practice outside the state system being altogether prohibited). At the same time, in individual cases, legal help might be readier, or more effective, if the advocate knows he can expect a present. Some well-known advocates, anyway, will agree to act only in better-paid cases outside their obligatory consultation hours.

One legal service which poor people may require (or have forced upon them) is, however, charged dear. The minimum cost of 'drying out' at a sobering-up station was recently 25 roubles; medical care or overnight accommodation could take the total up to 50 roubles. If the incident is brought to the notice of the inebriated person's employers, these fees, too, may be deducted from his wages.

CONSTRAINTS ON TIME USE

Categorising an individual's daily use of time is no easy matter, and measuring it is even more difficult. The problem of analysis increases when social parameters are brought into the equation. Nevertheless the topic is important and requires attention. For the purposes of this section we shall concern ourselves only with the use of 'free' time, taken to mean that which is left over after certain common daily functions, namely: sleep, meals, ablutions; daily travel to work, and work itself, have been excluded.

Of all the 'inbuilt' demands on the daily fund of hours, activities such as sleeping, eating, dressing, washing, etc., are least amenable to modification. The Soviet urban adult male, according to recent sociological surveys, required between 8 hours, 15 minutes, and 9 hours a day to effect them: his mate managed with half an hour less. It remains to be seen how far the march of science will permit further regulation and reduction. Working hours, by contrast, are delineated by law, and even if this is sometimes disregarded, Soviet workers and employees (but not peasants) are still in a fairly satisfactory position. By 1980, according to official sources, the average basic working week was 39 hours, 24 minutes, while most industrial workers did 40 hours, 36 minutes. Working time has, in fact, shown a tendency to fall since the labour reforms of the mid-fifties. Certain categories of workers – juveniles, persons employed in harmful environments, invalids, part-time students, and in some circumstances, women – have long been entitled to a shorter working day.[15]

Overtime, it would appear, is fairly limited, at least for most non-agricultural workers. Extra hours are not normally revealed in

Soviet labour statistics, but sociological studies have indicated rates of about two a week.[16] Our emigre survey results suggested that poor people in fact did less: work 'on the side' was not in most cases time-consuming either. It would seem, therefore, that the urban poor did not end up with significantly *less* free time than their richer neighbours.

The peasants' pattern of time use is considerably less favourable (although this is not a matter we can pursue in detail here). They enjoy neither state-approved limitations on working hours, nor, for that matter, a guaranteed holiday. Control of their labour is in the hands of the collective farm administration, and the depressed state of agriculture leaves little room for relaxation. The private plots (owned by virtually all peasants) have continued to be extremely demanding in terms of time-input.

The 'free' time which remains for the use of the average adult may be subdivided, for our purposes, into three categories. The first is time spent performing mundane, domestic tasks like running a home, shopping, looking after dependants, local travel, etc; the second is leisure time, to be enjoyed according to taste and circumstance. The third category which warrants separate consideration is the annual holiday.

Domestic and other chores

For the average Soviet citizen, domestic chores intermesh closely with other aspects of Soviet reality. On the one hand, some are known to be very time-consuming. Shopping is an arduous, daily operation, while warm-up and convenience foods are little in evidence. Sophisticated, time-saving equipment (like the micro-oven) is lacking, and the sharing of kitchen facilities usually takes extra time. On the other, people may be less demanding, and the housing shortage inevitably limits the burden of housework. An intense concern with the home, which characterises consumer societies in the West, is absent.

The time spent on tedious household chores has been studied less than leisure, but over the years a few revealing figures have been published. The average weekly input, as revealed by an investigation of life-styles in Taganrog in 1978, was (exclusive of child care) 26 hours, 25 minutes for women and 11 hours, 10 minutes for men. Figures available for rural localities are much higher, reflecting the fact that many country people live in small wooden houses without modern conveniences. They still need to carry water, get fuel for their stoves, clear snow, do their own major repairs, etc. These magnitudes seem to be fairly typical. Nevertheless, there is some evidence of a significant fall in such time use between the early sixties and late seventies, mainly as a consequence of improved consumer services.[17]

As for the poorer householders, several of the time-use budgets published in the late sixties indeed showed that low-paid, less skilled and less educated people carried a heavier domestic burden than others. A study conducted in a Moscow district indicated that the poorest families spent only a fifth as much money on state repair services as the most opulent, implying not only lower standards, but more personal labour at home. There was also evidence that the woman's burden increased relative to that of her partner as one moved down the socio-occupational scale. Discrepancies were, however, numerous, and we found no coherent analysis of the perceived imbalances.[18] Since then, evidence of further improvement is hard to come by, and judging from the figures available, the gap between the sexes has in general hardly narrowed.

The data from our emigre sample seems to confirm the maintenance of earlier patterns. Virtually all the women were involved in shopping and housework at an average rate of 21 hours a week. The time input for men in the same activities came out at only 12 hours. However, the two rates were not strictly comparable, in that whereas most women worked steadily, some men were heavily involved at weekends, and others not at all. In general the men who *did* participate spent just as much time as the women shopping, and about half as much time doing housework. Interestingly, less than half of the women entered a figure for child care, either because they had no small offspring to look after, or because they relied on the services of another member of the family. Husbands were much more likely to do this. Obviously, one should avoid too simplistic an interpretation of such differences: much would depend on the situation in any given family, particularly the presence of a helpful grandmother, and the nature of the housework involved.

Time spent on travel to and from work is akin to a domestic chore in that it is a necessary, but not particularly pleasurable, part of the daily round. In the larger Soviet towns commuting tends to be long. Cars are the prerogative of a very few, public transport tends to be inadequate, and housing shortages, or residence restrictions, may oblige people to live in surrounding villages. Commuting does not have social connotations which are tractable within the confines of this study. We do need to note, however, that poor people in general benefit from the system of nominal fares. Further concessions, up to free travel, are available for invalids, pensioners and school-children.

Some leisure patterns

Of all time uses outside the work-place, leisure has been most studied in the USSR. The reasons for this lie in its essentially positive nature (it is neither a physical necessity nor a chore) and in its apparent amenability to social engineering. The authorities attach considerable importance to their cultural policies, and proof of positive impact is sought precisely in popular leisure patterns. Successive studies reveal gradual increases in the amount of leisure time available, together with an ever more 'cultured' and 'active' use of it. At the same time higher skill levels, educational achievement, participation in production campaigns, and membership of the CPSU, are held to improve the leisure patterns of the people involved.

No Soviet study of poor people's leisure pursuits has ever, to our knowledge, been published. But some convincing evidence that workers in 'lower' occupational groups use their leisure in a less creative and satisfactory manner is yielded by a recent survey of some 1,400 mine-workers in the Donbass area in 1976. The questionnaire was formulated so as to permit comparison with another applied ten years previously.[19] Mine-workers were presumably chosen for investigation because they are held to be leaders of the Soviet working class, and exhibit many exemplary traits. They are certainly among the highest-paid manuals.

The author of the study, V. A. Chulanov, provided comparative breakdowns of leisure pursuits by education and skill group. True, there was no specific control for age or income (both of which might have explained some of the differences). The categorisation of activities was very generalised, and omitted drinking and other socially undesirable deeds, important and time consuming though they must have been. Yet if we cautiously assume that the age-mix was approximately similar in each of the groups compared, and that the better educated, and highly skilled were also the highest paid (which was likely), then the results may be taken to illustrate how leisure patterns change as one moves through a workers' occupational

Table 4.2. *Leisure use among Soviet miners (per week)*

	Highly skilled				Unskilled, Low skilled			
	1966		1976		1966		1976	
	hrs.	mins.	hrs.	mins.	hrs.	mins.	hrs.	mins.
Study and preparation for lessons	5	12	7	00	0	30	1	30
Social work	2	11	3	17	0	48	1	13
Art	0	13	4	49			1	05
Scientific and technical hobbies	1	10	2	47			0	20
Public shows	4	20	2	25	5	06	4	00
Radio and television	8	36	9	30	12	06	18	10
Reading	9	06	5	12	5	18	3	12
PT and sport	1	14	3	07	1	00	1	15
Rearing children	5	34	5	55	7	06	8	16
Relaxation and amusement	2	18	3	20	6	00	6	35
Other activities	3	00	4	28	3	12	3	48
Totals	42	54	51	50	41	6	49	24

Source: V. A. Chulanov, pp. 154–5.

hierarchy. Considerations of space prevent us from adducing all of Chulanov's tables, but his findings for the two extreme groups by skill-level are reproduced in Table 4.2.

The figures are interesting in many respects, but here we shall comment on three. Whereas the more skilled workers devoted considerable amounts of time to 'active' forms of leisure, such as study, reading, social work, artistic, scientific and technical hobbies, and sport, the least skilled spent considerably more on 'passive' past-times like public spectacles, radio, television, relaxation and amusement. Only in attention to children, which is an active pastime with very specific connotations, did the least skilled group outdo the most skilled. We may add that by and large the same distinctions were apparent in Chulanov's breakdown of leisure by educational level.

Observed change over time is another matter of interest. Between 1966 and 1976 the weekly fund of leisure enjoyed by workers in the sample increased by between eight and nine hours, with the highly skilled group gaining most. All patterns showed some improvement in the quality of leisure use, though this change may have been more apparent than real (effected, for example, by re-categorising 'reading' as 'study'). Apart from that, much of the *extra* leisure available to the unskilled was devoted to TV and radio, or undefined 'rest and amusement', rather than to more 'improving' pursuits. Finally, the configuration of the data makes it quite possible to argue that the differences in leisure use between skilled and unskilled have actually been growing over the years (witness reading, public spectacles, sport). This has long-term implications for the elimination of social differences in general.

The impact of such factors as party membership and involvement in production campaigns has been investigated in a number of other studies. We would not wish to pursue this intricate and often tedious topic here, but may note that such involvement is usually more frequent amongst people with higher skill and educational levels, which again implies more active leisure patterns. People in lower-grade occupations, as we shall see, join the party less often, and get less involved in production campaigns.[20]

Leisure in rural areas must of necessity differ considerably from that in the towns, if only because of dissimilar work requirements and fewer amenities. But here, too, socio-occupational groups diverge markedly. The figures adduced by V. S. Tapilina from studies conducted in the villages of the Novosibirsk Oblast in 1972 and 1977 (covering, it would appear, agricultural workers, but not collectivised peasants) speak for themselves (Table 4.3). 'Developed' and 'highly developed' forms of leisure were defined as the 'rational coordination of multiple interests, participation in the more complex forms of social activity (artistic and technical creation, social activities, self-education)'. 'Undeveloped', or 'poorly developed' leisure was, on the other hand, characterised by 'monotony, and paucity of means', and included 'family contact, amateur labour, interspersed with either non-active rest (sleep, 'not doing anything') or a narrow circle of amusements'. Tapilina affirmed, on the basis of these findings, that leisure pursuits 'fit' people's jobs, rather than serving as a compensatory, or levelling, factor between them: in her own phrase, 'as work, so leisure'.[21]

Leisure usage is not only a matter of time use, socially or culturally conditioned. Some activities, like attendance at theatres, cinemas and games, are open only to limited numbers, and in most countries, cost money. It remains for us to add a few words on Soviet practice in so far as it concerns the poor.

When such activities are highly commercialised and expensive, as often happens in the West, poor people avoid them, turning to free, or virtually free, pastimes, like radio, television and popular sports.

Table 4.3. *Distribution of rural occupational categories by type of leisure* (*Novosibirsk Oblast, 1977; percentage figures*)

Occupational groups	'Under-developed' 'Poorly developed'	'Average'	'Developed' and 'Well developed'
High-grade managers	4	29	67
Middle-grade managers	23	42	35
Specialists, high and middle-grade	9	46	45
Other white-collar staff	27	50	23
Workers	44	38	18
Unskilled workers, low-grade service staff	53	39	8

Source: T. I. Zaslavskaya, L. A. Khakhulina, p. 78.

However, it would seem that money is less of a barrier to attendance in the Soviet Union. What might be called 'ticketed' culture is normally subsidised and offered at nominal prices, while facilities belonging to trades unions, sporting and other organisations are free of charge to members. There is still a broad public interest in the cinema, which always has cheap tickets. Difficulties remain mostly with regard to admission to prestige spectacles, leading theatres, or facilities which have an administratively restricted clientele. Tickets for such events may have to be procured on the black market: scarcity, as usual, generates its own prices. There is no lack of evidence, however, that people low in the socio-occupational hierarchy are little attracted by the more demanding cultural fare. A widely-based study of RSFSR theatre attendance which we analysed a number of years ago showed that although tickets were cheap, workers were under-represented in the audience, (as compared with their weight in the population) by a factor of four, and not a single person admitted to the status of peasant.[22] At more sophisticated and technical levels, the known deficits of motor cars and boats; workshop, radio and hi-fi equipment; the difficulties of acquiring exotic pets, or of pursuing esoteric hobbies restrict such activities to the higher echelons of society.

Annual holidays

In capitalist society organising an 'annual' holiday is regarded as a
purely private matter, and the holiday sector is by and large left to
the attentions of commercial agencies. State or local authorities
intervene only indirectly, through the provision of general amenities,
leasing of buildings etc. Rarely do they offer organised holidays
themselves. The Soviet authorities, on the other hand, have long
concerned themselves not only with providing facilities, but also with
arranging holidays for large numbers of citizens. The major facilities
comprise some 13,000 state-owned institutions – rest homes, sanatoria,
and camps – which are controlled or administered by trade unions,
ministries and sports societies. In 1980 over 40 million people were
said to have been accommodated for holidays lasting more than two
days. Additionally, about 27 million children and young people stayed
in summer camps and other youth holiday centres.

Extensive though these efforts may appear, they presumably left a
huge potential demand. In the same year only a small proportion of
adults, perhaps one in four, could make use of state services for a
reasonable length of time (though about half of the 5–17 age group
were provided for). In these circumstances other would-be holiday-
makers – or some of them – must make do with private rooming
(which is legally tolerated), holidays with relatives, or less organised
camping and hiking. Ordinary hotel rooms, which might seem to offer
an obvious 'overflow' solution, are not necessarily expensive, but are
difficult to reserve without an official order.

Unfortunately, very little is published about the sociology of
holiday-making; it also appears to fall outside the compass of Soviet
time budget studies. Yet there is little doubt that access to holiday
facilities, as to so many other things, is socially much differentiated.
Generalisations on the extent to which the poor use them must be
attempted on the familiar nexus of cost, availability and
attractiveness.

Although the state institutions are funded from official sources,
they are not free; in fact, prices vary greatly. A voucher for board and
lodging at prestigious sanatoria, located in popular holiday areas like
the Caucasus or Black Sea coast, was in 1983 reported to cost nearly
300 roubles per person for a stay of one month. Ordinary sanatoria
cost 120–220 roubles, while rest homes charged 80–160 roubles.
Camping sites and similar centres usually charged a few roubles a

night. Fares in all cases would have been extra. This range would in itself suggest considerable hierarchisation of usage, in so far as a senior official would not normally choose a mediocre trade union rest home, while a low-paid worker or employee could not afford the best institutions. He might find, moreover, that places in them had been reserved for the management, or persons with labour awards. The cheaper and more frugal establishments are another matter. 'Putevki' or holiday vouchers for them are usually made available at the work place, through trade union committees. The more attractive vouchers are commonly much sought after, and indeed may be a focus of some tension. This subtle, but still uninvestigated, process operates rather to the disadvantage of the less privileged employees.

Their lot, however, is somewhat ameliorated by a system of subsidies. Regulations still in force in 1972 stipulated that 20% of vouchers for recuperative holidays, and 10% of those for rest homes, were to be issued free. A proportion of vouchers to rest homes is made available to trade union members (i.e., the overwhelming majority of the work-force) at 30% to 50% of the nominal cost: individual enterprises or unions may give further help if social funds permit: and the less popular holidays may be sold at a discount. Costs may, of course, be further reduced by shortening the stay. In 1980, according to official sources, some 13 million people had subsidised or free holidays of one kind or another. In addition, 10% of all vouchers for young pioneer camps were issued free, and the remainder sold below their formal price.[23]

In similar fashion, the poor derive some benefit from the government policy of low fares. This is important, since great distances separate many of the larger centres of population from the most valued recreation areas. A return air ticket from Leningrad to Sochi, for instance, covering an overall distance of some 2,000 miles, recently cost only 31 roubles and 50 kopecks, while the 'compartment' and 'common' class tickets on the train cost respectively 26 roubles and 17 roubles. Given the long distances, and poor roads, bus travel is less practicable.

Further indication of poor people's holiday arrangements, particularly what was done outside the state sector, may be gleaned from the responses to our emigre survey. This provided data on a possible total of 400 adult, and 495 child holidays, spread over two years. As for the adults, the patterns were remarkably consistent for married couples in any given year. Just over half of them went away, in the great majority of cases for two or three weeks. The cost varied greatly according to the type of holiday taken, but some three-quarters of those who went spent between 20 and 100 roubles per adult (including travel and pocket money). The cheaper holidays were obviously subsidised, or taken at someone else's expense. The most frequent type (taken by 36% of the holiday-makers) was in fact a stay with relatives or friends, though 25% went to rest-homes. Some 14% of the respondents rented private rooms. The latter practice cost up to 10 roubles a day, but sharing, or the negotiation of more favourable rates, could make it a viable option. Of the adults who did *not* go away during the two years in question, 60% gave lack of money as the main reason, and only 8% said they stayed at home voluntarily. Most of the remainder were deterred by family circumstances.

Regardless of their social status, most parents make a special effort to keep their children happy. Of all the possible child holidays yielded by the sample, we find that just under three-quarters were taken up. About 12% of the children could not go for family reasons, or did not want to, and about 12% were prevented by parental inability to pay. These holidays lasted mostly three or four weeks, at an average cost of 10 to 25 roubles. Over half of the children went to camps; 20% or so to relatives and friends; and a similar percentage shared private lodgings with adults.

It might be assumed that families poorer, or less responsible than those in the sample would have worse patterns. The mass of the peasantry, for example, was for decades too poor to contemplate anything like an organised 'holiday' anywhere, except possibly with relatives living in crowded conditions in the towns. They also had to contend with the seasonality of their work, and (until the early seventies) their virtual exclusion from the trade union movement. Possibly, their rising standards of living, and admission to union membership have since somewhat alleviated their position.

5

WORK AND SOCIAL SECURITY

———————— ⌖ ————————

For most people, satisfactory employment is central to personal well-being. While able-bodied, they expect their labours to ensure a reasonable standard of living (though things may not always work out that way). They also reckon to maintain, either from their own purse, or with state help, dependents who are unable to work. When they are old or ill, they may well believe that earlier contributions to family and society give them a moral right to adequate sustenance. It would appear that these principles are generally accepted in Soviet society.

The Soviet authorities, for their part, have always displayed a particular sensitivity towards labour, both because it lies at the heart of Marxist theory, and because it serves as a good instrument of social control. They also lay great stress on the excellence of state provisions for people who are unable to work. So it behoves us to consider, in a little more detail, the main relationships between labour, social security, and poverty in the Soviet context.

We shall examine, more specifically, the laws by which Soviet citizens are encouraged to maintain themselves, and their families, through honest labour: and the arrangements made to help those who, for various reasons, do not work, or work enough. No analysis of poverty in the USSR would be complete without some account of government intervention in this sphere.

WORK AS A RIGHT AND AS A DUTY

The Soviet Constitution of 1977 contains some far-reaching undertakings with regard to labour. Like the document which preceded it, it lays considerable emphasis on toil both for the good of society and the benefit of the toiler. According to Article 40, citizens have 'the right to work (that is, to guaranteed employment and pay in accordance with the quantity and quality of their labour, not below the state-established minimum)...' The formulation is firm and reassuring; but constitutional declarations are rarely what they appear to be, and we must ask how this one is implemented in practice.

The right to work implies, in the first place, protection against dismissal. The rules for dismissing workers and employees in the USSR are certainly explicit, and protective of their interests. Though short-term contracts are available for seasonal and temporary employment, most hiring is in this sense open-ended. Once a normal contract has been signed, a management can terminate it only on the basis of closure or staff reductions; revelation of the employee's unsuitability through lack of training or failing health; systematic failure to fulfil work obligations (after certain warnings have been given); drunkenness; long-term illness; the reappearance of a person formerly employed in a given post; and absence from work without good cause. Dismissals must normally be approved by a workers' council, and can be a subject of appeal in a court of law.[1] These provisions are supposed to be strictly supervised, and the management bears the onus of proving its case when they are disputed. Security of employment is possibly further enhanced by the fact that the closure of enterprises and organisations, or reduction of their staff, are a function of state planning, which may tolerate labour surpluses more easily than the market forces operative under capitalism.

The right to work, however, cannot possibly include an absolute guarantee of non-dismissal. In practice pretexts are not difficult to formulate, and the threat of dismissal, or transfer to a lower paid post (as a milder sanction) may be used to strengthen work discipline. The rule permitting dismissal as a result of absence from work contains no provision for other, less serious, forms of punishment, while a USSR Supreme Court ruling of 26 September 1967 actually gave managements the right to dismiss an employee for a *single* infraction of this kind.[2] One finds, indeed, when talking to Soviet workmen, that the ability of the management to sack them, if need be, is simply taken for granted. Drunkenness, which carries penalties of its own, is often mentioned in this connection.

A judgment on the frequency of dismissals or demotions is difficult to reach, as no comprehensive figures are published. Common wisdom suggests general observance of the constitutional declaration. Provided an individual works well, does as he is told, and avoids controversy, he enjoys a fair level of job security.[3] As for the poor, dismissal was hardly known among the families covered by our survey. It may be that since poor workers are less able to sustain income loss, they hold on to their jobs more firmly: or that managements find it harder to fill lower-paid jobs, and act more leniently towards those who do them.

Ironically the constitutional guarantee of employment serves to justify one of the most startling gaps in the Soviet social security system, namely the absence of unemployment benefit. As we indicated in Chapter Two, unemployment has its place in Soviet reality, so there is no need to reiterate the argument here. The present policy was launched on 9 October 1930, when the People's Commissariat of Labour published its decree 'On the Immediate Placement of the Unemployed and the Cessation of Unemployment Insurance'. The title of the document accurately described its content.[4] Despite innumerable changes in the labour market over subsequent years, the authorities have never admitted that unemployment exists, nor reinstated the benefit. Possibly the closest approach to a recognition of need among people who lose their jobs is the statutory issue of two weeks' severance pay and the availability of a retraining allowance. The latter, however, is restricted to those who need to master new technology, usually in the same enterprise, or are unable to keep their job for medical reasons. It is payable at the rate of former earnings over the three-month period normally considered adequate for redeployment.[5]

Labour is defined by the Soviet Constitution not only as a right. 'It is the duty of, and a matter of honour for, every able-bodied citizen of the USSR to work conscientiously in his chosen, socially useful occupation, and strictly to observe labour discipline' states Article 60. 'Evasion of socially useful work is incompatible with the principles of socialist society...' Children, according to Article 66, must be 'train[ed] for socially useful work, and rais[ed] as worthy members of socialist society...'

The definition of work as a constitutional *duty* permeates Soviet labour law, and underpins ubiquitous references to 'discipline'. (The Russian term, *ditsiplina*, which has the same connotations as the English, is used for the purpose.) The standard Soviet 'work rules', for example, place considerable emphasis on the need for strict observance of it. Workers and employees are required to 'work honestly and conscientiously...observe labour discipline...arrive punctually, observe working hours, use all of these hours for productive labour, carry out the instructions of the management promptly and accurately...'[6] The wording leaves no doubt about the level of official expectations, and reveals, incidentally, a clear difference between Soviet and capitalist concepts of relationships at the workplace. Few Western trade unions would consent to so rigorous a formulation. The constitutional definition is also used to justify 'work input' rather than 'proven need' as a basis for assessing most social security payments, a matter to which we shall return in a moment.

The emphasis on discipline has varied with the views of the leadership and economic circumstance. The industrialisation of the thirties involved the introduction not only of the workbook, a kind of labour passport, but also of a series of sanctions, from reprimand to dismissal and imprisonment, for such misdemeanours as arriving twenty minutes late, leaving early, or loafing on the job. Labour protection was in many respects reduced and output norms raised. Between 1940 and 1956 workers and employees lost the right to change jobs without the consent of their managements.[7] With his enforced induction into the collective farm, the peasant soon lost virtually all possibility of job choice. Laws passed in the thirties and forties subjected him to what amounted to forced labour in the public sector, on a residual wage, and with stringent punishment for labour violation. Pressures were considerably eased on worker and peasant alike during the liberalisation of the mid-fifties, and although 'efficiency' remained a constant theme, under both Khrushchev and Brezhnev, there was no return to the draconian measures of Stalinism. But the constitutional requirements are still there to be invoked: the collective farm rules remained oppressive; and laws passed during the brief advent to power of Yuri Andropov gave clear indications that a return to the rigours of earlier days was not beyond the bounds of possibility.

WORK AS SOMETHING BEST AVOIDED

Every society, however regimented and dedicated, contains able-bodied people who prefer, for one reason or another, not to work. Since Soviet society is composed of normal human beings, it has its share of them. We may safely presume that they include the genuinely work-weary; the disillusioned; people psychologically incapable of effort; layabouts, young and old; those who take a conscious decision, for good reason or bad, to manage without a job, sporadically or permanently; and some types of criminal. Having chosen to forfeit the benefit of an income from regular employment, they comprise, in a sense, a 'voluntary poor'. We cannot estimate how many there are. But in a society where work is both a right and a duty, we must at least ask how they cope. One can postulate for them two on-going problems: daily sustenance, and the avoidance of prosecution.

As we have seen, the only regular income which Soviet citizens may receive must be legally earned, or emanate from officially-approved sources. Non-state earnings which are tolerated (but only when declared and taxed) include the return from one's own labour, provided as a personal service or by contract (most domestic workers, tutors, doctors in private practice, and creative artists are in this category); part-time and seasonal employment, particularly in agriculture; and the income from private garden plots, or home work-shops (producing mostly simply artifacts and folk art).

There are, in addition, a few types of income which are legal, but do not involve regular employment. Living space may be let for gain, but the 60 square-metre limit on most dwellings, the prohibition on the ownership of second houses, and heavy taxation of declared rents do not encourage the practice. Interest may be earned on savings accounts, though this can amount to no more than 2–3% a year on capital. Rich parents may support adult children over a period of time, though the number in a position to do so is certainly tiny. Wealth may be inherited with comparative ease, as 'death duties' are normally no more than 10%, and there is no law preventing a beneficiary from realising an inheritance little by little. But since the means of accumulating wealth are limited, and accumulation usually requires many years, few people can be in a position to benefit from such a practice. Royalties for artistic work of most kinds are payable to direct descendants of the creator for a maximum of fifteen years. In any case, dependence on unearned income would show up as gaps in an individual's work record, as noted in his work book, and endanger pension rights in later life.

Living without a regular state income may also imply an existence of dubious legality. The authorities have always evinced profound disapproval of personal reluctance to work for the state, and this was reflected, particularly under Stalin, in a long series of unpleasant (and often unfair) sanctions against work-dodging.[8] True, the Khrushchev legislation of the mid-fifties removed the most oppressive of them, but it continued to discriminate against persons fully and voluntarily unemployed. As early as 1954 Khrushchev personally began a press campaign against school-leavers who did not want 'dirty' manual jobs – the so-called 'white hands' – and used the phenomenon as a major argument for educational reform. He encouraged efforts to keep young villagers at work on the farm, and to improve job-placement procedures for young people generally.

By the early sixties the drive developed a more ominous character. On 4 May 1961 the Supreme Soviet of the RSFSR passed an edict entitled 'On intensifying the struggle with persons who refrain from socially useful labour and lead an anti-social parasitic way of life.' Similar measures were soon introduced in other republics. Refraining from 'socially useful' labour was now defined as 'parasitism', and categorised with such misdemeanours as illegal employment, 'speculation' (buying and selling for personal profit), begging, the use of private transport for personal gain, the unregistered renting out of living space. A legal dictionary published in 1965 added 'living at the expense of relatives, obtaining unearned income from garden plots or privately-owned buildings, drawing a high wage for an insignificant amount of work...enrichment at the expense of superstitious people (for example, fortune-telling) and so on'. Punishments ranged from a public warning to exile for between two and five years, with obligatory labour and the confiscation of goods obtained 'without the application of labour'. Exile could be ordered not only by a local court; incredible though it may seem, public meetings and the extra-legal 'comradely courts' (whose decision required only confirmation by the local soviet) were also granted this power.[9]

The main 'Brezhnev' contribution to the campaign was a much-publicized decree of 23 February 1970. Noting that refusal on the part of 'individual citizens' to participate in socially useful labour, together with parasitism, drunkenness and amoral behaviour, were becoming ever more intolerable, the enactment enjoined local authorities 'to ensure the systematic and rapid discovery of persons who refrain from socially useful labour, and ensure that they are put to work...' The Central Statistical Administration, Gosplan, the Ministry of Internal Affairs, local employment committees, and other offices were ordered to keep count of able-bodied persons not actually employed, and investigate the reasons for their inactivity. The administrative organs (i.e., police) were to apply the power of the law more decisively against 'malicious parasites', and assist local authorities in finding employment for them and re-educating them. Extra powers of detention were granted for the purpose.[10] Although the February decree contained no reference to other legislation, a 1980 commentary indicated that the measure was regarded as dependent on an old article of the RSFSR Penal Code (No. 209) which covered persistent vagrancy and begging. These activities carried a maximum penalty of two years' hard labour. Under Andropov, who headed the CPSU from February 1982 until his death in November 1984, pressures not only on loafers, but also on employees who 'slacked' on the job, were considerably increased.[11]

It is clear that such laws could scarcely be implemented in a pluralistic society. They function in the Soviet Union thanks to the existence of the internal passport system, the necessity for urban dwellers to register their place of residence with the militia or a housing office, and the lack of privacy in communal housing. Long-term concealment of voluntary unemployment is correspondingly more difficult. The number of would-be 'loafers' who were prepared to face the difficulties raised by so hostile a world can only be a matter of conjecture: but the severity of the laws themselves indicates a significant social problem.

The relationship between poverty and crime, in a more general sense, is shrouded in secrecy. Discussion of it, let alone statistical correlation, seems to be virtually excluded from Soviet sources, in contrast to crime and drunkenness, which are referred to frequently. Given the nature of the evils, this practice needs no explanation.

Such indications as are available, however, show a pattern familiar in 'bourgeois' society. An analysis of a large body of crime and labour statistics referred to in the spring 1983 issue of the journal *Sotsiologicheskie issledovaniya* demonstrated, it would seem, that persons with unskilled, unmechanised, and relatively undemanding jobs were far more likely to indulge in criminal activity. The poorly paid also appear to attach more importance to high earnings. Soviet analysts usually attribute crime to such factors as unsatisfactory family circumstances, alcoholism, and failures of local administration.[12]

INABILITY TO WORK AND SOCIAL SECURITY

We now turn to the matter of the assistance which the state offers to persons who are, for one reason or another, incapable of earning a normal wage. The technical intricacies of the Soviet social security system lie beyond the scope of our study, but we do need to review its principles and the main changes effected in it during the Brezhnev years, because these changes were important for large numbers of the poor. In the account that follows we do no more than consider the most general provisions, in non-technical language, eschewing the legal formulations and detail of the official texts.

The system is unitary in the sense that it covers, in one form or another, all Soviet citizens, leaving no place for private schemes such as exist in the West. Since it is also non-contributory and (when possible) service-linked, the individual employee cannot easily influence the size of his entitlement, other than through his work record. The recipients of benefits fall into five broad, and sometimes overlapping, categories, namely: the aged, the disabled, surviving dependents, women who are pregnant or need assistance for family reasons, and minors who lack proper guardianship. We shall have something to say about all of these categories.

Old-age pensions

Any discussion of Soviet social security should begin with old age pensions. Not only did these pensions take up the greater part of social security funding, but the modifications they underwent reflected government thinking on state maintenance in general. We shall comment primarily on eligibility and minimal payments, since these are the matters most relevant to persons in poverty.

The Khrushchev pension law of July, 1956 is as good a starting point as any for analysis. It effected major improvements in regulations going back to 1928, while retaining certain central principles.[13] Thus it stipulated that old-age pensions were payable as a right to 'workers and employees', and also to servicemen, until death ensued. (The peasantry, it will be noted, were not mentioned at this point.) Eligibility for a full pension started at the age of sixty for men, providing they had not less than twenty-five years of service behind them, and fifty-five for women, after twenty years of service. These starting ages were, by international standards, relatively low. A

minimum of five years' service, including three uninterrupted, immediately before retirement, was set as an additional condition of
eligibility for a 'full' pension. Any shortfall in the regulatory service
provisions brought a partial pension with a proportional reduction in
the rates payable. Persons formerly receiving certain other types of
pension had the right to switch to an old age pension if they thought
it beneficial to do so.

The rate of full pensions varied, with some exceptions, from 100%
of the lowest wage bracket to 50% of the highest, with a normal
maximum of 120 roubles. An applicant was allowed to propose the
years when he earned most, so as to obtain for himself the most
advantageous rate possible. No Soviet pension, incidentally, was
subject to income tax (though most would have fallen below the tax
threshold anyway). Lower starting ages, or augmentations were
available for people in onerous jobs; working invalids; mothers of large
families; persons with outstanding work records, and a few others.
There were supplements of 10% for one dependent, and 15% for two
or more. Rates for workers and employees living in rural areas and
involved in agriculture were, however, 15% below the urban norms.
A separate, but similar system of 'long-service', rather than 'old age'
pensions was retained for military, academic, teaching and medical
personnel. Applications for entitlement were normally handled by
commissions attached to the social security departments of local
soviets.

The tie between pension rights and regular employment in a state
(or cooperative) organisation naturally posed a problem for persons
whose work record was interrupted or incomplete. The pension then
payable was commensurate with the years of service, subject to a
minimum pension of *one-quarter* of the full rate. The least fortunate
pensioners could therefore receive a rate as low as 11 roubles and 25
kopecks.[14] The Soviet authorities have never recognised the concept
of 'national assistance ', i.e., maintenance payments based solely on
assessed need, so inadequate pensions could not be supplemented by
this means. A minority of housewives, mothers and persons with
unusual career patterns who might not ever have had a formal job,
and seemed likely to fall in this category, clearly had an interest in
justifying their lack of state-employed status by medical or family
circumstances, so as to qualify for payments of other types. Able-bodied
people who earned a living by private practice, contractual work, or

other marginal activity were generally left outside the provisions of the state system.

The main changes in the provision of pensions between 1956 and 1979 contained a mixture of positive and negative features. Under the 1956 law the minimum pension was set at 30 roubles a month, which more or less equalled the September 1956 minimum rates of pay for workers and employees (i.e., 27–35 post-1961 roubles, depending on type of work and locality). This minimum remained in force until June 1971, when it was suddenly hoisted to 45 roubles. So great an elevation was to be welcomed, as it betokened a big improvement in the living standards of the poorest pensioners. At the same time it posed two questions, which, as far as we are aware, have never been properly answered. The first was why the rise was so abrupt, after fifteen years without change. It would surely have been fairer to increase the rate gradually, as funds became available. Secondly, the new minimum was now significantly below the current minimum wage of 70 roubles, which cast grave doubt on its adequacy.

The 45-rouble minimum itself lasted a decade, being raised only in January 1981 to a modest 50 roubles. In relative terms it had fallen from 36% to 26% of the average wage over a decade, still leaving the urban pensioner with an income slightly below the old, 1967 family-based poverty threshold. Given the Brezhnev leadership's much-publicised concern with living standards, its record in so malleable a matter was most disappointing.

Furthermore, the standard provisions concerning length of service, and the percentages of pensions payable for dependents, remained unchanged. A new pension law promulgated in August 1972 was designed more to systematise post-1956 rulings than to effect significant improvements. The most noteworthy changes effected subsequently (in February 1976 and June 1977) involved raising maximum pensions to 140–160 roubles for some personnel in the more arduous sectors of mining and metallurgy.

Over-age employment, which was actively encouraged by the Brezhnev leadership, could be either on a full or part-time basis. The 1956 pension law had not forbidden this, but stipulated a much reduced pension of 15 roubles for those (the great majority) who earned up to 100 roubles a month, and no pension at all for those who got more. The result had been a sharp fall in the number of working pensioners and, presumably, an increase in poverty among old people.

A series of measures passed between 1963 and 1979 eased these restrictions. The decree of September 1979 which brought most of the new rules together, allowed over-aged workers in production, trade and the service industries to draw between 50% and 100% of their normal pension on top of their salary. Most pensions payable subsequently, on cessation of employment, were subject to a ceiling of 150 roubles a month, though war invalids were more favoured. In addition, rules were introduced under which each extra year worked *without* a pension brought an augmentation of the pension, when paid, of 10 roubles, up to a maximum of 40 roubles. Pensioners who wanted to go on working thus had the choice of earnings supplemented by a partial pension, followed by a full pension on retirement; or earnings without a pension, followed by an augmented pension on retirement.[15]

The scheme, as we saw in Chapter Two, proved exceedingly popular, and was taken up by several million people. Its introduction can be most readily explained, from the point of view of the authorities, by the increased number of people in the upper age groups, continuing labour shortages, and need to control a rising pension bill. The policy also justified, albeit indirectly, the low minima we have just examined.

The peasants require a separate commentary. For three decades after the establishment of the collective farm there was no other institution they could turn to for support in old age. The relevant regulation in the 1935 Model Statute stated that the farm should, 'in accordance with the decision of the general meeting, create funds to assist disabled, old or sick people, and the poor families of the Red Army soldiers, and to support crèches and orphans'.[16]

These funds, however, were not to exceed 2% of total annual production; and since most farms had many old people in their labour force, and were almost permanently bankrupt anyway, real help was usually out of the question. The fact that the peasant was expected to feed (through taxation and obligatory deliveries) the state-insured worker, was one of the worst ironies of Soviet reality. In general, elderly farm members had to live off their private plots, or rely on the generosity of relatives and friends.

Although much was done to ease pressures on the peasants and improve their living standards after the death of Stalin, Khrushchev showed a curious reluctance to move on pensions. A scheme for peasants was announced only in the summer of 1964, a few months before he fell, and a central pension fund was established for their benefit on 1 January 1965. The coverage it provided was still inferior to that enjoyed by workers and employees. The 'length-of-service' requirements were the same, but men became eligible only at 65, and women at 60. The range of payments was 12 to 102 roubles, entitlement being calculated at 50% of former earnings up to 50 roubles, and 25% of the remainder. There is little doubt that the modest income of most collective farm members, and their known reluctance to work in the communal sector, kept average pensions close to the bottom of the scale.

The Brezhnev years brought a series of improvements. In 1967 the ages of eligibility were lowered to match those of workers and employees: mainly as a result of this, and the ageing of the collective farm population, the number of pensioners rose from 7 million initially to 10 million by 1980. In June 1971 the minimum pension was raised to 20 roubles and the maximum to 120 roubles. More flexibility was introduced into the provisions for determining individual rates; collective farm personnel resident in the less hospitable parts of the country were given the favourable conditions of eligibility and rates hitherto reserved for state personnel in the same areas. In July 1978 the peasant minimum pension was raised again to 28 roubles. All these improvements obviously alleviated the hardships faced by the elderly in the farms, but still left them significantly worse off than workers. The unspoken supposition was that village society, being more cohesive than urban society, would provide the extra support needed, and that the elderly would continue to live off their private plots. The Bolsheviks' long-standing distrust of the rustic toiler had cast a long shadow.

The provision of old-age pensions for persons – workers, employees and peasants – hitherto unreached by any pension scheme was one of the positive features of the decade. We have noted that this unhappy contingent evidently fell from about 2 million in 1970 to a matter of thousands in 1980. It is unlikely that the system of old-age pensions, given its long-term inflexibilities, will be extended to the most marginal categories of need in the foreseeable future.

The system as it developed in the seventies was admirable in that it envisaged relatively low retirement ages, and the retention of a high proportion of former earnings. The main reason for its failure to remove the fear of poverty amongst the aged lay in the exceptionally modest minima, the dependence of pension rights on the recipient's previous earnings, and the generally low level of those earnings. Had the government willed it, the system could have been improved much more quickly, and been made more supportive of old people in distress, regardless of how they had spent their younger days.

Disability and survivor pensions

Disablement and survivor pensions bear many similarities to old-age pensions, though the complexity of the rules for issuance, and the lack of detailed figures, make analysis even more difficult. Between 1966 and 1980 the number of persons receiving non-retirement pensions throughout the country remained approximately stable, at about 16 million. Some 7.6 million of these (to judge from a note on the 1979 Population Census returns) still derived their *main* income from other sources, presumably full or partial employment.[17] No proper statistical breakdown of these large contingents has, to our knowledge, been made available.

The 1956 law on state pensions confirmed that all Soviet citizens in the working age groups had the right to maintenance in the event of *illness* or *disability*.[18] Long-term disability (which is all we shall consider here) was categorised according to severity (from 'total' in group one to 'partial' in group three), and also according to origin (i.e., work-related or personal). Pension entitlement for the first group, when the injury was sustained at work, was set at 100% of wages up to the first 50 roubles, plus 10% of the remainder, within overall limits of 36 to 120 roubles. Pensions for the other groups of work-related injury were set within limits of 29–90 roubles and 21–45 roubles respectively. Persons who were incapacitated from childhood, or for reasons unconnected with their employment, had somewhat lower rates, ranging from 30–90 roubles in group one down to 16–40 roubles in group three. Dependents brought the same augmentation as with old-age pensions – 10% for one, and 15% for two or more – but only with regard to invalids in the first two groups. The recipients of lesser disability pensions were expected to supplement them by earned income whenever possible.

The system was not ungenerous insofar as the minimum rates for a fully incapacitated person equalled or surpassed the national minimum wage. Yet it contained four sad disadvantages. Firstly, the minima were still exceedingly low in absolute terms. Secondly, pensions for work-related disability again depended on the length of service, and payments in some circumstances could go down to a quarter of the full rate. Thirdly, persons in the second and third groups could have their entitlement reduced if their wage from a subsequent job, combined with their pension, raised their total income above what they earned before disablement. Finally, these benefits, like old-age pensions, lacked a mechanism to provide rises in the rates of existing pensions as the years went by.

The pattern of development here roughly paralleled that of old-age pensions. The principles of eligibility remained unchanged for most categories of workers and employees, but the amounts payable were significantly increased in December 1964 and November 1973. The latter improvements, which were valid until 1981, brought the minima up to 70 roubles for group one, 45 roubles for group two (both work-related and otherwise), and 25 or 21 roubles respectively for group three. The 'best' minimum therefore continued to equal the state minimum wage. Amongst other detailed changes was the payment of 15 roubles a month to group one recipients for home help.

Special efforts were made to improve the lot of military and certain other categories of personnel invalided in the Second World War. In May 1970 they were promised better housing, cheap tickets on rail and river transport, priority in using sanatoria, and in some cases even free motor cars. A law of November 1973 provided special minimal pensions (no less than 90, 70 and 33 roubles for work-related disablement, 70, 45 and 21 roubles otherwise), a little more money – up to 20 roubles a month – for home help, and improved rates for dependents. In April 1975, on the 30th anniversary of Soviet victory in the Second World War, they were afforded a 50% reduction in housing costs, free medicines (medical care being free anyway), free local transport (except in taxis), and a new 300–rouble maximum for earnings and pensions together. Benefits for their survivors were also slightly improved.[19] These policies may be explained either as an instance of concern for ageing veterans, or a spin-off from increasing militarisation.

The peasants once more had their own regulations. The 1935 Collective Farm statute lacks specific reference to this matter, the implication being that the sick and disabled, like the aged, were to be maintained from the farm's own resources. The 1964 regulations on state pensions introduced coverage closely resembling that enjoyed by disabled workers and employees. However, benefits were payable only to peasants in the first two disability groups, and the rates were much lower. The minima ranged from only 12 to 18 roubles, according to category of disablement. Judged against the current minimum wage of 60 roubles these sums were, of course, little more than nominal. There was no provision for supplementation in the case of dependents.[20]

Gradually, improvements took place. In September 1967 the minimal rates were raised, and pensions were introduced for 'group three' invalids, with a minimum of 12 roubles. There were further improvements in June 1971 and July 1978, by which time the minima rose to 45, 28 and 16 roubles respectively. Disabled peasants were by this time entitled to the same maxima as workers and employees resident in rural areas.[21]

Under the terms of the 1956 pension law for workers and employees, *survivors* were generally defined as persons immediately related to, and entirely dependent upon, a deceased and pensionable individual, the definition of 'death' being supplemented by 'proven disappearance'. There were three main categories of survivors: (1) children up to the age of 16 (or 18 if they were still at school); (2) a surviving husband, wife, mother or father when they became of pensionable age, or if they had to look after a child less than eight years of age; and (3) a grandmother or grandfather, if they were left without means of sustenance. Children who lost one of two working parents could also benefit, even if the second parent continued to work; those left without anyone at all were considered to be entirely orphaned, and eligible for full state maintenance.

It will be evident that this categorisation left an awkward gap. Adult survivors who had *not* reached pensionable age, and had *no* young children to look after, were quite without cover. Clearly such adults – among them many housebound mothers with children over eight – were expected to find employment in an expeditious manner. The 'survivor pension' system was evidently designed to encourage active employment for all able-bodied adults, even though this could entail hardship in some cases.

The size of pensions depended on many factors, but basically, there were three levels, covering respectively one, two, and three or more dependents. The 1956 minima were 16, 23 and 30 roubles respectively.[22] The low minimum payments and the 'three or more' formulation obviously implied great difficulty for the larger families. Survivors reaching retirement age had a strong incentive to switch to an old-age pension, if their work-record entitled them to do so. The system remained stable throughout the seventies, and there occurred only two kinds of modifications of concern to us here.

The first involved the levels of payment. As with other pensions, the minima were raised twice, in December 1964 and in November 1973. By 1973 they had reached 23–70 roubles, and that is where they stayed until late in 1981. Interestingly, the maximum rate payable for dependents – a total of 120 roubles – remained unchanged for nearly a quarter of a century. The rates for survivors of military personnel were a few roubles higher. On the whole, the minimum rates of survivor pensions were raised more than those of the disability pensions; but an only child could still receive as little as 23 roubles a month, and would have required help from elsewhere to raise his income to a realistic subsistence level. Even a child on the *maximum* rate received only 40 roubles.

The other principal modification, effected in 1964, was the extension of such pensions to the peasantry. The categorisation of 'survivors' was the same as for workers and employees, and the rates were likewise dependent on former earnings. The minima, however, were set at 9, 12 and 15 roubles a month for one to three or more persons. Such miserable sums suggest that the authorities wished to introduce the principle of payment without facing the financial implications of practice. Improvements did, however, follow, and by July 1978 the minima were 20, 28 and 45 roubles. The maximum rates were again the same as for survivors of workers and employees resident in rural areas.

Family allowances, child and other benefits

The best known payments of this type are doubtless the monthly child allowances for mothers with large families – defined as four or more offspring. The system has remained largely unchanged since its establishment in November 1947.[23] The rules, as valid in December 1979, stipulated that the allowance first became payable when the eligible child was one year old, and ceased on his fifth birthday. Rates ranged from 4 roubles a month for the fourth child to 15 roubles for the eleventh and any others. Mothers of five or more children who reared them to the age of eight could claim earlier receipt of an old-age pension. The production and successful rearing of ten children brought the honoured title of 'Heroine Mother'; instituted in July 1944, this has always entitled the bearer to extra pension, accommodation, and other benefits. Lesser degrees of reproductive prowess (from the fifth child up) are marked by the 'Order of Maternal Glory' and the 'Maternity Medal'. All 'large family' payments are made regardless of income.

These benefits seem to be consistently the lowest of any provided by the Soviet state. Four roubles is a dismal starting point, especially when judged against the wage levels of the seventies: supplements of one rouble for each successive child are laughable. It is not easy, given the steady, if modest, improvements in the pension system, to explain such unrelenting stinginess. No official explanation has (to our knowledge) been proffered. Possibly the decision-makers thought improvement unnecessary in view of other developments (which we shall discuss in a moment) and the more general rises in state maintenance programmes.

The long-standing policy of strengthening family bonds included help for unmarried mothers. Under the 1947 law just mentioned unmarried mothers were entitled to monthly grants for each child up to the age of twelve. The payments were again very low – 5 roubles a month for one child, 7 roubles 50 kopecks for two, and 10 roubles for three or more. In this case, too, the same sums were still being paid in 1980. Single mothers were, however, entitled to have their children maintained free in a state home, should they have so desired, and got a 50% reduction in kindergarten charges if their monthly income was below 60 roubles.[24]

It was, perhaps, the almost nominal character of these payments which prompted the introduction, in 1974, of a separate system of child allowances specifically for low-income families. On 25 September of that year, in accordance with the Directives of the 24th Party Congress, families whose average monthly income was 50 roubles per head or less were given the right to draw 12 roubles a month for each child up to the age of eight.[25] The new law embraced not only families of workers and employees, but also those of peasants and military personnel. According to regulations published subsequently, entitlement to the benefit was interpreted in a relatively broad way, provided that at least one adult was already eligible for social security, though most kinds of income, over and above the basic wage or salary, had to be taken into account. Applications and payments were normally channelled through the enterprise or organisation where the applicant worked.

No provisions were made for reduced payments – it was either 12 roubles per child or nothing – and applications had to be renewed annually. The authorities apparently decided that greater flexibility would be administratively impracticable, and that the resulting anomalies should be ignored. As we indicated in Chapter One, the introduction of this measure was one of the clearest ever official indications that poverty was still a widespread problem.

The long-standing system of maternity benefits and birth grants also underwent some development. A law of March 1956 envisaged, basically, 112 days of maternity leave for mothers employed in the state sector, including 56 days before the anticipated birth and 56 days after. Limits were placed on the nature of the work which could be undertaken in this period. The rate of payment depended principally on the mother's work record, but the requirements were lax and apparently allowed a majority to claim full pay over all, or most of the leave. In July 1973 full pay was extended to virtually all working mothers, regardless of their length of service. Peasant women were included in the scheme by a decree of 4 November 1964; payment in this case depended on their degree of involvement in kolkhoz labour, and was subject to a minimum of 40 kopecks a day (or some 10 roubles a month). The 1973 law extended the equivalent of full pay to these women as well.

Provisions for feeding babies during working hours had long been part and parcel of the Soviet maternity laws. The culminating measure in this instance was the granting, under the terms of the 1970 Labour code, of up to one year's leave for child care at the request of the mother. Such leave, however, was to be unpaid, and it is unlikely that many mothers took full advantage of it. Managements were forbidden to dismiss pregnant women, nursing mothers and mothers with children under one year of age, if they had no prospect of employment elsewhere.[26]

The removal of the long-standing ban on abortion in November 1955 presumably helped families who were not in a position to feed an extra mouth. In January 1957 normal sickness benefits were extended to women who required abortion for reasons of health. Soon afterwards working women who had abortions on their own volition also became eligible, provided that they earned less than 60 roubles a month.[27]

State maintenance for the children of broken marriages also has a history of several decades. According to the principle enactments, a parent held responsible by a court, be he worker, employee or peasant, must pay a quarter of his usual wage for the upkeep of one child, a third for two, and a half for three or more, until the unfortunate offspring reach the age of eighteen. In certain circumstances other family members – a disabled spouse, for example – may be eligible for maintenance. Payments may be made voluntarily, or as compulsory deductions from a wage packet. Interestingly enough, under the decree of 16 April 1945 the fathers of progeny born out of wedlock bore no obligations in this respect.

Finally, a word on death grants intended primarily to cover funeral expenses. These payments, which have evidently remained unchanged since November 1945, vary from 10 to 20 roubles in town, and 5 to 10 roubles in the village, depending on the age of the deceased.[28]

So much for the most general provisions of Soviet social security. what is one to make of it in practice? Obviously, there can be no shortage of recipients, especially in the higher income brackets, who have good reason to be satisfied with their lot. The Soviet newspaper, *Golos rodina*, distributed free among Soviet citizens living abroad, is, for example, often replete with the glowing testimonies of old-age pensioners in the Homeland.[29] At the same time there can be no doubt about dissatisfaction with the payments at the lower end of the various scales. It has been voiced with great acerbity by emigres and the authors of samizdat documents, some of which are included in Appendix 1. Professor Bernice Madison, in a recent survey of 103 emigre old-age pensioners, found that all of them regarded the minimum of 45 roubles a month as 'utterly insufficient to provide even a humble existence'. Only 2% conceded that a pensioner could survive on 52–70 roubles, (circa the poverty thresholds) while the great majority thought the minimum should be in the 100–150 rouble range. Supplements for dependents, survivor and disability pensions were also considered to be inadequate. Strangely enough, there was criticism of the (relatively liberal) retirement ages, while the years-of-service provisions raised few objections.[30] Most pensioners believed that they did not get enough assistance from the local social security departments, particularly in finding suitable housing, work and home help.

Our own assessment of Soviet social security, based on a perusal of its main provisions, cannot be particularly positive either. It is true indeed that some categories of recipient had few grounds for complaints. Both the Khrushchev and Brezhnev leaderships made numerous improvements in the amounts paid, and in the complex matter of eligibility. The rising average wage caused commensurate rises in the average rates of pension (though no meaningful figures are published). One cannot, moreover, expect splendid social security benefits if real wages are too low to support them.

But having said this, there is no doubt that most of the changes we have enumerated were long overdue, and failed to remedy a number of inbuilt shortcomings. There was, by and large, no departure from the stultifying centrality of the work-record as a determinant of eligibility and level of payment. There was no state assistance based solely on need, or on an inability to obtain work. The minimal levels for full and partial pensions were miserably low, and lagged far behind the sums needed to surpass the putative poverty thresholds. Most child benefits were nominal or sadly inadequate: several types of payment fixed in the 1940s were left unchanged. Finally, the peasants, though brought into a state-administered scheme in 1965, remained subject to a distressing degree of discrimination.

For the great majority of people, therefore, recourse to social security meant an inevitable lapse into poverty. Successive Soviet leaderships have obviously not been able, or willing, to save them from a fate all too familiar to recipients of state benefits under capitalism.

6

POVERTY, POLITICS AND CHARITY

—————— ·◇· ——————

In pluralist societies the problem of poverty is usually the focus of much comment and political activity. This takes the form of national debate about economic policies and efforts on the part of the government to raise living standards, protect the interests of the poor, and ensure a 'fair' distribution of goods and services. Political parties may monitor the well-being of the least privileged groups in society, and espouse their cause.

The matter is not, however, dealt with only at a government or party level. Trade unions endeavour, through collective bargaining or other means, to obtain the best possible wage rates for all their members, including the poorest. Major churches may have poverty alleviation programmes. Other voluntary organisations, large or small, may play an important charitable role, enjoying financial support from local authorities or the central government itself. A recent US handbook of voluntary associations, for example, listed some 1,300 concerned primarily with social welfare, and many more with peripheral involvement. According to US official sources, in 1981 some $54.1 billion were donated to various types of charity, in great part by private individuals. The War on Poverty Program of 1964 was an example of massive support through US government funding. In the UK a comparable directory of voluntary effort contained about 1,000 entries, and a large proportion of the organisations named were directly involved in researching poverty or fighting it. A Low Pay Unit, founded by the government in 1974, provided 'information and background data for independent members of wage councils, briefings for MPs, trade unionists...', reported to 'relevant bodies of individuals', and provided 'an advisory service for the general public'. Of course, the USA and the UK are in this respect only akin to other industralised states in the West. The poor, in other words, have both a legitimate political voice, and some opportunity of obtaining help from non-government agencies.[1]

The centralised and unitary character of the Soviet state has engendered a very different administrative response. The poor, as such, can claim no place, or hardly any, in party-political literature; they have no lobby, and no legitimate champions. But since poverty exists, the authorities and larger social organisations must take some account of it. This chapter is an attempt to summarise the extent to which existing bodies may serve the interests of the poor, and conversely, how far poor people may penetrate them or use them for their own benefit. The story is, alas, one of exclusion, rather than participation: much of it will cover ground familiar to observers of the Soviet political system, albeit from a particular angle. We will begin with the central organs of power, and work, as it were, outwards.

POVERTY AND THE ORGANS OF GOVERNMENT

The fate of the Soviet poor, as of any social group, is ultimately decided by the Politbureau of the CPSU, which stipulates the direction of all national policy – economic, political and social. The deliberations of the Politbureau are secret, and we have very little indication of how often it considers poverty-related problems. Its thinking on social matters is best monitored through brief reports of its meetings, the published speeches of its acknowledged leader – the General Secretary – or those of other members. These stalwart figures may let it be known that they are themselves of humble origin, but their ascension to the pinnacle of power means that they have joined a specific elite, and have little contact with other groups in the community (not least for security reasons). In modern states all major social legislation normally falls within the parameters established by national leaderships. The uniqueness of Soviet practice lies in the degree of centralisation, in the isolation of the leaders and in the secrecy with which major decisions are made.

Below the Politbureau come the Secretariat and the Central Committee. The former is a small body of 'secretaries' (ten in March 1981), including some Politbureau members, who provide the Politbureau with administrative backing, handle the nomenclature and

Table 6.1. *Central Committee membership, March 1981 (selected groups)*

	Full members	Non-voting members	% of total membership
Workers	11	7	4.2
Peasants	2	6	1.7
Employees (low grade)		2	0.4
Trade Union officials	4	3	1.5

Source: XXVI S'ezd KPSS, Stenograficheski otchet, Vol. 2, p. 249ff; Vol. 3, p. 289ff.

other organisational matters, and act as a link with the Central Committee apparatus, of which more in a moment. There is no evidence of the Secretariat being directly concerned with social problems as such.

The Central Committee of the CPSU, as an elected (or more accurately, selected) body comprised, in March 1981, 472 members, of whom the overwhelming majority held high, influential office throughout the Soviet system. Its plenary sessions, usually biannual, are extremely important events in the Soviet political calendar: they allow the party leaders to address the political elite in camera, and keep it up to date on party policies. The universality of censorship, and wide territorial dispersion of full-time officials add significance to the gatherings. There is little or no evidence of spontaneous debate at them, and it would normally be unthinkable for Central Committee members to use them as an area for the expression of any ideas unacceptable to one leader or another. The formation of a 'lobby,' in any active sense, could be categorised as an infringement of Lenin's March 1921 ban on factions.

In any case, Central Committee members who are likely to have contact with the poorer sections of the community are in a tiny minority. According to our analysis the current Central Committee, elected in March 1981, contained only eighteen workers, of whom eleven were registered as brigadiers or foremen (Table 6.1). Since five more were highly skilled manuals or machine-tool operators, and presumably well-paid, only two – a weaver and a field worker – were left to represent (in some sense) the lowest paid artisans. There were also only eight peasants and (it would seem) two low-grade white-collar employees. The seven trade union representatives were professional officials, while V. G. Lomonosov, the head of the State Committee for

Labour and Social Questions, could be identified as the lone official spokesman for all such matters. The Central Committee of 1981 resembled its predecessors in the weight of representation afforded to the lower orders of society. The same situation, it would appear, exists in the (considerably less powerful) bureaus, secretariats and Central Committees of all the union republics.

The Politbureau relies for the implementation of its decisions, via the Secretariat, on the so-called Central Committee apparatus, a body thought to comprise some 2,000 full-time officials in Moscow. This monitors and supervises the state executive, headed by the Council of Ministers, the hierarchy of full-time party offices throughout the country, and most, if not all other official organisations. It is, in fact, the linchpin of the administrative structure (though its actual relationship with subordinate bodies is the subject of much debate among outside observers). All the more striking, therefore, is the fact that none of the twenty four departments known to have existed in it in 1981 was primarily concerned with labour, wages, or social security.[2] Neither were these matters, as far as we can tell, handled by sub-departments or sections. The same gap existed in party offices down to local level. Presumably the existing departments (of industry or agriculture, for example) would have an occasional interest in employees' welfare. But the absence of named units gives a fair indication of the low priority afforded to social problems in party work, contrasting starkly with the attention paid to economics and ideology.

Turning to the state executive, the most authoritative body at a national level is the USSR State Committee for Labour and Social Questions. This operates as a 'union-republican' entity, insofar as it has a central office in Moscow, and subordinate committees in each of the republics. Its head in 1981, V. G. Lomonosov, was a member of the USSR Council of Ministers (as well as of the Central Committee). Its history provides another indication of the cautious attitude of the leadership towards social problems in general.

We have already noted that the People's Commissariat for Labour was effectively abolished in 1933, when its functions, were either transferred to the trade unions, and/or simply abandoned. Only in 1955 was it resuscitated, and then as the less influential State Committee for Labour and Wages attached to the USSR Council of Ministers. As such it lacked offices at the republican or lower levels, and seemingly relied on the trade unions for the implementation of its policy.[3] It was renamed the State Committee for Labour and Social Questions in 1976, with specific responsibility for 'the management and coordination of activities relating to the organisation, payment and conditions of labour, the rational use of labour resources and the solution of other social problems', based on the 'single unified policy of ministries and administrations'.[4] The committee also assumed responsibility for social security throughout the country. The existing republican ministries of social security, mentioned in Chapter Five, had until then lacked a coordinating office at the centre. It is relevant to note that ministries most concerned with the well-being of the public – food, clothing, education and health – are traditionally of union-republican, rather than all-union, status. Public amenities, housing and local industry are handled at the republican level only. The strong centralising tendencies observable in the state bureaucracy during the Brezhnev years hardly reached the consumer sector.

Of the three nominal pillars of Soviet governance – the Party, state executive, and legislature, the last (i.e., the Supreme Soviet), is most attuned to social matters. But it is politically powerless; proceedings last only a few days a year, and are scripted in advance. Problem-orientated debate is, as such, unknown, and every single vote has been unanimous since the first session was held in 1936. In August 1966, however, as part of a drive to strengthen the impression of democratic participation, the Brezhnev leadership made certain limited structural changes. These involved the establishment of new permanent (or standing) commissions for 'Health and Social Insurance', 'Education, Science and Culture', 'Trade and Public Services', in each chamber of the USSR Supreme Soviet. Commissions for 'Youth Affairs' and 'Consumer Goods' were registered in July 1974, Commissions for 'Women's Labour, Living Conditions and the Protection of Mother-hood and Children' were added two years later. (Comparable bodies, it must be added, had long existed in local government, but these need separate consideration.)

Some assessment of the activities of the commissions at Supreme Soviet level may be made from brief reports published in the Supreme Soviet journal. Each consisted of between thirty-one and fifty-one deputies with professional interests in the given field. During the years 1979 to 1981, which we may take as typical, they met only one day a year though after, it was said, 'considerable preparatory work', by their members. During its session a commission usually heard reports from selected officials, usually ministers, and approved declared party policy. Some critical comment was in order, and sessions usually ended with a number of 'recommendations' directed to the administrative offices concerned. Criticism could be more stringent and pointed than was normally permitted on the floor of the chamber, and may have served mainly as an incentive to officialdom to work better. Thus several speakers at a joint Youth Commission meeting on 21 March 1980 criticised 'a series of substantial shortcomings and gaps in the organisation of labour and life, which often caused young people to leave the village. The main thing was the low level of mechanisation…the pay received by young workers and collective farmers in some farms remained low… it often happened that young people starting work did not get the jobs they were trained for, nor the benefits and labour protection granted by law.'[5]

In the context of Soviet bureaucratic realities the new commissions could not serve, in any realistic sense, as a vehicle for poverty interests, nor have much impact on the functions of the Supreme Soviet itself. If impact there was, it was due more to the nominally prestigious level at which they operated than to the powers granted them. Serving members continued to be bound by the stringent de facto rules covering all Soviet deputies, and persons of real authority rarely, if ever, attended their sessions. The publicity devoted to the establishment of the permanent commissions at the Supreme Soviet level has caused some observers to exaggerate their importance.

Below the central executive and legislative bodies there lies, of course, the broad net of local government. This comprises the local legislatures (the soviets, understood as groups of elected deputies) and the permanent departments which serve them. These in turn intermesh with the local party offices, certain ministries, and the higher-level soviets.[6] Obviously, the departments most concerned with the well-being of the populace include social security, housing, local amenities, labour and employment, education, health and local trade. In addition, departments of internal affairs (principally the militia) maintain order and implement the all-pervasive passport regime, while legal advice for the public is issued by juridical consultation points.[7]

Obviously, insofar as poverty is a national problem, local government can at best play a minor, alleviative role. Even so, most studies of the local soviets suggest that they are but poorly equipped to lessen distress within their territory. Their lack of political autonomy needs no further comment, and they have in any case suffered long periods

of neglect. As to finance, virtually all of their powers are highly
circumscribed by the centre. They cannot insert un-authorized budget
categories, while their use of funds is monitored by several agencies,
including the local party offices. Of the 50,600 or so local soviets
operating in the mid-seventies, almost 45,000 were said to be 'economically insignificant,' accounting for only 10 % of all local spending;
large cities were, of course, the main exception.[8] Generally, local
government is regarded primarily as an instrument for the detailed
implementation of centrally-approved policies, rather than as a
channel for mediating the desires of any groups of electors.

The ordinary citizen who wishes to indulge in political activity may
do so most easily by joining one of the local permanent commissions.
In 1977, for example, the local soviets used the services of 329,052
commissions, with a membership of approximately 1,800,000 deputies
and over two million activists. Although 45,822 of these bodies dealt
with matters pertinent to poor people (as may be surmised from the
names listed below) the figures themselves show that most local
soviets had to manage without them. Futhermore, it seems unlikely
that such matters monopolised any given commission's activities.

Name of commission[9]	Number
Health and Social Security	14,870
Youth affairs	12,288
Housing	10,326
Local amenities	7,260
Women's labour, living conditions, protection of maternity and childhood	1,070
No. of local soviets	50,602

The commissions are usually described as links between the soviet
on the one hand, and the public on the other, though their role as
truly 'popular' organisations may also be emphasised.[10] They operate
with more flexibility than the local soviet which ideally has to debate
a wide range of topics in a more formal setting. The commissions are
by nature suited to pinpointing more specific problems. Formally they
are empowered to prepare proposals for discussion in the full soviet;
provide it with information; implement the decisions of the full-time
departments; and organise approved campaigns. In rural areas,
where local village soviets are understaffed, the commissions (though

voluntary in character) may be required to shoulder some regular administrative burdens. Despite these advantages, however, the commissions serve primarily as instruments of political mobilisation, or channels through which individuals may gain 'perks' or further their political careers. The commissions have not shown themselves capable of overcoming the well-recognised inflexibilities of Soviet local government, or of gaining recognition as a vehicle for expressing the interests of the under-privileged sectors of the community. The establishment of commissions specifically for that purpose is, in the context of Soviet polity, quite impracticable.

The trades unions embrace nearly all of the labour force, but are also ill adapted to articulate the interests of their poorer members. The government is virtually the only employer outside the cooperative sector, and the country's twenty-nine trades unions (1980) are all thoroughly statified. Wages are not subject, in any true sense, to negotiation, and union policies hardly reflect what we would understand as popular pressure from below. The proof of the pudding is in the eating; and since the early twenties, there has never been any public evidence of dissension, let alone confrontation, between ministries and unions over the level of wage rates. The negotiations themselves are entirely unpublicised, and the modest wage levels agreed speak for themselves. Trade union officials may, it would seem, express disquiet, but how far they do so is a matter of conjecture. New wage agreements are submitted to the USSR State Committee on Labour and Social Questions, or its republican equivalents, for approval and implementation.[11] Significantly, trade union documents list the need to protect workers' rights and interests *after* the encouragement of increased output.

Trade union committees within any given enterprise may be able to assist poor employees insofar as they may bear a somewhat circumscribed responsibility for enterprise housing, and the use of limited funds for social amenities. Although the committees may also have small sums of money available for personal loans and socio-political activities, they exercise no charitable function as such.

THE POOR AND THEIR ELECTED DEPUTIES

Under the terms of the USSR Constitution, every Soviet citizen who is of sound mind has the right to be elected as a people's deputy, provided he or she is aged eighteen or over (for republican and lower

soviets) or twenty-one for the Supreme Soviet of the USSR. There is
no system of deposits to deter the impecunious, and electoral expenditures are covered by the state. At the same time the selection process
at all levels, from local to republican, is very stringent, and effectively
exludes representatives of any unauthorised groupings. A candidate
may be proposed by the CPSU, the trade unions, the Komsomol,
cooperative and other social organisations, labour collectives and
military units. 'Social organisations' is a loose term, but includes only
large, officially-registered bodies. In accordance with long-standing
practice, each electoral district has its own (hierarchically-controlled)
selection committee, which chooses a single candidate to run for its
seat.

The post of deputy (formally held, at the local level, for a term of
two and a half years, though a majority of deputies serve longer) is
somewhat prestigious, and brings significant advantages. There is thus
an in-built tendency for it to go to persons who are known for their
political conformism, enthusiasm at work and involvement in
approved activities. Selection for a candidacy (and the virtually
automatic election which ensues) is in itself a sign of success, which
poor people would not normally enjoy. Such data as is available on
the social configuration of the deputies accordingly show that even at
the lowest levels they are much more likely to be members of the party,
and have higher education than the population at large (Table 6.2).
They are also more likely to do white-collar work, hold a professional
party post, and have some form of decoration. Already in lowest rural
and urban soviets they form a sort of popular elite: the winnowing
process, as the table shows, intensifies at higher levels of the system,
raising greater obstacles to penetration by the less favoured citizens.

A clearer idea of the impact of this process on the chances of
different socio-occupational groups achieving deputy status may be
gained from some of the figures provided by the Tuva sample which
we considered for other purposes in Chapter One (Table 6.3). Thus
the percentage of people who were deputies fell from 27.1% among
the highest managerial staff to 0.7% amongst the lower grade
manuals. Most likely to provide deputies, after the managers, were the
two categories of specialists. In all, the three groups of responsible
personnel provided 70% of the deputies in the sample: to put it
another way, a manager had thirty-eight times as much chance of
becoming a deputy as did a low-grade manual. Occasional socio-
political involvement, particularly in trade-union duties and one-off

Table 6.2. *Distribution of deputies by selected social characteristics (1977, unless otherwise indicated; percentages)*

	Party members	Specialists with higher education	White-collar employees	Professional party officials	Persons holding various decorations
Executive committee members					
Krai, oblast	93.0	88.8	81.4		
Village	68.0	30.5	62.9		
Other deputies					
USSR Supreme Soviet[a]	67.2	52.2	50.6	16.6	
Krai, oblast	55.3	44.8	43.9	8.8	61.2
Rural district	49.1	36	37.0	5.6	44.9
Urban district	47.4	33.2	38.8	4.7	39.1
Town	46.6	29.6	37.7	3.6	39.0
Village	41.0	16.7	28.0	1.4	26.8
Public at large[b]	9.3	8.7	26.3	[0.2]	

[a] Elected February 1980
[b] Relevant age groups, and employed persons, as applicable. Professional party officials estimated at a quarter of a million.
Sources: Itogi vyborov i sostav deputatov mestnykh sovetov, 1977; Nar. khoz. 1978, pp. 365, 377 (calculated); *SPR, 1978,* p. 367; 1981, p. 506.

tasks, is rather more evenly apportioned. But this does not affect the central question of access to deputy status.

The publication of such detail is, as we have indicated, a rarity in itself, and this instance covers only a small ethnic group in a remote town. Nevertheless, sociological samples are usually constituted to investigate common phenomena; and this one was no doubt chosen so as to reveal practices common at least among national minorities.

We have argued so far that Soviet deputies can do little to influence the government's social policies at any level, and that poor people are unlikely to achieve deputy status. Many electoral systems are weighted against the poor, though the Soviet Union, as the world's first socialist state, might be expected to exhibit an exemplary flexibility in this sphere. Beyond this point there lies the question of how far deputies, once elected, may respond to instances of personal hardship. The Law on the Status of People's Deputies in the USSR, passed in September 1972, assigned to them a very caring role. They were supposed to be

Tables 6.3. *Socio-occupation groups and election of local deputies (Tuvan urban dwellers, 1977)*

	No. in group	No. elected as deputies	% elected as deputies	% of all deputies	% Involved in 'one-off' political activities
Managerial staff, administrators	70	19	27.1	24.1	17.1
Production specialists	99	7	7.1	8.9	22.4
Non-production specialists, cultural employees	250	30	12.1	37.9	17.4
Other white-collar employees	171	8	4.7	10.1	27.8
Workers in (mechanised) jobs	304	4	1.3	5.1	27.2
Manual workers (higher grade)[a]	294	9	3.1	11.4	26.5
Manual workers (lower grade)[a]	296	2	0.7	2.5	25.3
Others[b]	80				
Totals	1,564[b]	79		100	

[a] This distinction is not explained in the text, but the high-grade manuals are more likely to be in partly mechanised jobs and have higher wages.
[b] The 53 pensioners and 27 persons whose occupation was not known, provided no deputies, and were only marginally engaged in 'one off' activities.
Source: V. I. Boiko, p. 141.

The absolute figures are reconstituted from percentages to one decimal point of the total sample of 1,564, and accurate to about 0.5%

extremely accessible to electors, responsive to the emergence of local issues, and active in decision-making within the soviet itself.

The major institutional channels through which deputies may be involved in local issues were, according to the American scholars Stephen Sternheimer and Carol W. Lewis, the presentation of public reports on their work; receipt of constituents' instructions (*nakazy*), complaints about administrative behaviour, or legislative inquiries (*zaprosy*); and the conduct of local social surveys. Sternheimer and Lewis concluded, however, that Soviet local government was still, in 1979, a long way from ensuring 'citizen access'. The most formidable barriers lay, they thought, not in institutional obstacles, but in the government culture itself. Soviet adminstrators at the local level did not value citizen participation highly, and the limits on it were probably very similar to those existing in the USA.[12] At the regular sessions of the soviets it is those deputies who are furthest from the experience of poverty, the better-educated holders of white-collar jobs, who are most likely to make their voices heard.

Yet it would be incorrect to conclude that the poorer electors have no feed-in at all. The deputies' contact with the full-time apparatus, on the one hand, and their participation in the permanent commissions on the other, give them some elbow room. There is nothing to stop a deputy from responding to requests for help from the needy, and using what influence he or she has to obtain a more advantageous interpretation of existing rules. Such responses lie in the sphere of personal, rather than socio-political, activity, but may not be negligible. The responses to our emigre survey showed that some 8 % of the respondents knew their local deputy personally, and another 37 % knew him or her by name, which indicates some degree of exposure to public scrutiny.

One point needs to be made in conclusion. Political scientists in the West generally prefer to study movement, rather than stagnation. When systems of government present considerable evidence of the latter (as happens with the USSR), there is a common inclination to seek evidence of movement through informal 'pressure groups' which may mediate known interests, and strive to achieve their objectives by manipulation of individual contacts. True, the Soviet government has been moved to respond to poverty over the years. But how far these responses were altruistic, and how far they were prompted by pressures from below, it is hard to say. The continuing existence of poverty, and the governments's need of alleviation, suggest that such pressures, if exercised at all, have not been very effective.

MEMBERSHIP OF THE COMMUNIST PARTY

If the poor people are remote from the centres of power in the USSR, and face extra difficulty in rising through the state elective system, we may ask how they fare in the most obvious remaining avenue of advancement, the CPSU itself. The total membership of this body is considerable: in January 1981 it stood at 17.4 million, or about one in ten of all persons in the relevant age groups.

The question is particularly intriguing in view of the Party's professed aims and objectives, which since its earliest days have harboured an internal contradiction. On the one hand it was supposed to contain the most perceptive and active Marxists, that is, people who could lead the feckless masses to a socialist way of life. On the other it aimed to unite the poorest and most exploited folk, especially among the urban proletariat, who saw membership in it as their best chance of salvation. The fact that the Party, by 1917, was still a tiny group of political activists, whose views were far from universally popular, did not deflect its leaders from their idealistic beliefs.

Over the decades which have passed since, official ideology has retained both of these concepts, but they have undergone a subtle, and perhaps unavoidable mutation. The leaders, by now all born or raised in the Soviet state, have turned into a professional bureaucratic elite, with a considerable degree of social exclusivity. They are drawn from the better-educated, white-collar groups, with a clear tendency to self-propagation. At the same time the growth of party membership and increasing *proportion* of each age group joining the CPSU, has not ensured the induction of the poor and under-privileged. The reason is simple. The party was transmogrified, to quote its 1977 statute, into 'the tried and tested militant vanguard of the Soviet people, which unites, on a voluntary basis, the more advanced, politically more conscious section of the working class, the collective farm peasantry, and the intelligentsia of the USSR'.[13] Thus it developed, rather than shed, its exclusive character, and was soon different indeed from the political haven which the most exploited members of Soviet society may have dreamed about earlier. Stalinist ideology recognised no poverty or exploitation in the USSR anyway.

In practice, enrolment of 'the leading and most conscientious' toilers has come to mean, rather as with the local soviets, admitting people who have a good work record, enthusiasm for socio-political involvement, and a good chance of obtaining responsible, senior, and hence better-paid jobs.[14] Conversely, membership itself facilitates promotion, so once in the stream, as it were, the chosen individual is more likely to be upwardly mobile. Party membership is recognised as being the prerogative of, and providing access to, the middle and upper ranks of the labour hierarchy. Better wages achieved through party membership improve pension entitlement and reduce the chances of poverty in old age.

Admission to the party is not merely a matter of personal desire, be it on the part of rich or poor. Detailed control over the selection of new members is openly admitted. 'The party organisation cannot allow spontaneity [*samotek*] in the question of growth (stated a recent handbook). 'The party committee or bureau and the secretary of the primary organisation must be well aware, when making selections for party membership, what sectors of the enterprise and what individuals are to be kept in view, and who is preparing himself (or herself) for admission.' Candidates who are thought to be suitable are told to apply through the primary organisation (formerly known as the 'cell') at their place of work, but their applications are then vetted by 'commissions for the preliminary examination of admission' at the local party office.[15] Any socio-occupational mix specified by the leadership is thus to a great extent ensured at the point of entry.

There is, it would seem, no deliberate *exclusion* of the poor from the party ranks. Indeed, ambitious individuals from deprived backgrounds may make extra efforts to enter them and make a career in them, precisely because they see this as a good way of escaping the poverty state. But the lower-paid worker, lacking a key post, or appropriate enthusiasm, is less likely to have the necessary personal contacts. It may also be that the poor are, on the whole, simply less ambitious in this respect. 'Workers' living standards have a definite effect on their degree of social and political activity, although this influence is not in itself decisive...' wrote V. Chulanov, with regard to a large sample of miners (themselves a workers' elite) studied between 1972 and 1979.[16] 'Among workers earning on average up to 100 roubles there were five times fewer activists than in the group with earnings of 250–300 roubles.' The non-activist will have difficulty in finding sponsors (of which no less than three, each of five years' standing in the party, are needed). And unless he has good personal relations with the secretary of the enterprise party organisation, he may be told that there are too many other applicants, that his work record must be improved, or that he has not been active enough in other ways. The level of demand for admittance to the party has never been revealed, but it would seem most secretaries have a choice of genuinely eager applicants.

The mass membership in the primary cells forms the base of a well-defined organisational pyramid. Party members elect, by indirect voting, territorial committees at the district, town, province, territory, republican and, of course, all-union levels. In 1980 there were in all some 429,000 'elective positions' of this type (with formal re-election every two to three or five years, depending on the level). Beyond this, each party committee has its full-time apparatus, manned by career

Table 6.4. *Characteristics of elected CPSU Personnel, 1980–81 (percentages)*

	White-collar employees	Persons with higher education
Union Republic, Krai, oblast committees (territory, province)	68.9	69.3
Town, district committees	57.9	54.8
Mass membership (total)	43.8	28.0
Krai, oblast secretaries		99.9
Town, district secretaries		99.7
Primary cell secretaries		54.0

Source: KPSS, Naglyadnoe posobie po partiinomy stroitel'stvu (relevant tables); *SPR*, 1981, pp. 500, 501.

officials. The election process here, as in the soviets, is in fact controlled through an extensive nomenclature system.[17] While the more promising party members are given ordinary seats on the various committees, full-time officials are 'elected' to the more senior positions, thereby ensuring the implementation of decisions from the centre, and their own predominance in local affairs. At this point, ironically, practice may slightly favour persons who were originally of worker or peasant background, and who have thus succeeded in bettering their lot.

The official statistics on party membership provide a little firm evidence of social differentiation in the party hierarchy, to the expected detriment of poorly-educated manuals (Table 6.4). The successive campaigns by the leadership to increase the proportion of workers, and to a lesser extent peasants, in the primary organisations do not seem to have had much impact on the occupancy of the elective posts, while full-time officials in the apparatus are by definition white-collared. Detailed information on party mobility of this type would be interesting indeed, were it available. Soviet sociologists are obliged to avoid serious study of such differentiating mechanisms, but a rare breakdown of party membership among different groups of factory personnel in Leningrad, published by O. I. Shkaratan early in 1967, is of special interest. In a sample of just under 3,000 respondents he found that the proportion with CPSU affiliation fell from 16.2% among skilled manuals, fitters and welders to 3.7% among unskilled manuals.[18]

The difficulties poor people may have in gaining admission to the party, or promotion inside it, do not, of course, mean that all party members are free from the spectre of poverty. Their material well-being must to some extent mirror that of society as a whole. Thus the youth of some members, and the pensioned status of others, inevitably mean low incomes. In January 1977, nearly a million members were under twenty-five and two million were over sixty years of age. Some members doubtless suffered from low pay in the enterprises where they worked: in the same year there were nearly a million in the worst-paid branches of industry, while half a million had field jobs in agriculture.[19] There is little doubt, however, that the prospects of the young were better, and the pensions of the retired somewhat higher, than those outside the organisation. Our discussion leaves little doubt that even in low-paying enterprises party members tended to earn more than their non-party workmates.

VOLUNTARY HELP AND CHARITY

We have already noted that voluntary charities, in the forms familiar to us, are hardly known in the Soviet Union. The inhabitants of the land doubtless have a fair share of charitable impulse: but official practice is to direct this into centrally monitored, and at times highly politicised channels.

Russia, to digress for a moment, has a history of social concern stretching far into the past. Local authorities were legally obliged to make some provision for the destitute under the governance of Peter the Great, and this was continued, through aid committees and workhouses, in the eighteenth and nineteenth centuries. The main political movements of the second half of the nineteenth century were charitable in conception, and encouraged self-help. The various churches, though lacking teaching and nursing orders, helped poor parishioners. Such efforts were but small salvage in the ocean of poverty, but they were of great moral consequence, and still await the attention of a committed social historian.

By the beginning of the twentieth century the new industrial bourgeoisie, was also involving itself in charitable activites, at least in the larger towns. The 1896 Moscow city budget, for example, allotted about 246,000 roubles to such assistance, of which personal donations and contributions amounted to 126,000 roubles; 'charity evenings' provided 15,000 roubles, and the interest on capital sums donated for the purpose yielded another 37,000 roubles. The residue of 68,000 roubles was presumably provided by the city duma.[20] The tsar himself set an example by assisting many institutions from his personal (and not, it seems very great) allowances.[21]

The Bolshevik government's attitude to the question of charity was at first heavily coloured by its own ideology. The continuing existence of bourgeois charitable institutions was quite unacceptable, so they were quickly dismantled. Existing state institutions, principally the offices of social security, were incorporated into new people's commissariats: the church lost its entire possessions by nationalisation; and other charitable bodies were either thoroughly bolshevised (with the attendant reorientation of their activites), or closed down altogether. Of course, the seizure of personal and institutional wealth; state control of financial transactions; the nationalisation of the means of production; rampant shortages of food and consumer goods; and hyperinflation together created a situation in which old-fashioned charitable functions became almost unthinkable.

At the same time, the new leaders felt a moral obligation to help people who were devoted to the new Bolshevik cause, or particularly vulnerable to poverty. Help of this kind took the form of officially-established funds for assisting hungry children, victims of 'counter-revolution', families of Red Army soldiers, etc. The movement was not really voluntary, however, for many of the contributions were the subject of state regulation.[22] The most spectacular reversion to charity of a more genuine variety was the establishment, in July 1921, of the All-Russian Committee for Aid to the Hungry, to assist millions starving as a result of harvest failure.[23]

As a kind of economic normality returned to the country, the Bolsheviks found it desirable to set up a few organisations which, if not primarily charitable in character, still helped people in obvious need. The best known were the Society of Old Bolsheviks (1922 to 1935), the Red Cross Society (closed after the Bolshevik coup, and reopened in 1923), the Red Crescent Society in the 'moslem' republics (1923), together with the republican societies for the Blind, and for the Deaf (founded in 1925 and 1926 respectively). These grew to be very large, with branches up and down the country. Societies devoted to specific spare-time activities may also have had small ad hoc arrangements for assisting old or distressed members.[24]

The churches, of course, were never allowed to regain their charitable role. A law of 29 April 1929 (still valid in substance) prohibited religious associations from 'setting up funds for mutual aid, cooperatives or associations of producers' and from 'granting material aid to their members'. Amazing though it may seem, the common Russian word for active charity, *blagotvoritel'nost'*, was redefined in Soviet dictionaries as 'bourgeois', the granting of 'material help by private persons to the poor out of demeaning kindness'.[25]

Local party bodies, the Komsomol trade unions, army units and other entities were increasingly called upon to fill some of the existing voids. This became a well recognised, though subordinate activity for all of them, specific initiatives usually being thought up by responsible officials. Plans of campaign are embodied in written resolutions, or if they are sufficiently long-term, built into a statute.

The activites vary enormously in character and extent. Often the aim is to supplement state services, thereby reducing the costs of official intervention. Involvement may be described as 'socio-political tasks' (as we have just noted in our treatment of Soviet deputies) and attributed to large numbers of people. How far the participants are moved by truly charitable feelings, or obliged to act as they do, can hardly be determined. Russians themselves use the ironic phrase 'voluntary-obligatory' to describe it.

Two examples of such activity may serve by way of illustration. The post-Stalin years, as is well known, saw many efforts to imbue new life into the trade unions. In November 1976, the Presidium of the All-Union Council introduced, as one such measure, 'Commissions for Cooperation with the Family and School and in Bringing Up Children and Adolescents'.[26] The statute governing these commissions (which functioned under the aegis of enterprise trade union committees) stipulated that they were to help schools in organising labour training and vocational guidance for the pupils; promote training inside the enterprise; help repair schoolbuildings and check equipment; organise links between sections of the enterprise and individual classes; cooperate with libraries and clubs in providing leisure and sports facilities; cooperate with other bodies (the Komsomol, health and sporting organisations) in arranging summer holidays; and run various publicity campaigns. Other regulations reveal that enterprise managers were empowered to use part of the Material Incentive Fund for such purposes.[27] Clearly, it would be in the interest of any potential recipient (school, hospital, etc) to be associated with as large and successful an enterprise as possible.

A decree of the Secretariat of the USSR Komsomol Central Committee dated January 1970, enjoined the Komsomol organisation of the Smolensk oblast to help war veterans 'as a gesture of filial gratitude'.[28] Each organisation and pioneer group in the locality had a duty,

> to create an atmosphere of constant care and attention around invalids, families who lost members in the war, and parents with children serving in the USSR armed forces... Komsomol members and Young Pioneers [the text continued] should establish links with all such people employed at enterprises, state and collective farms, etc., with schools, and with veterans living in the same district, so as to locate people needing constant care, and encourage young workers, collective farmers and pupils to help them.
>
> It is essential for the Central Committees of republican Komsomol organisations, local committees, Young Pioneer councils, together with local military offices, war invalids' committees, social security and health offices, to give them practical help...in solving their household and day-to-day problems...

Activities of this kind may be admirable insofar as they go. One must, however, bear in mind that the party, Komsomol and other 'social' organisations, are designed for quite other purposes and are ill adapted to charitable work as such. It is likely to be sporadic, and devolve on largely inexperienced helpers. There can be none of the consistency and professionalism characteristic of specialised voluntary bodies in the west.

Nevertheless, there has over the years been a tendency for the authorities to use this mechanism (usually known as *sheftstvo*, from the word for 'chief') almost as an arm of local administration. Extreme examples are still to be found in the sphere of collective farm management. Farms have long been expected to support local village communities, and even build roads and schools. The director of the village school would thus look to the farm for help in keeping buildings and equipment in order, heating them in winter, and housing the teachers. The farm in turn would expect the school children to labour in the fields as part and parcel of their school programme. The farm chairman might for his part look to a large industrial enterprise for physical assistance, or a labour draft to help with the harvest. In a situation like this truly charitable impulse may all too easily be stifled. Some people participate in official campaigns because they think it will benefit their careers as 'activists', others may fear some kind of sanction if they do not. But yet others may genuinely want to help their fellow beings. The emigre survey indicated that end-of-the-month loans of a purely personal character, within the family, and among friends, were common among poor people. Soviet law has not yet produced a prohibition on gifts between individuals, and even giving money to beggars is legal, though begging is not. The amount of charitable help Soviet citizens afford one another by all of these means, formal and informal, must be vast, and remains one of the great imponderables of the Soviet social system.

POVERTY AND DISSIDENCE

The difficulties poor people in the Soviet Union face in furthering their interests through legitimate channels prompts the question of how far they have become involved in political dissidence. In Poland widespread unrest over low living standards fused with political dissatisfaction to form a powerful popular movement. Except for a few local riots and strikes, however, overt political opposition in the Soviet Union has been restricted to very small groups of people, operating more often than not in isolation from one another, and able to make their views known only by word of mouth, or through illegal information sheets. Judging from this source, which now comprises several thousand documents, poverty as such has not generated a distinctive brand of dissidence. The main dissident themes have been the defence of human rights, particularly political freedom; protest against religious repression; demands for the proper protection of ethnic minorities; appeals for the relaxation of censorship, and for more contact with the outside world. Though thousands of men and women have braved prosecution for expressing unorthodox views, it is difficult to name many who have made poverty a principal focus of complaint.

There are, it would seem, several plausible explanations for this. The first is that many poor people believe that they are not too badly off, at least in comparison with their fellow citizens (see p. 153 below). A second explanation certainly lies in their greater economic vulnerability. Involvement in the dissident movement may provoke accusations of anti-Soviet activity, loss of employment and residence rights, exile, internment or other highly unwelcome contingencies. In a sense, the poorer the family, the greater the financial disaster threatened. Thirdly, a greater concern with earning a living, or narrower cultural horizons may dis-incline poor people to struggle actively for betterment. The great majority of those who figure as activists and *samizdat* authors are, understandably, of educated, white-collar background and tend to be more taken up with moral issues. The few known to have been workers apparently came from the better-paid and more skilled groups, while the peasants have supplied very few recruits indeed. Poor people, when they get involved at all, are more likely to be found in movements for religious freedom and the protection of minority rights. They may have large families, or have been subject to intolerable discrimination.

Having said all this, however, there is no question but that poverty, in the broader sense of low living standards, has had a marked influence on the programmes of several dissident groups. The few trade union associations known to have existed since 1977 have concerned themselves not only with bad working conditions, infringements of workers' rights, and the difficulties of effective protest, but also with inadequate pay, non-observance of overtime rates, and violation of work regulations.[29] Groups established to monitor Soviet implementation of the international accord on human rights signed in Helsinki in December 1977 have also exhibited a sympathetic awareness of low standards of living. The Moscow section, for example, has expressed concern with numerous infringements of labour law, low pay, shortages of consumer goods, restrictions on the movement of workers, and most important, the lack of instruments for the effective defence of workers' interests. A movement launched in 1978 by the Initiative Group for the Defence of the Rights of Invalids has a close interest in the well-being of the poor, insofar as most invalids may be so categorised.

The firmest relationship between poverty and political protest in the Soviet Union is, ironically, an inverse one, in that active dissent of any kind may cause loss of employment, or other repressive action against the individual concerned and his family. The mechanism for dismissal in politically tinged cases, incidentally, is rather curious. It usually takes the form of fabrication of pretexts like refusal to work overtime: disruption of the production process: absence without leave (taken perhaps to appear without one's workmates' knowledge at militia or KGB offices); dismissal may also be covered by reference to planned redundancy, or an intention to transfer the employee to unacceptable lower-paid work. The managements involved may be advised to act in this way by outside authorities, or may do so spontaneously. The latter response is most likely to be prompted by a desire to avoid the unwelcome attentions of the security organs. The demands of a local party organisation, or a desire to display overt concern for the ideological well-being of the work-force, may also come into play.

The flood of *samizdat* material which has become available since the early sixties has thrown much light on social conditions. The documents presented in Appendix 1 may be regarded, in a sense, as the little-heard voice of the poor, or at least of people closely aware of their problems. Contributing to *samizdat* outlets requires great courage (especially when a signature is appended), so bitter criticism of Soviet reality is only to be expected. We have, nevertheless, chosen texts which are thoughtfully composed, and offer generalisations going beyond individual experience. In many cases they graphically illustrate points from our argument. The authenticity of the material is beyond doubt, while the situations described in it are often poignant. We leave the reader to draw his own conclusions on its value as a mirror of Soviet poverty in the late seventies.

7

SOME FURTHER DIMENSIONS

———————— ·◇· ————————

There are certain aspects of Soviet poverty which, though of great importance, are difficult to assess, even by Soviet standards. Three which we have chosen for consideration, by way of conclusion to our study, are mobility into, or out of, the poverty state; the degree to which poverty has haunted the Soviet-controlled states of East Europe; and prospects for the Soviet poor during the current decade. Although detailed analysis is not possible at this point, and would require several volumes anyway, the obvious importance of all of these topics makes it inappropriate to pass them over without comment. We need scarcely add that state censorship, limited indigenous investigation, and the absence of forthright statistics again hamper attempts to draw clear conclusions.

SOCIAL MOBILITY AND THE POOR

All poverty is to some degree binding upon those who experience it. Where it is limited in extent, or relatively mild, there may be comparative ease of escape, ensuring a tolerable turnover of those afflicted. On the other hand, it may be so common or specific that generations of families are destined to know nothing else. When this occurs, it is usual to describe the situation as a 'poverty trap'. At a national level, whole socio-economic groups may be released from, or engulfed in, poverty, as a result of over-riding changes in the economy, without themselves being 'socially mobile' at all. The term thus covers numerous dimensions of a temporal and special character.[1]

Let us begin with the matter of social theory. It is quite arguable that with the passage of time Soviet Marxism–Leninism has become less sympathetic to upward mobility among the poor. After the Revolution the Bolsheviks envisaged a massive uplift of the needy and exploited, together with the suppression of the former exploiters. Most of the social measures of War Communism were directed to improving the well-being of the poorest classes, and assisting their upward mobility within the framework of what was possible at the time. The fact that these policies were propounded by middle-class intellectuals, and executed by a minority of politically active, but not necessarily poor, workers did not seem to matter. This overt emancipationism, however, soon disappeared, and by the mid-thirties the authorities had ceased to admit that social mobility was needed at all in an avowedly socialist society composed of homogeneous and friendly classes. Indeed, the term itself was for a time discarded on account of its antagonistic and hierarchical associations.

At the same time Stalin and subsequent Soviet leaders encouraged varying degrees of social differentiation, which implied that mobility, though not openly admitted, was both benign and justified in a socialist framework. Thoroughgoing egalitarianism of the early Bolshevik variety was now proposed only as an exemplar for capitalist or developing states. Yet social differentiation, even of a 'socialist' character, introduced a new ambivalence into official ideology. It meant, if anything, that persons who earned little enough to remain poor did so not because they were helpless victims of exploitative forces, but because they contributed least to society and state.

A second relevant factor is observed change in the real configuration of Soviet society as a whole. Such change was promoted most vigorously under War Communism, and again in the thirties as a function of industrialisation and urbanisation. The main objectives were the suppression of bourgeois 'exploiters' of all hues, the formation of a numerically preponderant working class, and of a new 'Soviet' intelligentsia. By the late thirties the old bourgeoisie (who had numbered, according to Soviet figures, no less than 26 million in 1913) had disappeared altogether, to be replaced by a group of 30 million or so white-collar and service workers. The working class grew to 55 million, while the great majority of peasants (some 81 million) were collectivised.[2]

Clearly, transformation of this order provided people at the lower levels of society with splendid opportunities for movement out of farm or unskilled manual jobs into new, higher-skilled, and better paid occupations in the 'upper' working class and intelligentsia. Both Khrushchev and Brezhnev claimed humble origins and were supreme examples of what could be achieved at the time.[3]

After the Second World War the change in class alignment became slower and more measured. The village yielded ever smaller amounts of manpower for other sectors of the economy, and the annual growth of the corpus of employed workers fell from just over 2 million between 1960–5 to 0.8 million in 1981. Over the same period the annual increments to white-collar employees fell from around 0.9 to 0.7 million. By 1981 the working class (as a social group) numbered 164 million, the various white-collar and service personnel 70 million, while the collectivised peasantry had dropped to 35 million. So opportunities for inter-class mobility of this kind became progressively less numerous.

The classes are also in some senses converging. It is arguable that mechanisation of agriculture tends to make it a little more comparable to industry; the gap between workers' and peasants' living standards is evidently narrowing; and some of the legal distinctions between them (particularly access to state social security and passportisation) have been largely erased. The peasant, however, still does not have a clear right to leave the farm at will.

One must bear in mind, moreover, that the worker or peasant who crossed a class divide in the course of these changes acquired no guarantee of improvement in his socio-economic status. Several Soviet studies have demonstrated that migrants from the countryside to the towns usually took up unattractive manual jobs, failed to get as much further training as they might have done, and faced a long wait for adequate housing.[4] Our discussion in Chapter Two has shown that a poor artisan may acquire advanced white-collar skills and still earn comparatively little. Many members of the white-collar group saw no significant improvement in their salaries for years at a time. Many people who changed their place of residence or job only changed one poverty situation for another.

Considerable mobility has always been possible *within* each of the major social groups, worker, white collar or peasant. The rise in living standards between the mid-fifties and the mid-seventies indisputably helped the poorest people in each of them. But here, again, retardative factors have become increasingly evident. Recent falls in the rate of economic growth, not least in the consumer sector, have meant that the poverty threshold has become harder to surpass. Wage and salary differentials, narrowed between the mid-fifties and early seventies, have since been broadened, providing more incentive to upward mobility, but also increasing the distance for the lowest earners to traverse. Efforts to modernise the occupation structures of the productive branches of the economy have had disappointing results. The drive to improve the career chances of young peasants by training them to become agricultural 'mechanisors' resulted not so much in a new, stable stratum of collective farmers, as in a flow of newly trained drivers into the towns.

The two major channels for movement into, and through the white-collar group are education and party membership. (Any administrative system may, of course, serve as a channel in itself, but adequate training and party membership would seem to be major prerequisites for success in the USSR.) We have noted that the education system reached an advanced level of maturity by the early seventies. However, poor people, for reasons we have discussed, tended to get less out of it than the more favoured groups in society; and even by 1980 it was still permitting up to a million and a half children, approximately a third of the age group, to leave school at 15 plus, either to start work, or take less ambitious courses in manual skills. Higher educational facilities remained highly differentiated, the less attractive being the usual lot of disadvantaged students. In rather similar fashion, political participation (in the Soviet sense) has expanded with the growth of the CPSU, and other officiose organisations, but this has brought little modification of the mechanisms which hinder the poor from gaining access to political power.

We would argue, therefore, that the possibilities for social mobility among poorer citizens are probably declining somewhat. The policies of the post-Brezhnev leaderships, with their emphasis on control and stability, would suggest a continuation of this trend for the present. But the future is another matter. Soviet society possesses massive potential for change, even within the existing political and economic framework. Its occupation structure is still relatively backward; considerable numbers of workers are still in manual, low-skilled jobs; a large proportion of its work-force is still employed in agriculture; and its peasantry is still numerous and poor. The entire consumer sector of the economy awaits upgrading, with consequent benefit for its employees. Beyond these structural possibilities, there is the potent matter of popular conception. The efforts of official ideologues to popularise jobs at the bottom of the occupation hierarchy appear to have been relatively unsuccessful. If this is so, there must be a common desire among the lower orders, who (despite all the drawbacks) have benefited from the existing educational facilities, for both personal betterment in the more modest posts, and for advantageous movement beyond them.[5]

Our poverty survey provided some interesting insights into mobility among individuals, even when allowance is made for the smallness and rather specific nature of the sample. Firstly, it provided a positive illustration of *inter-generational* mobility. As compared with a parent of the same sex, about 49% of the men, and 62% of the women moved up the occupation hierarchy (categorised in eight steps), this being respectively twice and three times the proportion who moved down.[6] The overall improvement was about one category: it must be borne in mind that since most respondents were workers in mid-career, some had opportunity for further advancement. Inter-generational improvement in educational levels was no less striking: in this case 80% of the men, and 76% of the women moved up (mostly by two or more out of eight educational categories) while only 8% and 4% moved down.

But respondents' own career patterns (reflecting *intra-generational* mobility) were more sombre. Only 14% perceived improvement in their position over the five years preceding the one in review; some 74% said there was no change, and about 11% claimed deterioration. The pattern was substantially similar for a subgroup already in their forties.

Promotion, of course, depends both on personal proclivity and the availability of jobs. The desire for advancement was not particularly widespread, for less than half said they had had an interest in it. But 57% of the respondents considered that no real opportunity existed anyway; 31% thought the opportunities to be average; and only a little over 10% considered them good. Among those who were interested in promotion, but had failed to achieve it, the most diverse reasons were given, including antisemitism (55%), lack of personal training (43%), absence of suitable posts (40%) and family circumstances (23%). Of the women, 22% blamed lack of promotion on their anatomical nature. In a more general, socio-economic sense, the possibilities of moving upwards were thought to be limited in Soviet society. Some 55% of the respondents believed that it was harder for the poor, as opposed to the well-off, to better themselves, and only

3% believed it to be easier. The remainder of the sample did not express an opinion on this point.

It is noteworthy that marriage appeared to offer rather better possibilities for intra-generational mobility. Of all working spouses, 53% and 64% were in the same, or immediately adjacent occupation and educational categories respectively. In the many cases of discrepancy, the wives tended to be rather worse employed, but better educated, than their husbands.

The degree to which poor people in the Soviet Union *feel themselves* to be a group apart bears an obvious relevance to mobility problems. Apartness, in a deprecatory sense, is something which few people are willing to admit, and may strive to overcome. In fact, only a quarter of the sample declared that they thought the urban poor to be, in a general sense, a separate group in Soviet society. A third thought the opposite, while the remainder had no particular opinion. Only 2% of the sample admitted to being 'very poor', and 21% to being 'poor', themselves. Nearly all of the rest considered that they were not poor at all (regardless of a low income), or made no clear response. When asked to state whether they ever experienced a condescending attitude from officials, 3% replied 'often'; 18% replied 'sometimes'; and the remainder either had not, or had paid no attention to the matter (which implies the same thing).

A further explanation for unwillingness to admit personal poverty emerges from the opinions expressed on the *extent* of the evil in the Soviet Union, as subjectively perceived. About 75% of the respondents believed that poverty was widespread (involving between one and four-fifths of the population) while no less than 99% of them estimated the average wage to be significantly lower than the official published figure. The median sample estimate was 129 roubles, as against published figures of around 160 roubles (depending on the year chosen). This implied either a popular overestimation of the extent of poverty, or unrealistic official data, or both. Poverty in the village lay beyond the bounds of the survey, and many respondents did not comment on it, but most of those who did equated it to poverty in the towns. Since the peasantry had been desperately poor for decades this assessment presumably reflected a rise in their income.

If the urban poor indeed experienced no clear cut or pervasive feeling of apartness, such perception can be explained by the nature of Soviet society itself. We have often argued that this society is far

from being homogeneous, and there is little doubt about its hierarchisation. But at the same time it lacks the variety which political
freedom, pluralism and market forces engender. Perhaps, indeed, the
shared limitations of Soviet reality induce in Soviet man feelings of
'belonging' which are absent in less oppressive lands.

To what do poor people in the USSR themselves attribute poverty?
In order to elucidate opinions of our sample on this point, we proposed
twenty-six possible causes, divided into two broad categories; those
which accounted for poverty in general, and those which explained
it in personal or familial terms. Respondents were asked to state which
causes they considered 'very important', 'important', or 'unimpor-
tant', with an extra option added for indecision. The configuration
of the first two options, which may be combined for the sake of
convenience, is somewhat surprising.

A series of economic failings ranked highest, including unjustified
high prices for consumer goods (94.8%), official neglect of agriculture
(82.5%) and wrong wage policies (81.9%). Alcoholism also came
very high (87%), seemingly confirming the importance we attributed
to it in earlier pages. Soviet aid to developing countries was blamed
by 86.2% of the respondents. Among the rather less important factors
were an absence of material incentives (72%), popular unwillingness
to work (67.6%), the consequences of the Second World War
(70.2%), geographic and climatic factors (66.5%) and militarisation
(56.1%). General factors entered by far fewer respondents were
dysfunction of a 'good economic mechanism', a 'real need' to
strengthen national defence, Russia's historical backwardness, and
the hostility of the West (19%–35%).

The personal factors mentioned with greater frequency were family
size (75.6%), the choice of a poorly-paid trade or profession (52.2%),
and lack of education or training (37.6%). About a quarter admitted
an unwillingness or inability to find extra income, hindrances to
promotion at work, and health. It is hardly surprising that few
respondents were willing to admit lack of knowledge of other sources
of income (12.4%), or an inability to handle money (6.1%). Relatively few attributed their material hardship to a lack of desire to
make a career in the USSR; overt criticism of Soviet power; or a lack
of interest in material things.[7] Only a handful of respondents entered
factors beyond those listed.

Mention was made on p. xiv above to our earlier study of privilege in Soviet society. It is worth noting, to conclude this section, some curious similarities between the Soviet elite, as a social group, and the Soviet poor. The existence of each of them strongly contradicts the socialist ethic, and the central aim of the 1917 Revolution. Both groups are virtually unmentionable in official Soviet sources, and difficult to study: both have acquired, over the years, their own bodies of legislation, replete with promise and circumlocution; both have proved incredibly resilient to corrective pressures.

Furthermore, each is, in its own way, essential to the functioning of the Soviet state. Behind the humanitarian affirmations of the Soviet Communist party there lies, we would argue, a profound understanding of Soviet man's day-to-day expectations and requirements. Privileges are needed to stimulate effort and provide an exemplar of the good life attainable under Soviet power. Poverty, on the other hand, may well serve as a baleful warning to those who neglect their civic duty to labour. The curiously functionalist character of Marxism-Leninism in post-revolutionary conditions places low wages beyond any real criticism, and treatment of many citizens has in the past been extremely harsh. Public fear of downward mobility into the poverty state, and the known difficulty of escaping from it, may still be considered by a secretive and cynical leadership to have its uses. We would not go so far as to say that this attitude has completely crystallised out, or that it will always obtain. It was clearly stronger under Stalin than under Khrushchev, or even Brezhnev; the Andropov emphasis on labour discipline suggested that it could have hardened again. But there is no doubt whatever that while elitism is protected, the elimination of poverty continues to receive a rather low priority. The ambivalence of official attitudes to both of these unsocialist phenomena is profound indeed.

POVERTY IN EAST EUROPE

Our study so far has been concerned with the characteristics of Soviet poverty, and the problem of how far it has changed in recent years. Given the political and economic similarities between the systems in Soviet-controlled states, it is logical for us to review poverty in them, from the same perspective. We shall comment on the German Democratic Republic, Czechoslovakia, Poland, Hungary, Roumania

Table 7.1. *Population and GNP, East Europe, USSR, USA*
(in constant 1981 dollars)

	Population (millions) July 1981	Gross National Product (per capita)		
		1965	1975	1981
GDR	16.7	6,011	8,398	9,731
Czechoslovakia	15.3	6,278	8,387	8,958
Hungary	10.7	4,122	5,426	5,943
Poland	36.1	3,552	5,481	4,986
Roumania	22.4	2,306	3,636	4,238
Bulgaria	8.9	2,363	3,578	3,825
East Europe	110.1	4,080	5,818	6,109
USSR[a]	264.5		5,430	5,863
USA[a]	266.5		11,290	12,661

[a] 1980: the SAUS figures for Eastern Europe diverge slightly from the T. P. Alton, and others estimates.
Sources: Statisticheski ezhegodnik S. Ch. E. V., p. 7; T. P. Alton and others, p. 22 (GNP for East Europe); *SAUS,* 1985, p. 846; *Nar. khoz. SSSR,* 1980, p. 7.

and Bulgaria only. The 'socialist' governments of Yugoslavia and Albania have been subject to quite different developmental pressures, and may be justifiably excluded from consideration.

Let us again begin with the problem of average living standards. The figures available for any given country are often conflicting, depending on the source, but recent America dollar estimates of the respective Gross National Products provide a reasonable basis for comparison (Table 7.1). These show that by 1981 most countries of East Europe still lagged far behind the USA, and consequently behind the most advanced lands of the West, but surpassed the USSR itself. At the same time there were great differences between them. Bulgaria, Hungary, Poland and Roumania formed, as it were, a lower tier, while East Germany and Czechoslovakia formed an upper one, and enjoyed living standards much closer to those of the advanced industrialised nations. In the absence of freak income distributions, poverty must have been more widespread or intense in the countries with the lowest averages.

A second dimension is that of change over time. Figures from the same source indicate strong growth rates for most states between 1965 and 1975, though Bulgaria and Czechoslovakia appeared to falter

Table 7.2. *Average annual GNP growth rates (per capita,*
at constant prices; %)

	1965–70	1970–75	1975–80	1981
GDR	3.2	3.8	2.5	2.4
Czechoslovakia	3.2	2.7	1.3	0.1
Hungary	2.7	3.0	2.0	0.6
Poland	3.0	5.7	−0.1	−7.5
Roumania	3.2	5.2	3.0	0.3
Bulgaria	4.0	3.9	0.9	2.8

Source: T. P. Alton and others, p. 24.

after 1970 (Table 7.2). However, all rates dropped badly afterwards, with the partial exceptions of East Germany and Bulgaria, in 1981. Poland registered an absolute and potentially catastrophic decline. Separate estimates available for 'real personal disposable money income', adjusted for price changes, largely confirm this pattern, in so far as they show growth easing or ceasing in the late seventies in all countries except Roumania; but Roumanian figures are in any case thought to be among the least reliable.[8] We may well conclude, therefore, that up until the mid-seventies poverty was receding in most countries, but that afterwards this movement was reversed.

Some generalisation is possible regarding the sections of society most affected. Nationalisation of the means of production, and the sovietisation of management, have promoted wage distributions by branch of the economy broadly similar to that existing in the USSR. In fact, in all of the six countries under review, the same branches usually paid the lowest wages, although the order varied somewhat from one to another (Table 7.3). It is noteworthy that the biggest inter-branch differentials were recorded for the Soviet Union itself, and the smallest for Roumania. All countries of the Soviet bloc have graded their wage and salary payments in a functionalist manner, so that the least skilled manuals and service workers get the lowest rates, subject to various supplements and incentive bonuses. Yet as in the USSR, a specialist, white-collar job carries no guarantee of an above-average income, and many of the less favoured personnel in health, culture, agriculture, etc., may well find themselves among the poor.

During the seventies, all countries operated a minimum wage,

Table 7.3. *Lowest-paid branches of East European economies*
(1981, average monthly pay, local currencies)

	GDR	Czecho-slovakia	Hungary	Poland	Roumania	Bul-garia
All industry	1,055	2,772	4,163	7,821	2,342	207
Agriculture	1,010	2,621	4,071	8,167	2,286	181
Housing and public amenities	n.a.	1,991	3,706	6,938	2,067	176
Trade and delivery services	927	2,280	3,664	6,360	2,023	174
Education and culture	n.a.	2,456	4,010	6,013	2,320	176
Health, social services, tourism	n.a.	2,522	3,838	5,805	2,190	174

Sources: Statisticheski ezhegodnik S. Ch. E. V. M. 1982, pp. 391–4; *Statistisches Jahrbuch der DDR*, 1984, p. 127.

Table 7.4. *Minimum wages in East Europe (as a percentage of the average wage)*

	1970	1975	(1980)
GDR	39.7	39.2	39.4
Hungary	37.6	36.0	n.a.
Poland	40.7	33.9	38.0
Roumania	55.8	60.8	63.7
Bulgaria	52.6	54.8	46.6

Note: All figures for 1970 and 1975 from M. Pohorille. No data has been found for Czechoslovakia. Figures in the third column (circa 1980) are from different sources, as noted, and may contain some discrepancies. Data on wage rates is not regularly published in all cases. Years as follows: GDR – 1979; Poland – 1982; Roumania – 1980; Bulgaria – planned for 1980, against a minimum of 80 leva.
Sources: M. Pohorille, p. 295; *Statistisches Jahrbuch der DDR*, 1984, p. 127; D. Michev and others; *DDR Handbuch*, p. 728; P. Pissulla in H. Höremann, p. 259

though as may be seen from Table 7.4, most of the minima were exceedingly modest. Given what we know about living standards, the sums involved afforded but little protection against poverty. A combination of economic pressures and the Stalinistic wage reform effected in Roumania in September 1983 (for instance) cast doubt on the continuing validity of the minimum wage, while inflation and shortage has consistently robbed it of meaning in Poland.

A great deal of evidence in all cases shows that despite equal pay legislation womens' average earnings were significantly lower than men's. The greater likelihood of women being employed in the lower-paid branches of the economy, their exclusion from certain types of well-paid but onerous work, interrupted career patterns and other social considerations explain what appears to be a common differential of about 30 %. There is no consistent evidence that the gap between the earnings of the sexes has been closing over time.[9]

Soviet-style economics have always ensured a marked degree of disadvantage for the peasantry, which is still numerous throughout East Europe. (In Czechoslovakia, which had the smallest agricultural sector, it recently comprised 9 % of the total population, while the figure for Roumania, at the other extreme, was 30 %.) Nearly all peasants were collectivised after the Soviet occupation, and obliged to labour under harsh administrative regimes, with under-capitalisation of farming and low prices common. The principal exception was Poland, but in this case standards of living were depressed by other government restrictions, and by the small size of the plots. Peasants tend to do better under the more liberal regimes, when the threat of poverty recedes or when food shortages force up prices of garden produce; for the relatively small territory of the states under review facilitates access to urban markets.

Like most modernising societies, those of East Europe have witnessed a marked growth in the proportion of citizens receiving some form of social security. This is due not only to the planned extension of benefits to people formerly ineligible (particularly peasants), but also to a marked ageing of the population. All of the social security systems bear a close resemblance to that of the USSR. On the positive side there is the fact that coverage exists at all: for many people, the statification of social security after the Soviet occupation brought a degree of well-being which might otherwise have been unattainable. The new systems bore a strongly egalitarian character, in that the differential between the highest and lowest rates tended to be narrow, and manual workers came under the same regulations as white-collar personnel. Retirement ages were relatively low, at about fifty-five to sixty years for women and men respectively; the principal exceptions were Poland and East Germany, where in the 1980s the ages were still sixty for women and sixty-five for men. Pensions were all non-contributory (again with the partial exception of East Germany) and, when possible, earnings-related. The point has now been reached where

Table 7.5. *Pensioners and pension rates in East Europe (1980–81)*

	Pensioners as % of population	Average pension as % of average wage	Minimum pension as % of average wage
GDR	16.7	30.0	23.3
Czechoslovakia	15.3	44.8	23.2
Hungary	10.7	56.9	32.9
Poland	13.2	46.3	31.0
Roumania	7.4	58.1	46.7
Bulgaria	22.7	37.0	24.0

Note: The figures in the first and second columns are for 1981 and derived from data in *Rocznik statisticzny* 1983. Those in the third column have been assembled from the other sources, and although every effort has been made to effect a correct alignment, they should be regarded as indicative only. The figure for Czechoslovakia in this column covers the years 1976–9, and that for Bulgaria – the late seventies. Pensions are considered to be 'full', as paid to workers and employees (in cases where other social groups, for example peasants, have different rates).

Sources: Statisticheski ezhegodnik S. Ch. E. V. M. 1982, p. 422. Rocznik statisticzny 1983, p. 503. Poland, Statistical Data, 1983, pp. 30, 32. Porket (1981), p. 298. RFE Situation Reports (Cyclostyled), Hungary, 5th December, 1979; Roumania, 29th January, 1983. DDR Handbuch, p. 904.

eligibility for social security has been extended, like the franchise, to virtually all citizens, provided they fulfil the requisite conditions of service and disability.

At the same time, the drawbacks of the Soviet exemplar are no less evident. The ubiquitous earnings-related principle has deleterious effects for those who lack the necessary years of service. By 1981 average pensions varied between 30% and 58% of the average wage, but minimum pensions were exceedingly meagre (Table 7.5). An absence of 'national assistance' for the needy meant that family size or circumstance could easily take per capita income below local subsistence levels. None of the systems, with the partial exception of Hungary, appear to be index-linked, so recipients suffer from inflation. 'Second' economies, with their customary high prices and disadvantages for pensioners, have flourished, especially in Poland and Roumania. Women, who are likely to have lower earnings, retire younger and live longer, are most vulnerable in these circumstances. It is noteworthy, too, that the various peasantries, as in the USSR, had to wait until the late sixties or early seventies to be brought into the state schemes.

OVERT RECOGNITION OF POVERTY: POLAND AND HUNGARY

Public discussion of poverty in East Europe has, on the whole, varied in inverse relationship to the stringency of regime. The more rigidly controlled states – East Germany, Roumania and Bulgaria – have consistently banned all but the most indirect reference to the problem. Most comment here has centred on the implementation of minimum wage rates, and the operation of social security systems. In Czechoslovakia there was considerable interest in poverty at the time of the 1968 'thaw', and an extensive survey was conducted into popular attitudes to the problem. About a third of the population had failed to achieve a 'poverty line' established at that time, and two-thirds were below a line of 'minimal material comfort'. Since then, silence has again been the rule. A rare discussion published in 1979 claimed that the relative proportions had fallen to 2% and 10%, but the performance of the economy made such a claim dubious.[10]

The two countries where the most overt and objective analysis has been attempted are, not surprisingly, Poland and Hungary. We shall conclude with a brief review of some of the more accessible information on them.

Poland

As we have noted, throughout the seventies Poland occupied a middling position in East Europe in terms of living standards, as personal consumption rates rose and then fell sharply. But thanks to its tradition of independence, the country retained a degree of political freedom rare in East Europe, and its recent social history has been quite unique. Thus we have seen episodes of overwhelming social and economic turbulence, including popular uprisings at Poznan in 1956, Gdansk and Szczecin in 1970, Ursus and Radom in 1976, and on a more widespread scale in the summer of 1980. Overt discontent caused the displacement of no less than four national leaders – Bierut, Gomulka, Gierek and Kania. It has profoundly affected government policies towards pricing in the consumer and other sectors, and forced the incurrence of an enormous foreign debt.

Most observers agree that the causes of popular frustration lay in opposition to political and religious repression, anti-Sovietism, shortages of goods and the material hardship which, despite improvements in economic performance, continued to occur. These difficulties were made less bearable by perceived corruption and the patently unfair distribution of goods by administrative order. The consumer also suffered from the highest admitted rate of inflation in East Europe – prices, even by official estimates, rising by 71% between 1970 and 1981.

Not surprisingly, the economic difficulties of daily life attracted a great deal of attention, both among respected academics and in the less respected official media. Three income minima were commonly recognised: the *minimum exystencji*, which was unacceptably low; the *minimum socjalne*, which marked a barely acceptable level; and the *minimum spoleczne*, or public minimum, which permitted a slightly more generous life-style, with less frugality. Of these the *minimum socjalne*, or social minimum, came to be used as the commonest touchstone.

A revealing, and apparently reasoned, analysis of the decline in living standards was provided by Professor A. Rajkiewicz, Director of the Warsaw University Institute of Social Policies, in a lecture given in November 1980, and summarised in the newspaper *Dziennik Baltycki* a few days later. In 1970, he said, the social minimum had been set at 1,515 zloty for a single person, and 4,210 for a family of four. With the average wage in the socialised sector of the economy standing at 2,497 zloty up to a third of all Polish families apparently did not achieve this minimum. But because improvements in living standards early in the decade were palpable, the contingent of poor people undoubtedly fell. Rajkiewicz claimed that by 1980 some 6.2 million people, or 18% of the population, were still below the social minimum, about half of them being rural dwellers.

The economic breakdown which followed the disorders of 1980, however, caused a massive fall in living standards. Food prices, for example, increased 2.4 times between the beginning of 1982 and the middle of 1983. The increased stringency of the censorship following General Jaruselsky's accession to power hindered assessment of the poverty situation; but Dr J. Auleytner of the Warsaw Institute of Labour and Social Affairs stated in a March 1982 interview, that between 9 and 10 million people, or at least a quarter of the population, were by then failing to achieve the social minimum. According to Solidarity Trade Union sources, by the spring of 1983 this minimum had been raised to 5,500 zlotys for family members and 6,000 zlotys for individuals, while between 30% and 40% of working families, and 60% of all pensioners were below it. These estimates seem reasonable enough, given that the average monthly wage was 8,424 zlotys, and the minimum basic was 3,300 zlotys. The minimum retirement pension was, incidentally, only 2,300 zlotys.[11]

The problem of the consumer not only fuelled the Solidarity movement, but remained a central object of its concern. A recent list of complaints drawn up by the union included: low minimum pay; the inadequacy, and sometimes unfairness, of 'compensatory' payments to balance increased food prices; the unfair use of piece rates; oppressive employment rules; absence of index-linking for pensions; infrequent recalculation of the social minimum; inadequate control of prices; discrimination against farmers; the encouragement of new forms of privilege, and a 'retreat from many aspects of the social policy of protecting the poorest'.[12] Solidarity writers emphasise the need not only to protect toilers' interests, but also to effect far-reaching changes in the pattern of remuneration, social security benefits, and the supply of consumer goods. Solidarity is, of course, strongly socialist in orientation; anti-government criticism of a non-socialist character has been expressed in the underground journal *Niepodległość* (Independence).

A second response to economic difficulty has taken the form of charitable help, with the active involvement of the Catholic Church. The so-called 'Primate's Committee for Helping One's Neighbour' was established in Warsaw many years ago to encourage and coordinate such activity at a parish level. We have no precise estimates of its extent, but it was certainly considerable. The mechanism may be illustrated by a few extracts from a recent 'Solidarity' report.[13] As a result of a sermon by Bishop Tokarczuk at Jasna Gora, the diocese of Przemysl organized the collection of farm produce for 'the most needy inhabitants' of the towns.

About 270 tons of food were collected [mainly potatoes, apples, vegetables, nuts, dairy products, eggs, etc.]...The real and inestimable value of this collection was the fact that it created solidarity with the most deprived workers...It was discussed at a meeting of the Communist Party in Katowice, and several persons involved were interrogated by the police...In exchange for [fresh] food, the following goods were received: religious books, jubilee calendars, tinned food, fats, sugar, washing powder...13 tons of coal, 22 tons of coal dust...quantities of cheese and flour...Eight doctors from Katowice examined 1,000 patients and performed 220 minor operations...and medicines to the value of 60,000 zlotys were dispensed free of charge on prescriptions...As the needs of the town in the forthcoming years will not diminish, it would be desirable to arrange regular food deliveries earlier, and with greater care...

Exchanges such as these clearly require a strong charitable impulse on both sides, since no individual can be sure of avoiding loss. The recipients, it would appear, were known to the local priests or church authorities, but the strong ties between families in town and country undoubtedly facilitated matters. Assistance of this kind has been supplemented by the large Polish community abroad, on both a personal and a communal basis. Solidarity members have started special arrangements to help political prisoners and their families.

Hungary

With a population of less than 11 million, Hungary is the second smallest state in the Soviet bloc. Up to the mid-seventies (as may be seen from Table 7.1) its estimated per capita GNP came close to that of Poland. It experienced, like Poland, a massive anti-Soviet revolt in 1956, but its subsequent economic development has been amongst the smoothest and most successful in the bloc. Indeed, the relatively satisfactory supply of consumer goods engendered the term 'goulash communism'. The slowdown in the growth of living standards after 1980 would appear to have been less traumatic than that experienced elsewhere. Although the means of production have been nationalised, economic planning is less detailed than in the USSR, and market forces are allowed some play in the consumer sector. Politically, the atmosphere has been liberal and relaxed by East European standards, and anti-Sovietism (which is so imbedded in the Polish consciousness) is much less evident.

The configuration of poverty in Hungary has been the subject of a number of articles, both in the popular press and in learned journals. One of the more academic analyses was published by Dr Zsuzsa Orolin in the journal *Szociologia* in January 1980. Adopting what might be described as an almost critical approach, the author maintained that poverty, even in socialist Hungary, was a 'specific way of life', which established itself as a result of low income, insufficient education, unwillingness to work, unfavourable family composition, poor health, bad housing conditions, or faulty cultural tradition. She quoted (but did not name) an economist who claimed that 3% to 5% of the population had no regular home or adequate income, while a like number, though housed, had incomes which were below the subsistence level. Against this, a report published in August 1979 claimed that between 8 % and 15 % of the population (i.e., 800,000 to 1,500,000 people) did not achieve a 'comfortable living standard'. These comprised, it would appear, unskilled labourers in industry and agriculture, pensioners, families with two or more dependent children, single-parent families, and an unknown number of vagrants, alcoholics and dispossessed individuals. The country's important gypsy population (numbering 320,000 in 1971) is said to be particularly vulnerable to poverty, in so far as it has lost most of its traditional means of support, yet cannot be easily integrated into a socialist economy.[14]

Social security is another focus of analysis. In a recent article devoted to the development of the system, the sociologist Zsuzsa Ferge presented state policy not merely as a means of 'improving the wellbeing of the people' (in the hackneyed Soviet phrase), but as one of 'countering the inegalitarian effects of the private market', reducing important or 'inbred' social inequalities, and promoting 'positive discrimination in favour of worse-off groups.[15] This is almost the language of social reformers in the west. Ferge implied that the slowdown in economic growth was caused by, or closely related to, a concern for full employment which was supposed to 'automatically yield an acceptable income level for all'. However, the continuing demand for security to help the needy demonstrated the fallacy of this belief. 'Full' employment promoted intramural unemployment and lax work discipline, leading to loss of self-esteem and job satisfaction. Many social security provisions (child-care, the minimum wage, retirement pension rules) were actually aimed at encouraging people to take full-time jobs which, she implied, might be unrealistic. Ferge referred to a category of 'really unemployed' people without exploring the matter further. Her article offered no simple solution for the problem of hidden unemployment, and stated that the fate of the least fortunate groups over the next ten or twenty years was hard to predict.

The cautious analyses published in official sources may, however, be compared with the forthright comments of an unnamed Hungarian dissident recently interviewed by a Polish Solidarity activist in Budapest. Prices, he claimed,

are rising all the time: meat by 20 %, cooking oil by 50 %, transport, preserved food, i.e., everything that hurts the poorest people most. State compensation payments, at one per cent, are laughably low. This is, as it were, the other side of the economic reform. Twenty years ago things were bad for everyone, and everyone was in that sense equal. Since then enormous differences of income have appeared which in practice are not compensated by anything. The effect is catastrophic. Anything can be bought for money, but on the other hand you have to pay literally for everything. State social policy [i.e., security] in the sense of free medicine, care for the old and poor, has in general disappeared. Persons who have no opportunity to participate in the second economy are much below the social minimum, and real income differences are even greater. Seventy per cent of all pensioners cannot live on their pensions.[16]

In Hungary, too, poverty has prompted some public charity. In the mid-seventies a group of eight intellectuals associated with the sociologist Istvan Kemeny started a kind of unofficial counselling service for the needy. It was relatively successful, and in 1979 adopted the title of the 'Foundation for Assistance to the Poor' (under the Hungarian acronym SZETA). The Foundation was said to be the first truly independent organisation in communist Hungary. Its aim was to collect precise information on the poor, to make small gifts of money, clothing and household goods to families in need, and to offer advice on the use of legal, medical, educational and housing services.[17]

SZETA, by the nature of things, had to operate in an overt manner. The authorities adopted a negative attitude to it from the start: but since poverty had received some official recognition, private, and apparent innocuous attempts at alleviation were not entirely prohibited. Thus while a fund-raising concert openly advertised in the local press in September 1980 was disallowed, an auction of graphic art organised for the same purpose proceeded without let or hindrance in December. The number of persons involved in SZETA rose to a peak of 120, and included, it would appear, a Methodist minister. The Solidarity upsurge, however, frightened some participants, and the roll fell back to about thirty. At the time of writing the future of SZETA is in considerable doubt.

We have noted that Zsuzsa Ferge was not able to predict sure progress in the elimination of poverty in Hungary. Given current trends, few uncommitted observers would be prepared to do so for any country in the Soviet bloc. Developments since the Second World War, would, indeed, suggest that the imposition of the Soviet-style economics is unlikely to provide a satisfactory solution anywhere.

The Soviet government prides itself on its ability to plan social and economic development throughout the land. Yet all Soviet central planning is to some extent unrealistic. It is bound by the official 'cult of optimism'. So massive failure cannot be admitted; solutions must fit an established mould which seems to change but little over the years; and anything involving radical reform of the political or economic system seems unlikely to find expression. Within these limitations the eleventh Five Year Plan, covering the years 1981–5, and certain advance proposals for the decade up to 1990, may be taken as an official response to the social problems of the early eighties, including that of poverty. The promises it contains for the less favoured sections of society form a suitable conclusion to our study.

Personal income and consumption

The main problem, given the nature of Soviet economics, lies in the prospects for the consumer sector in general. The plan, as finalised late in 1981, stated that the growth of consumer-related branches of the economy (the so-called sector B) was to be 26.6 % over the five years, equalling, or slightly exceeding, that of heavy industry (sector A). The relevant figures have been analysed by Professor G. Schroeder, and some of her comparisons are shown in Table 7.6. Although this priority was new in the practice of five year plans, it nevertheless involved a fall in the *rate of growth* of consumption; indeed, national income as a whole was planned to grow more slowly than in the previous five-year period. Consumption as a proportion of national income was to rise to 78 % by 1985, as opposed to 75.3 % in 1980, which still left a relatively high rate of investment.

Real per capita income, the average state wage, and the collective farm wage were (as the table shows) all set to rise, but again by lower percentages than in the preceding five-year period. Retail trade, light industry, consumer durables, and housebuilding were to grow at approximately the same rate as before; repair and other services were to improve rather less quickly. At a more detailed level, a big rise was envisaged in the growth rate of the food processing industries, and figures (not adduced in the table) showed that like movement was envisaged in the production of clothing, certain domestic requisites, and such 'quality' foods as meat, fruit and vegetables.[18] The 'social

Table 7.6. *Growth rates of consumer-related branches of the economy*
(% increase over period indicated)

	Reported growth 1976–80	Planned growth 1981–5
Industrial output		
Group 'A'	26	(26–28?)
Group 'B'	21	26.2
Real per capita income	17.7	16.5
State wage (average)	15.8	14.5
Collective Farm wage (average)	26.1	20.0
Social consumption fund	29.3	23
Retail trade	24	23
Light industry	18	19
Consumer durables and related goods	41	40
Housing construction[a]	(530)	(530)
Food processing	7	22
Personal and repair services	43.3	40

[a] Millions of square metres of useful space, absolute figures.
Source: Extracted from Table 4, G. E. Schroeder, 1982, p. 384.

consumption fund', used for financing state benefits, health, educational and cultural services, etc., was to suffer a significant cut in its growth rate, but this may only have been a reaction to an earlier expansion demanded by extra provision for the peasantry (amongst other things). It must not be forgotten that any planned overall increases have to be set against a projected population growth of perhaps 5 % over the five-year period.

Foreign observers expected Soviet economic growth to be no more than 2% or 3% annually through the 1980s, as various strains, particularly in the supply of labour and capital stock, made themselves felt. If living standards increased proportionately, the average citizen would find himself (according to these estimates), one-eighth to one-quarter better off by 1990. A rise of this magnitude would still leave the USSR well behind its main capitalist rivals, even in the unlikely event of the latter making little or no progress themselves. It would also have only a marginal impact on the poverty problem. As it is, the agricultural failures of recent years, and the disappointing economic achievements of the early eighties, have already cast doubt on the viability of these objectives.

No less relevant is government policy in the sphere of income distribution. As we noted in Chapter One, the Khrushchev years brought a retreat from Stalin's elitist social policies, reductions in bonus payments, and a gradual narrowing of pay differentials among workers and employees. These changes, together with the consequent increases in real wages, benefited the lower-paid. The same policies were, at first, maintained under Brezhnev; but the directives of the tenth Five Year Plan, published in 1976, suggested that there was a renewed interest in incentives. Pay rises stipulated for middle-paid, white-collar employees benefited the topmost earners as well. The directives of the eleventh Five Year Plan retained the same emphasis, and required 'an increase in the dependence of wages and bonus payments received by every working person on his personal contribution, and on the final results of the work of the collective; an increase in the incentive role of wages and bonuses, a rise in productivity, an improvement in the quality of goods, and in the careful use of resources; perfection i.e., improvement of the system of wage-rates and labour norms'. The wages of various categories of toilers were to be 'perfected...taking into account the complexity of work, the responsibility it entailed, the conditions and intensity of labour', while wages were also to be perfected by branch of the economy and region of the country. As for the peasantry, their remuneration was to be made more dependent on the 'final results of their work, their productivity and the quality of their production'. Both the text of the eleventh Plan, and more recent legislation, show concern with encouraging people, when possible, to do more than one job.[19] The idea behind such proposals is that the stimulation of economic growth is more important than equal pay. Differentiation of this kind, together with the apparent development of the second economy, may operate to the disadvantage of the poor (at least until the day when improved output results in higher standards of living for society as a whole). The niceties of Marxist prognostication are once more being subordinated to current economic necessities.

The eleventh Five Year Plan, however, follows others in raising the wage 'floor'. 'As the conditions are created, and resources become available' the minimum wage is to be raised 'gradually' to 80 roubles a month, initially in the production branches of the economy. This cautious undertaking is followed by the proviso that the funds needed for increases should come from higher productivity. The previous minimum of 70 roubles took, it will be recalled, about a decade to creep through the economy, and there is little indication that this one will move faster. No minimum is mentioned for the peasant, but his pay is to be raised to the level of that of the agricultural worker as his 'productivity, skills and rate of employment (on the communal fields) increase'. To conclude on a more optimistic note: at last, nearly sixty years after the appearance of the RSFSR 1918 labour code, the peasant is promised a paid annual holiday, matching the statutory provision so long enjoyed by workers and employees.

Pension arrangements

The text of the eleventh Five Year Plan contained a number of proposals regarding the pension system, the detail of which was set out in laws passed in January, February and September 1981. We shall use these as a basis for comment, taking the story forward from our discussion in Chapter Five.[20]

The decree of January established a new monthly minimum of 50 roubles for workers' and employees' old-age pensions, to be implemented in the course of 1981. The comparable minimum for collective farmers was to be increased to 40 roubles, and introduced gradually over five years, reflecting anew the official reluctance to treat peasant and worker equally. No less noteworthy was the promise to increase pensions granted ten years or more previously to levels 'approaching' those enjoyed by persons newly retired (from like jobs). Pensioners receiving less than 60 roubles a month were to benefit first. This was a new departure in republican legislation, and eased, at long last, one of the most unsatisfactory characteristics of the system. However, the new rule as drafted could only help the older pensioners with but few years to live. It did not affect persons who had been retired for less than ten years, and stipulated that the process was only to be *started* in the eleventh Five Year Plan. The network of homes for old people and invalids was to be expanded, and there was to be an increase of 20–25 % in expenditures on 'medicines, food, and other needs' for them over the first half of the decade. Efforts to encourage pensioners to work, particularly part-time or at home, were to be maintained.

Provisions for invalids and survivors were improved under the terms of a Supreme Soviet edict of 2 September. The minima for the three invalid groups rose by five roubles each to 75, 50, and 30 or 26 roubles respectively (as against the sums stipulated in the November 1973 legislation). Families of three or more survivors likewise had their minima raised to 75 roubles, those of one or two survivors to 28 and 50 roubles. A basic minimum of 20 roubles a month was stipulated for all children under 16 (including peasants) and pupils under 18 years of age, if their parent or guardian had not worked the number of years required for a full pension.

Particular attention was again paid to the well-being of war veterans and families of soldiers who had been killed in action. A statute of 23 February afforded this group priorities in medical treatment and recuperation, some travel benefits, priority in housing, 50% rent reductions, special help in finding jobs, and other unspecified aid. The military had, of course, enjoyed superior provision for many years, and these improvements are best explained in terms of further rises in its influence and prestige.

The new measures fitted the government's long-term policy of improving pensioners' well-being, while the new Five Year Plan presented an apt opportunity for publicising them. The current stagnation in living standards possibly made them more needful. However, most of these improvements fitted the pattern of earlier years in that they were small and rather slow in coming. As will be evident from a reading of Chapter Five, the system itself was left almost unchanged. The automatic increase of pensions of ten years' standing was possibly the best indication of structural improvement in the future.

Help for poor families

A number of changes were proposed in state support for working and single mothers, poor families with children, and large families, while new provisions were introduced to help young couples setting up home. These measures were embodied in laws passed between January and October 1981, in some cases accompanying new pension provisions.[21]

The principal changes may be summarised as follows. Pregnancy leave for working mothers was increased to 70 days, and the first three days' absence after an abortion became payable. Birth grants were raised to 50 roubles for the first child, and 100 roubles for others, while mothers who had been at their jobs for a year acquired the right to eighteen months leave for baby care. Pay could now be claimed at the rate of 35 roubles a month throughout the first year, which was a great improvement on the year's unpaid leave available hitherto. All of this still, of course, betokened an exceedingly pinched lifestyle. The authorities promised to improve benefits in the second half of the decade.

Working mothers gained a few new concessions at their place of employment. There was to be 'wide implementation' of part-time working with flexible hours, faster release from 'heavy or unhealthy work', and a significant reduction of the numbers on night work(!). Those with children under twelve became eligible for an extra three days' holiday a year, priority in choosing the dates, an extra two weeks for child care (but this was unpaid, and available only if administratively practicable). Up to fourteen days leave could be requested, partly at half pay, for the care of sick children, and mothers of five or more could apply for early pensions. We have not, however, found any notice of increase in the tiny payments for the children of 'Heroine' and other decorated mothers.

Pre-school institutions, on which working mothers were particularly dependent, were to be improved over the decade. Families with four children or more had their fees halved, and those with a per capita income of less than 60 roubles (sic) were released from payment altogether. Such families were likewise entitled to free use of boarding establishments, which were also to be upgraded. Improvements were promised in the output of partly prepared foods, shop and home delivery services, and in the supply of children's goods.

We noted earlier that single mothers could claim a maximum benefit of only 10 roubles a month for three children or more. The new law raised the maximum substantially to 20 roubles per child up to the age of sixteen (or eighteen, for pupils without state stipends). Child allowances for poor families were retained at the 1974 rate of 12 roubles, but families living in the Far East and the North would now qualify for them with a per capita income of 75 roubles of month. All students who had children became automatically eligible for grants, without a means test, provided they passed their exams. Further unspecified improvements in child benefits were promised for the second half of the decade.

In an apparently new departure (at least, we have seen no earlier reference to such provisions at a national level) families with children and newly-weds were to be given preference in certain housing matters. People under the age of thirty who were getting married for the first time, and who needed living space, were to be allotted, 'as a minimum, a room', and if they had a child within three years, 'a separate, one-roomed flat'.[22] These new rules were to be introduced fairly quickly, over a six-month period, starting in the peripheral areas of the RSFSR. Hostel accommodation (occasionally used by newly-weds) was also to be improved.

Young couples (though hardly the poorest) may have benefited from a new policy towards private housing. This practice had had an uneven history in the USSR, but the January 1981 decree gave young families priority in the purchase of cooperative flats, and reduced down payments.[23] It must be remembered that loans normally bore an interest charge of only 2%. Young parents with good work records could also claim interest-free loans for home improvement (and, it would seem, construction). A peculiar aspect of the scheme was a permitted write-off of up to 300 roubles if the borrowers had a second or third child. House buyers in capitalist lands might well envy such opportunities, although the quantity and quality of Soviet housing would satisfy few. The loan scheme was to be introduced by stages, and also start in the least hospitable regions. An extra gift to young couples was the promise of exemption from income tax during their first years of conjugal living.

So broad a range of improvements in state provision for the poorer families introduced (if not implemented) in a short space of time may have been prompted by acute unease on the part of the authorities. If this was so, the falling birthrate, high infant mortality, increasing divorce rate, and the economic necessity to keep parents employed were the most likely explanations. The establishment in 1976 of permanent commissions for the 'Women's Labour, Living Conditions and Protection of Motherhood and Children' at the Supreme Soviet level was an earlier indication of concern. In any case, the modest role played by the poor in Soviet politics makes it hard to believe that the changes were brought about by pressures from below.

Reviving the village

The eleventh Five Year Plan dwelt specifically on the need to improve living conditions and amenities in the countryside. This policy was designed not so much to relieve rural poverty in itself, as to raise food production for society as a whole, and improve coordination between the agricultural and industrial sectors. The so-called Food Programme, launched in May 1982 and a series of associated measures filled out the general precepts of the plan. The more economic and adminis-trative implications of all this lie beyond the scope of our study; but aspects pertinent to the village poor certainly require mention.[24]

We have already noted that the eleventh Five Year Plan envisaged a significant improvement in peasant income. Subsequent measures made it evident, however, that this would be in a context of higher managerial pay, greater wage differentiation, and more emphasis on payment by result. A decree on improving the 'economic mechanism' in agriculture allowed for rises (from 15 January 1983) of 16 milliard roubles in the state prices paid for a wide range of animal and field products, together with state support for collective farm building (including houses, creches, clubs), equipment and certain types of insurance. Debts to the sum of 9,700 million roubles were annulled, and the repayment dates for another 11,080 million roubles were set back by ten years. This clearly betokened an easing of financial pressures on the farms and their employees. The Food Programme mentioned the need to heighten the prestige of agricultural labour, improve rational working and rest conditions, and close the gap between agricultural and industrial earnings.

There was further encouragement for the private plot. Despised under Stalin, tolerated by Khrushchev, it had continued to provide a large amount of the country's fresh vegetables and animal products, and save countless peasants from starvation. As a result of decrees passed in and after September 1977, it acquired a new-found respectability.[25] The Food Programme not only called for a 'significant' increase in production from this sector, but also for conditions which would allow 'each rural family to have its own garden plot, to keep cattle and poultry'.[26] For the first time in decades the authorities envisaged an expansion of the network of collective farm markets. The results of this policy seem to have been at best patchy. Reasons for continuing stagnation or decline in the private sector include the primitive character of the labour involved; peasant distrust of official policy, which was regarded as changeable; improvements in peasant income from other sources; and the introduction of social security benefits for the old and infirm, thereby reducing their incentives to labour.

Living conditions were dealt with in another enactment. One hundred and seventy-six million square metres of accommodation were promised for persons employed in all major types of agricultural enterprise, including collective farms. This compared with the 148.6 million built in rural areas under the tenth Five Year Plan, but still worked out at something less than two square metres per capita, *without* demolition of old structures.[27] Some 111,000 kilometres of hard-topped road were to be built, which meant about two kilometres per agricultural enterprise. This, given the catastrophic state of the roads, was not very much, but we may charitably presume it was concentrated in areas of great need. The rate of provision of public amenities like laundry and repair services was to be doubled; the village was to have its first public telephones, while the existing official and private telephone network was to be increased from a modest 3.9 million instruments to 7.2 million by 1990. The system of shops, medical services and water supply were also marked for considerable improvement. Proposals of this kind had, of course, found a place in Soviet economic plans before; new were the magnitudes involved, the apparent seriousness of intention, and the promise of effective financial backing.

Weighty promises were made in the sphere of education and culture. By 1985 about 1.2 million new places were to be provided in nursery schools, while an extra 2.3 million places in the general school would make it easier for children to complete their education in the villages where they lived, obviating the need for travel to the towns. New efforts were to be made to persuade young people to train for work in local health and cultural services. A big increase in the construction of clubs and 'houses of culture' was stipulated in the same context.

The extent to which the provisions of the eleventh Five Year Plan are implemented, both centrally and locally, remains to be seen. Yet there is no doubt that even full achievement of such objectives as raising the minimum wage, improving pension levels and other support schemes, will still leave the Soviet Union with a massive poverty problem. The plan may, or may not, be practical within the framework of the heavily militarised Soviet economy: but most of its social provisions are at best meagre. Few analysts would affirm, for example, given the pressures on prices, and all the other economic unknowns, that a minimum wage of 80 roubles, or a minimum pension of 50 roubles, will be worth more than the 70 or 45 roubles paid in the mid-seventies. The planned rises in many support payments will still leave many recipients well below the threshold we have discussed in these pages. Poverty, it would seem, will retain a prominent place in Soviet reality into the nineties and beyond.

POSTSCRIPT: TWELVE THESES ON SOVIET POVERTY

———————— ❖ ————————

(1) The existence of poverty some six and a half decades after the Revolution must be counted as a major failure of the Soviet experience. The central aims of the Bolshevik Revolution were not only the rapid establishment of a homogeneous society, but also the eradication of want. This failure has exceedingly negative implications for the practice of Marxism–Leninism elsewhere.

(2) The condition of the poor in the Soviet Union has been sadly neglected by Western observers, not least on account of the stringent Soviet ban on reporting. It is noteworthy that words like 'poverty' and 'slum' cannot be used in official sources to refer to any social condition in the USSR, and no official estimates are available. The contrast with the flood of information on poverty in other lands is stark indeed. Soviet poverty needs to be monitored by indirect methods; the difficulties of doing so should not be allowed to halt further research. The inability of Soviet power to eradicate poverty requires adequate illustration, both for Soviet citizens and the public abroad.

(3) Our analysis of Soviet data suggests that in the late seventies some two-fifths of the non-peasant labour force earned less than the sum needed to achieve a minimum level of subsistence proposed by Soviet scholars for small urban families. The incidence of poverty among larger families, peasants and pensioners was undoubtedly higher. Comparisons are hazardous, but about a ninth of the population of the USA was reported to be under the poverty 'cut-off' level in 1979. Moreover, a tentative cost comparison of the official US and 'academic' Soviet poverty thresholds indicates that the Soviet one is

much lower. Thus the application of American poverty standards to Soviet society would result in a far larger Soviet poverty contingent.

(4) The occupation groups most likely to be low-paid, and in poverty, comprise mostly unskilled manual and service personnel, recalling similar groups in Western society. However, many high-grade specialists are poor as well, and the actual earning power of women is significantly less than that of men. The great majority of pensioners evidently had incomes close to the state minimum. Despite their low income, the Soviet poor pay (by Soviet standards) significant amounts of income tax (up to 10% of gross pay). This, of course, is over and above the (relatively high) state mark-ups on consumer goods. A survey which we conducted amongst emigre families who were formerly poor indicated that there is much reliance on the 'second economy', most of it of dubious legality.

(5) Most supply failures, in so far as they inhibit purchase and affect prices, cause particular difficulty for poor people. That certain foodstuffs, especially meat and vegetables, are difficult to come by in many parts of the USSR is well known. Although appraisal in this sphere is also risky, the results of our survey showed that the quantities consumed recalled those claimed as national averages a decade and a half earlier. Many quantities (particularly meat, fruit and vegetables) did not reach the ideal stipulated for poor families by Soviet economists in the mid-sixties. Some products had on occasions to be obtained from collective farm markets, though prices there were significantly higher than in state shops. Overall, food costs absorbed nearly two-thirds of the total family budget, which is a well-recognised feature of poverty in capitalist society. There was also clear evidence of a shortage of heavy outer clothing.

(6) As for accommodation, we find that the Soviet poor lived in very cramped conditions, though average amounts of living space were not much less than among the public at large. Modern amenities were in many cases lacking, and tenants had to do a surprisingly large proportion of their own repairs. The cost of housing among poor people, even without repairs, ran at about 10% of income, and was far above the published national averages, contradicting the Soviet claim that rates are nominal.

(7) A key question in any assessment of poverty is the degree to which it is binding on those who suffer from it, in other words, whether a 'poverty trap' exists. The responses to our survey indicate that although respondents were upwardly mobile as compared with the

older generation, those who were in mid-career effected little substantive change in their own occupational status. This rather implies
that mobility has slowed, so that anyone starting a career in a low-paid
job has a good chance of staying in it. The poor have gained much
from the growth of educational facilities, but suffer from a palpable
discrepancy between educational achievement and occupational
status.

(8) To judge from the survey results, most people believed that
poverty was still widespread in the USSR. Its causes were thought to
lie mainly in the state's misdirected consumer policies, militarisation,
and, on a more personal plane, alcoholism and a failure to adapt to
circumstances (by obtaining for example, a better job, more education
or training).

(9) Although the condition of the poor in the USSR is, from a
western perspective, unenviable, they are in some respects less vulnerable than one might suppose. They avoid, it would appear,
unemployment (though were it to become a major problem we see
little reason why they should enjoy special protection). Their diet
might be far from satisfactory, but it is well above malnutrition. The
clothing situation, though difficult, is not disastrous. Most poor
people, by capitalist standards, have moderate housing costs and
considerable security of tenure. Many have benefited from the
house-building programmes of recent decades. Education and health
care are free and although the poor do not generally get the best, or
even adequate, service, the problem of fees does not in itself inhibit
access. The replies to some of the questions posed in our questionnaire
suggested that political pressures affected poor people's work and lives
less frequently than one might suppose. There is a fair degree of
adaptation to long-standing difficulties, no doubt encouraged by an
ignorance of the situation of the poor in other lands, and the feeling
that there is little to be done anyway. At the same time social groups
who are poorer than those in our sample may react differently.

(10) There are few grounds for believing that significant improvements have taken place in the living conditions of Soviet poor
between the late seventies and the present. Economic progress is
reported to be poor, there has been considerable agricultural failure,
and the expensive arms build-up has continued apace. It is likely that
the average standard of living in the USSR in fact fell further behind
that of the richest capitalist lands.

(11) The present leadership under Mikhail Gorbachev has up to

the time of writing (May 1985) given little indication of immediate concern with the problem of low income. In his speeches over two years before assuming the General Secretaryship, Gorbachev laid emphasis rather on improving productivity, strengthening discipline, and increasing the value of bonus payments. Such policies, if implemented, would probably lead to more wage differentiation, and could also promote unemployment, especially among the less skilled. At the same time Gorbachev's career in rural administration might mean a better deal for the village poor.

(12) The current generational change in the Politburo of the CPSU will doubtless give scope for new social policies. New leaders may well wish to develop their own public profile, and some movement in the social sphere is inevitable. But how innovative, or effective it will be remains a matter of conjecture. Poverty would seem to be too much a part of Soviet reality to be easily effaced.

APPENDIX 1

SAMIZDAT AND OTHER UNOFFICIAL DOCUMENTS RELATING TO POVERTY IN THE SOVIET UNION

———————— ∾ ————————

1 Poverty and working conditions in Siberia
2 Poverty and the large family
3 Problems faced by single parents
4 Communal living in Leningrad
5a 5b Poverty among invalids
6 Russian drinking habits
7 Poverty in Central Asia
8 Poverty and political persecution
9 Infringement of social and economic rights

Materialy Samizdata (Materials received from the USSR and made available to the public by the *Samizdat* Archive of Radio Liberty, Munich, henceforth 'MS', with numeration).

DOCUMENT I. *Poverty and working conditions in Siberia*

This document, part of an open letter addressed to the American Federation of Labour and Congress of Production Trade Unions in December 1977, describes working and living conditions in the hamlet of Chuna, Irkutsk province. The author, Anatoli Marchenko, is a worker, himself born in Siberia. Although the conditions described were no doubt typical for Siberia in the late seventies, they were probably inferior to those of the towns of European Russian. At the time of writing Marchenko was living in Chuna as a political exile. His account of his earlier experiences in labour camps, *Moi pokazania* (Frankfurt am Main, 1969), is valued for its restraint and evident veracity.

(MS, 3197, No. 14, 1978)

Translation from US Commission on Security and Cooperation in Europe, *Report of the Helsinki Accord Monitors in the Soviet Union*, 7 November 1978, Volume 3, p. 5.

It was not your fault or mine that I was unable to visit you. Still, I would like my short statement to be heard at your convention. And so let me tell you about the workers' life in a Siberian settlement, Chuna. Of course, I will not try to describe all aspects of this life; I will touch on three questions only.

The average pay of our workers is approximately at the level of the official average pay in the whole country, that is about 160 roubles per month. How does the worker earn this salary? In the drying section, the sorting and stacking of boards is done only by hand. Mostly women are used for this work. The damp boards coming in from the lumber mill measure five meters in length, and 19–20 mm. in thickness. The production quota for each worker, be it a man or a woman, is from 10–17 cubic meters per shift, paid for at the rate of 23–40 kopecks per cubic meter. A worker can make no more than four roubles per shift, or not more than 120 roubles per month (about $170 a month at the official exchange rate. There are one hundred kopecks in a rouble). Added to this is a premium of 20 per cent for working in a remote area. If the plan is overfulfilled (more than 400 cubic meters per person per month) a bonus is added. All this hardly reaches 160 roubles per month.

But this income is not guaranteed. In the first place, because of bad organization of labor the fulfillment of the plan does not at all depend on the worker himself. Secondly, the bonus is awarded only when the monthly plan is met by the whole section or shop, not just by the individual worker.

There are a thousand reasons why the section might not meet its plan, and these also do not depend on the worker. In order to fulfil the plan and receive the bonus, at the end of the month people have to work not one shift of seven to eight hours as established by law, but two shifts in a row, even on days off. These extra hours are not registered and no overtime is paid for them. The management of the trade union, together with the plant administration, organizes these illegal extra shifts...

I decided not to work additional shifts, and I was fired from the plant for 'violation of labor discipline' by decision of the union and plant committees.

The workers of the drying section work in any weather under an open sky, in winter in temperatures lower than −40. The law states that extra pay, the so-called 'cold-weather premium', must be paid under such conditions. But, with the knowledge and approval of the trade union, this premium is not paid to us.

Often the weight of the boards exceeds the maximum weight limit set for women or adolescents. Adolescents are put to work paired with adults, that is, on an equal basis with them. I refused to work with an adolescent and the shop foreman punished me by transferring me to other work.

In the settlement, many people come from other regions, for instance, from the Ukraine; a round trip takes from 12 to 14 days. Most of the workers at the plant receive 15 days paid vacation. This means that relatives may not see each other for years.

Except for the drying section, the whole plant works in two shifts. Women with small children, of whom there are many at the plant, also work these shifts. All the kindergartens and nurseries in Chuna are operated in the daytime only. In order not to leave the children alone, married people arrange to work different shifts, and they see each other only on days off. It is even worse for mothers without husbands: they are forced to leave their small children completely alone at night. An acquaintance of mine tells me that her children (aged seven and ten) don't go to sleep until she returns from the second shift, that is until two o'clock in the morning.

Women go to work under such conditions because a family cannot live on one average salary. (Incidentally, our statistics are silent about the minimum wages necessary to live in the Soviet Union).

Can a family live on 160 roubles per month? The following things can be bought for this sum of money: one round trip ticket from Chuna to Moscow by air; two tyres for the compact car 'Moskvich'; or three to five children's coats.

A kilogram (2.2 pounds) of meat in the store costs two roubles; a kilogram of dried fruit – 1.60; milk – 28 kopecks per litre (one quart); eggs – 0.90 to 1.30 roubles for ten; butter – 3.60 roubles per kilogram. But most of the time none of this is available in the stores. If one is able to buy anything privately, one must pay almost twice as much: a kilogram of pork costs four roubles; milk – 40 kopecks per litre.

Judging from all this, you can see how far our average monthly pay goes to cover the minimum needs of the family. We may not have unemployment, but the average pay of a worker here is probably less than your unemployment compensation.

It is said that our rents are the lowest in the world; rent for an apartment is only one-eighth or one-tenth of an average salary. My friend pays 17 roubles a month for his apartment. He and his wife, two working daughters, and a son, a high school senior, live in a two-room apartment (one: 170 square feet, the second: 130 square feet) with a tiny, hardly passable corridor, a cramped kitchen and a shared bathroom. Their multi-family dwelling has facilities: central heating, an electric stove in the kitchen, hot and cold running water, and indoor plumbing. That is the maximum of convenience known to us.

About a quarter of the Chuna population lives in such housing. Half of the two-story, sixteen-apartment buildings have no facilities: communal lavatories, cold wooden outhouses in the backyard, water at a street pump, stoves for heating. The rest of the people in the settlement live in their own or government-owned huts, also without any facilities whatever: often there is not even a water pump, only a manually operated well, several hundred yards from the house. We have no standards by which a dwelling can be condemned as a hovel unfit for habitation. If people live there, it means it must be usable.

DOCUMENT 2. *Poverty and the large family*

The following document is part of an appeal made by the Zherdaevs, an Evangelical Christian family, to leave the USSR in May 1979. The text speaks for itself. The family was fortunate in that a well-known dissident priest, Gleb Yakunin, publicised their plight and helped them get a renovated flat on the Mir Street in Moscow. In August 1980 the members were actually allowed to emigrate. There is no doubt that many Christian families suffer a certain degree of persecution, and are particularly subject to poverty as a result. An unwillingness to control family size is obviously an exacerbating factor.

Source: Samizdat Document, Centre for the Study of Religion in Communist Lands, Keston College, Kent.

We have six children. We are still living in a room of sixteen square metres, in a communal flat. We suffer greatly from overcrowding and damp.

The house was not heated for weeks during the winter, and we were unable to sleep, as we tried, somehow or other, to keep the children warm. They had coughs which sometimes caused vomiting. The cold, damp and stagnant air irritates their lungs, and no cure is possible in such conditions.

Our eight-year-old son, who had to be sent to a boarding school for lack of space and the absence of conditions in which he could do his school work, has been ill for over a year. A chronic infection of the ear has caused him to lose his hearing, but no effective treatment has been applied.

When we brought him home for some time, to prepare him for an operation, we were accused of breaking the law on school attendance, threatened with court proceedings, and obliged to put our son's health at risk again.

I am troubled by something else. In the morning the shops open, but I cannot buy milk for the children because I have no money. The tiny grant which we get from the state amounts only to 33 kopecks a day for each child. And today, as often happens, we have to wait for the second-hand bookshop to open, in order to sell books to feed the children with porridge without butter and criticise ourselves for wastefulness after spending only ten roubles on food...

In this country, from early childhood we heard only about children's happy fate and the state's concern for large families. But now we have to put up with mockery or empty expressions of sympathy. There is no help. The state is completely indifferent, our accommodation situation is very bad, medical services are unqualified, and even the most basic foodstuffs are lacking. If they do appear in the shops and we have money to buy them, we still have a long wait in a queue. People like ourselves, with small children, do not have the time for it.

As a result of this barbaric treatment we and our children often go hungry. This has affected their health – they are weak and often fall ill.

But the moral murder of our children worries us much more than our material needs. It is effected methodically, through the well-organised system of atheistic education...

Help us leave the Soviet Union, help us save our children before they are crippled permanently.

(Signed) Nadezhda Zherdeva
Moscow,
May, 1979.

DOCUMENT 3. *Problems faced by single parents*

The article from which these comments are extracted was, like Documents 1 and 2, written in the provinces, and describes what must be a fairly typical situation. The author, Vera Golubeva, lived in Arkhangel'sk (Archangel) and wrote for the first number of an underground almanach entitled 'A Journal for Women and About Women', dated 10 December 1979. The article contained, in addition to the text reproduced here, a harrowing account of conditions in a local abortion clinic.

(MS 3886, No. 10, 1980)

The greatest blessing nature has granted women is to fulfil her destiny as a mother. Only a woman who has experienced the feelings of motherhood is capable of understanding, feeling and appreciating all the indivisible responsibility for the life of a small being. The medal for Mother-Heroines does not exist for nothing.

But here we are concerned with the so-called single mother, who has the audacity to bear and bring up a child without a father.

Many women, when deciding on this courageous action, do not always realise what a thorny path they have chosen. Some of them have neither close relations nor even parents who are in a position to help them in difficult moments.

Nor can they expect much from society. The state allots 5 roubles a month for the upkeep of a child born out of wedlock. Even these 5 roubles have to be secured through numerous formalities and humiliations. You are not informed that you have any right to them, and they are not sent through the post; furthermore, it is impossible to live even two days on so ludicrous a sum.

But a single woman with a child, who has no one to rely on except herself, needs maintenance money for at least a year.

A woman can only survive comfortably for a year without working if she has carefully thought over and foreseen all the difficulties of life on her own, and has saved up some money in advance. But very few women are capable of doing it, because in practice it's extremely difficult to foresee what life will bring tomorrow...

Let us say the mother has taken care of her child for a year. From now on, of course, she is counting on the state and a place in a nursery. But here a new problem arises; how can she get one? To be sure of that, you have to be on the waiting list before the child's birth. There's one other solution; to leave work and take a job in the nursery, in which case the child will be admitted as well. If you have no medical training you will have to take on the dirtiest and heaviest work, and look after your child at the same time. That's quite important, since if you imagine that your child is going to be as happy in a state-run institution as he is at home you are greatly mistaken.

Nurseries and kindergartens are the most pernicious establishments in the country's public health system. The majority of the staff are middle-aged and elderly women. There is a small proportion of young women who take jobs as cleaners for the sake of their children. Most of the middle-aged and elderly staff have no children of their own. It's hard to say what brought them in to this flowery garden of childish innocence and spontaneity. But it is hardly likely to be a spirit of self-sacrifice and self-denial on behalf of weak and helpless babies, who need such careful tending...

Most of them are motivated by self interest. They know that these small, helpless creatures won't tell anyone what they see happening around them, since they are not yet capable of understanding or judging the actions of the adults who hold their tiny lives in their hands. People make use of this. I have had occasion to deal with such people. Never, anywhere have I come across such a heartless and quarrelsome lot. They come with a particular purpose in mind – to steal. They deprive the children of food, the basis of life. Half of the meat is replaced with bread; what a blessing it is that some clever cook invented meatballs and rissoles, gnocchi and patties. Milk and smetana can be mixed with water, which is also convenient.

In summer, when the children are taken out of town to the country, so they can get some fresh air and eat fruit and vegetables, there's another chance to make something on the side.

Fruit brought for the children by their parents is shared out between the staff, so the children are left with biscuits, sweets and other sugary things with no nutritional value.

The arrangements to keep the children clean are very bad. Girls are rarely washed, and are dried either with their own nighties, or with one towel for all. Their hands and feet are not washed at all often, either, and it's the same towel for everyone again...

The reason for the state of affairs must be sought in the origins of the public health system, and in the way the staff's work is organised.

The understaffing and high turnover is linked with the low rates of pay. Nurses are paid 80–90 roubles a month and orderlies 75.

The work of women who are called on to rear and care for the next generation, devoting their health and mental energies to it, is sadly undervalued.

DOCUMENT 4. *Communal living in Leningrad*

The main evils of the housing shortage in the USSR express themselves in 'multiple occupation' and substandard conditions. In this article, written for the second number of the underground journal 'Woman in Russia', Mrs Natalya Malakhovskaya describes with some irony the trials of cohabitation with difficult or rude neighbours, and the physical dangers of disrepair. The proportion of the writer's acquaintances living in communal flats in Leningrad late in 1979 was well above the official figure, possibly indicating that people who endured this misfortune tended to come from the same social group as she did.

(MS 4024; No. 28, 1980)

How do we live?

Can we describe our existence, if not as decent, then at least as tolerable?

To answer this question one needs to find out how many people live in separate flats, and how many in communal accommodation. Since the ordinary citizen has no access to [such] statistical information, we have to attempt a statistical analysis ourselves. Of all the families I know, thirty-one live in communal flats (I do not count the neighbours in my own) and only sixteen in separate flats. It is interesting to note that only one of the independent [i.e., dissident] journalists in our city lives in a separate flat (one small room shared with his parents).

So, on the basis of this reckoning, I have come to the conclusion that the problem of communal flats must interest many of our readers. It is certainly among the issues needing discussion in a women's journal; after all, the burdens of life in such flats fall mainly on the shoulders of the women. One sink among several families in the communal kitchen means that none of the women can wash to the waist at home, while the men can, even though it is women who need to observe the rules of hygiene most carefully. When there is one cooker for several families, again it is the women who come into conflict. This means that on top of the nervous, psychological and physiological overload described in my article 'The Maternal Family', there is another, often scarcely tolerable burden. The ease of entry into other people's living quarters encourages a huge number of crimes, the majority of which are, again, directed against women (rape, murder and attempted murder on the part of male neighbours who 'covet their neighbour's wife').

...very many flats in our city which date from the time of Dostoevsky are so dark that the electric light has to be on from morning till night. But we're lucky to have a flat that's light, because the windows face east. Again, most communal flats are over-crowded, with ten or even fifteen families in them: but there are only three families in ours. But day and night you are surrounded by a solid ring of people with whom you have nothing in common; they may be uneducated and pride themselves on their ignorance; they may have no inner life and profoundly despise any interests that are not intrinsically material. If you are educated, they will sarcastically call you an intellectual (which they regard as a terrible insult); if you have a drop of Jewish blood, you are called a yid. And all this goes on in your own home, when you are washing at the only tap, or cooking on the only stove in the communal kitchen. There are neighbours who will steal your letters from the letter box or open your parcels; some even amuse themselves by ruining your clothes with cat dirt, etc., etc. Each one has his hobby – after all, something has to fill the hallowed gap when there are no spiritual interests.

Don't let their apparent kindness in periods of 'peaceful co-existence' deceive you, when they make you listen to all their intimate secrets, or tell you what people are up to at work – illegal dealings, theft, or trade in spoiled goods...

True, the ceiling may fall in at any moment, but are you the sort of person to be frightened by such trifles? The floor is barely holding and the walls are no better, when someone started peeling the wallpaper off, bricks fell out. Do you know what they said at the housing office (which is supposed to look after repairs)? In the house next door all the ceilings are hanging loose on their supports, and in number 17 on our avenue the ceiling fell in and killed a woman. But we aren't dead yet, so what are we worrying about? It's interesting that we received the same kind of answer from the militia, when we went to complain about a neighbour who tried to kill us. 'You haven't been killed yet, have you? So what are you complaining about? When they finish you off come back and tell us.' You see, we're better off than a lot of people. Incidentally, the building where I work is also in a desperate state. [They told us officially six months ago that] the ceilings might collapse at any minute, but we go on working there, and no repairs are even scheduled; really, is it worth worrying about such a tiny thing?

Do you know how they are tackling the housing problem in our city? In order to deal with the waiting lists faster, they are offering families of three and four people who have been on it for more than ten years, not a self-contained flat, but another little room in the communal flat where they live. In this way living conditions which are incompatible with human dignity, contravene all standards of hygiene, and are often dangerous to life and limb, are perpetuated indefinitely...

But such matters as these don't really concern you. You are only worried that the rent of your flat is too high. You have to do without something. So do I. I don't know how you manage, but I, for instance, have to economise for several days, so as to buy toothpaste or soap. Both my son and I are obliged to do without essential foods, like fruit and vegetables, and sometimes to get by without meat and milk. Even those of my colleagues at work who earn

10 roubles a month more than I do often complain of feeling hungry. Although they work eight hours a day, they often have no money for breakfast or lunch. It's not surprising, for in our harsh climate you can't manage without warm clothing, and you have to deny yourself food to buy even a warm scarf. I know all too well what prolonged undernourishment can do to you; one soaking was enough to give me pneumonia. I didn't have ten roubles for an umbrella which would have protected me from the rain; as a result I had to spend seventeen roubles on medicine. Where did I get the money? From sympathetic relations who had some to give away, that is, by what we call charity. My clothing and footgear are either presents or other people's hand-me-downs, as well. Although I do a full day's work, I am not only unable to make a decent living, but also to protect my son and myself from cold and hunger...

DOCUMENTS 5A, 5B. *Poverty among invalids*

Invalid status is associated with poverty even in the most industrialised and wealthy countries. Relative to other Soviet pensions, provision for the disabled may seem reasonable, and in some way generous: but in absolute terms such people may suffer greatly. The following texts, taken from the underground 'Information Bulletin of the Initiative Group for the Defence of the Rights of Invalids', illustrate common complaints. The first shows how physical hardships may be exacerbated by the inflexibilities of the social insurance system, and the absence of a national body to represent their interests. The second deals with holidays, revealing some of the ways in which poor people may cut costs. The writers seem, alas, to have an exaggerated idea of the well-being of disabled people in capitalist lands.

(MS 3770, No. 41, 1979)

Document 5a

Among all the people of the USSR, the disabled, whose fate should evoke sympathy and pity, are most subject to cruel and refined exploitation, both economic and moral. Separated from the whole world, and from one another, they live pitiful, poverty-stricken lives. A sociological survey which we conducted among them showed that they live on the very verge of destitution. They are deprived of the right to education and skill, to enjoy culture, move about and have decent holidays, to labour, enjoy proper food, medical services, housing, clothes and sport, that is, the right to physical and psychological rehabilitation. It is difficult to imagine how an invalid can live on seventy roubles a month (the state pension for an invalid of the first group). But apart from that there are people who are invalids from childhood and who get only sixteen roubles a month. (By way of comparison let us recall that the cheapest car for invalids in the USSR costs between 4,800 and 5,200 roubles; a winter coat costs 200 to 300 roubles, and winter shoes 70 to 80 roubles.)

It is well-known that the level of consumption in the USSR has lagged behind that of developed western countries, in both the economic and cultural respects, by a factor of between five and six. Most striking is the fact that the level now is lower than in pre-revolutionary Russia. There is a serious shortage of essential goods. It would seem that no increase in the standard of living has been included, or will be included, in the plans of the ruling elite. To maintain the political regime, it is essential to keep society on the edge of destitution...

Invalids living in state homes find themselves in the most terrible conditions of all. They are completely dependent, and have no rights. stealing is widespread everywhere, telephones are cut off, there are reports of terrible beatings, and absolutely helpless, bedridden individuals being driven to suicide by the treatment they received. (Letters and eye-witnesses accounts are available to prove it.)

We have no organisations which protect the rights of invalids, on the contrary the so-called Councils of Invalids which have been set up in homes for the disabled, and whose decisions are binding on everyone, are there to restrict young people's activities. The Councils (groups of privileged and well-heeled invalids) merely follow the instructions of the management in all that they do. There is a system of punishment – from solitary confinement to the worst thing of all, the threat of enforced isolation, and transfer to one of the terrible psychiatric homes where incurable cases are housed. There is also enforced transfer to homes which are known for their strict regime.

...in 1956 the All-union Invalids' Cooperative, a network of large workshops for invalids was disbanded. Neither numerous demands nor protest demonstrations organised by the disabled in front of the Moscow Party Committee building had any effect. The journal 'Invalids Co-operative' was closed as well. Fairly recently, in 1977, a workshop which had begun to produce industrial output on a cooperative basis in Voronezh was also disbanded. Any initiative on the part of the disabled to create their own society is at present forbidden, and the KGB is threatening the people behind it with imprisonment and other forms of retaliation. For the moment more mild forms of repression are being used, like depriving invalids of their right to transportation, breaking up their vehicles (which is all they have) and taking away their driving licences. The militia may break into their houses and conduct illegal searches; their postal correspondence may be confiscated, etc...

Document 5b

As a rule invalids are not to be seen in the streets, and even more rarely in holiday areas. The pension of the great majority up to 1 January 1980 ranged from 16 to 70 roubles per month: now it ranges from 30 to 70 roubles. So naturally they have neither the money nor the opportunity to arrange a holiday for themselves. They are gnawed by a constant concern to make ends meet and stay alive. They are ashamed of their bad clothing and ugly, unreliable bicycles or motor-carriages. Invalids in these categories have no reductions on railway tickets in the summer months, only in the winter, autumn and spring periods, when roads are impassable. The cost of a journey from the central areas of the country to the southern coast (including a taxi to the airport, the flight, and a taxi to their destination) is almost twice as much as a group one invalid from childhood receives. (The most seriously disabled invalids cannot use railway transport because railway stations and the trains are totally unadapted to their needs.)

The number of places in the special 'reservations' for the disabled (the sanatoria in Saki, Sernovodsk and in the Baltic areas, etc.) is tiny compared to the number of people needing convalescence and a holiday. Many invalids have never been in these reservations at all; other have not been able to get tickets for six years or more... In other holiday resorts and zones throughout the country the local bosses don't even understand that they must take account of the needs of invalids, and create conditions for them to enjoy their holidays just like the able-bodied. At present holiday resorts are absolutely unadapted for invalids. The most beautiful and convenient places have signs prohibiting entry: there are closed gates, barriers and sentries. Of course, able-bodied people may freely pass through the gates, walk along the pebbly shore and over the hills, but how do invalids manage? In order to get permission for their special carriages to enter, they have to climb high administrative stairs, perhaps with a broken back, and possibly end up with nothing...

Let us take the case of a 'well-off' invalid who is in the first group. His pension is 70 roubles per month, and his mother gets 56 roubles, which makes 126 roubles in all. Let us say that as a result of fasting for 15 years, and saving up kopeks, the family has bought a car (the Zaporozhet designed for invalids costs 3,600 roubles). Sea and mud cures are an almost unrealisable dream for that man. He can't save anything, for nearly all his money goes on petrol, repairs and medicines anyway. He gets no compensation for increases in the price of petrol, repairs and spare parts. The journey from Moscow to the Crimea, which is 1,600 kilometres long, takes 120 litres of petrol. The return journey, plus travel around the Crimea takes, shall we say, 360 litres. At 15 kopeks per litre this works out at 54 roubles, plus 5 roubles for oil, 35 roubles for various services, including technical work at garages. So the journey alone, and the use of the car come out at 94 roubles. Of the 126 roubles that the couple gets, 94 roubles goes on these expenses, leaving 32 roubles. Unforeseen expenses for two work out at about 28 roubles. So only 4 roubles are left for food. Naturally, the would-be holidaymakers have to borrow 20 roubles – they can't ask for more, because there is no way of paying it back, and the car may need repair after the journey. The Zaporozhtsy are not very reliable, especially if they are old. So the couple have 24 roubles for food, or 40 kopeks per person per day. There can be no question of dining rooms, or fruit: they have to manage on bread, vermicelli and a primus stove. The disabled family, of course, is in no position to pay 2 roubles a day each for beds. The only way out is a tent – even for invalids! The 3 roubles and 20 kopeks registration fee for each person even as a backhander, so that no questions are asked about the tent or the car, equals the cost of food for eight days.

We think that extortions such as these from families with disabled members are shameful.

DOCUMENT 6. *Russian drinking habits*

There is little doubt that the Soviet Union has one of the highest rates of alcohol consumption in the world – a sad commentary indeed on six decades of communist rule. According to the best western estimates, the average family may spend an eighth of its income on alcoholic beverages. Heavy drinking may easily reduce a family to the poverty state. Further problems arise because Soviet towns have relatively few cafes, bars or beerhalls where such beverages may be legally consumed.

The following account of Soviet drinking habits was compiled from the statements of a number of observant, though abstemious, members of the BBC Russian service in London:

How much does an ordinary Soviet drinker consume? He makes every effort to drink a bottle, that is, half a litre a day. That's his ideal. But it's all a matter of money. Usually he can't make it because at seven to eight roubles a bottle, it costs too much. The most common thing is to split a bottle between three.

The way a person drinks on any given day depends on what happened the day before. If he drank a lot, he may try and buy more before he starts to work, to sober up. The easiest thing is to go to the wine department of the grocer's when it opens at 10 o'clock, and buy a bottle of port wine, which is strong but sweet. He will try not to drink vodka first thing in the morning, because if he does, that's the end of his day's work. Beer's better, of course, but you can't usually get it in the morning. There is usually a big queue at the beer booth, and people don't have time to wait.

A worker *can* drink vodka at lunch-time. That's sort of morally acceptable. If he shares a bottle with two others, they can have a glass each. Glasses are always a problem. In a factory you can get one in the cafeteria: in the street you can steal one from a water dispenser, or go to a public dining hall, say, and drink there. Drinkers usually buy a glass of stewed fruit, or a soft drink, and use the glasses for other purposes. But if you do that the vodka has to be poured out secretly under the table, because it's usually prohibited.

The lack of proper drinking places is a tragedy. It was only a couple of years ago that drinking halls appeared in Moscow (though they had always existed in Leningrad). You could buy vodka at them, but you had to have a sandwich as well. If a worker can't afford to use one of these halls (which are dear) he goes back to the old system of buying a bottle in a shop. Restaurants are usually packed, but they are expensive, too. The most popular places for drinking are doorways – they may be heated in winter. But people drink in shops and in the parks, or in the markets. Anywhere where there is no militia. The waitresses put up with drinking in the cheaper dining halls and cafeterias, because they hand in the empty vodka bottles left under the tables, and get a few kopecks for them. Everybody makes a bit of profit. Some war invalids who have no proper means of sustenance make a living by collecting bottles. They comb the parks, picking up the empties, and can collect up to three roubles' worth a day. That's enough to buy bread, etc., and save you from dying of starvation. All the parks in a town may be divided up like hunting grounds. Perhaps there will be less drinking in public places as the accommodation situation improves. Alcoholism is a favourite pastime in Russia.

Samogon is brewed mostly in the villages, but a few people in small towns also allow themselves to get involved in it. It's not done much among the great majority of drinkers. Your wife has to help, and you have to lead a stable family life to do it. Samogon can be made out of anything, particularly sugar, and costs very little. You can distil it easily with two saucepans – or you can get a glass-blower to make you an apparatus. Sometimes it is made at night, so that the smell doesn't reach the neighbours. It may be sold – it is much cheaper than vodka – but selling it is very dangerous.

You can use any occasion for getting drunk. Pay day is an obvious one, of course. But the process is so continuous it's difficult to distinguish one day from another. If, for example, someone had a birthday yesterday, and got drunk, he has to sober up next morning; to do that he may have to borrow money (because he spent all he had on vodka); when he returns the money, that is a pretext for having a drink with the lender.

Usually people start drinking at seventeen, when they start work. Sixteen is exceptional (although there are reports of drunkenness among older trainees in technical schools). The main drinkers are men. If a woman drinks she is regarded as an 'alcoholic', but if a man drinks himself to death, he is not.

Regional differences are important – people drink far less, and start drinking when they are older, in Central Asia; that's the influence of Islam. In Georgia they drink much more wine. The peoples in the Baltic Republics traditionally drink little, compared to Russia, the Ukraine, White Russia and Siberia.

If you are pulled in for drunken behaviour in public, you may have to spend the night in a sobering-up station. This is usually a large barrack-type room, with dirty beds, set up alongside a militia station. Usually the drunks are brought in unconscious, given a cold shower, and put to bed. A report is sent to their place of work. This is the most dangerous thing for the drunk. A charge is made for use of the establishment – it was about 15 roubles eight years ago in Moscow. It may be taken from the drunk's wage if he is a worker; but an engineer, say, will pay himself. If there was disorderly conduct as well, the drunk may face a formal court hearing (without witnesses) in the morning, be fined, and get fifteen days for 'hooliganism'. That has to be worked off in some job like street cleaning, building, etc. The nights are spent in police custody, or even in prison. A penalty of this kind is a very shameful thing, because the person has his head shaven, and when he returns to work everyone knows only too well where he has been. His reputation (if he had one) disappears, and the management is expected to keep an eye on him.

Over recent years drinking has got worse. Under Stalin there was a certain amount of food in the shops, but less money. Now people have money, but there are no decent snacks. Life has got freer and paradoxically, public drinking has become chaotic. The snacks and the old service, such as it was, have gone. Places where you could drink properly, by western criteria, were also closed down. A whole category of drinkers has disappeared as well. Years ago, in Marina Roshcha, a sort of Moscow East End, war invalids used to gather at the beer booth in the mornings, on crutches and trolleys. By the middle of the day they would be drunk, and start fighting, hitting one another as best they could. That's all gone now.

The difference between drinking in Russia and the West is that in Russia people (the intelligentsia, as well as workers) drink vodka rather than wine before meals, during meals and after meals. There is low consumption of dry wine, except in the Caucasus, and also of cognac, because it's expensive.

Then there is treatment of alcoholism. The hospitals, not to mention the research institutes, just could not cope with the wave of it. Between 1968 and 1973 the number of institutions for treating them increased by up to a third. Formerly alcoholics had been treated either in special wards of general hospitals, in republication, *raion* and urban psychiatric hospitals, or in special departments of research institutes. (The latter type was for privileged individuals, usually from distant regions, so that local people should not know about it.) In Latvia and in other districts, the authorites started to establish 'medical labour colonies for alcoholics', primarily for the poorer cases. Take a worker who cannot stop drinking: he has trouble with his wife and at work. He could be sent to one of these new colonies after consultation with his wife and doctor. There he gets an obligatory cure. But he has to work at the same time, doing simple loading or manual jobs, in the camp or outside it. He may be kept in for up to six months. The inmates must get up early, have injections, etc., and are subject to military discipline. Food is simple and primitive: all money earned is sent to their families. They are kept at subsistence level as it were, while they are being treated. The first colonies were established near Riga, Leningrad and in other places. They are, moreover, self-financing, with two bosses, one a doctor and the other an economic manager responsible for output and 'cost effectiveness'.

Drug addiction is not socially acceptable in the Soviet Union. It is insignificant in comparison with the West or Tangiers, but seems to have been growing since the sixties. 'Habits' are totally different anyway. There are bad cases of people who are in and out of hospital all the time. Heroin is not normally available, but of course you can get it on the black market. It is not produced in Russia (though perhaps there are one or two little workshops in Moscow). Addiction is mostly based on opiates from the Caucasus and Central Asia – though some (like morphia) are available from medical sources. Everyone is corrupt, so the National Health system is corrupt, too.

Hash is popular with young people in Moscow and Leningrad. It comes from Central Asia and is of slightly higher quality than in the West. The price is approximately the same, considering the price structure. Marijuana is not used at all, they don't smoke it even in Central Asia, where cannabis abounds. People don't seem to take cocaine: amphetamines are more easily obtainable.

DOCUMENT 7. *Poverty in Central Asia*

Although our main concern in this book has been to explore poverty among the Slavs and other European peoples of the USSR, the poverty experienced by the Asiatic peoples, particularly the 30 million or so Turkic muslims, needs due mention. This overview has been provided for us by Dr A. Donde, a social geographer who between 1976 and 1979 made a number of field trips to Tashkent, Samarkand, Bukhara, the small town of Shakhisyabs and other villages in the Central Asian republic of Uzbekistan. His observations on poverty in these localities, though (as he emphasises) casual, are penetrating and of undoubted interest. Dr Donde writes:

There is no doubt in my mind that the poorest people in Central Asia are those who live in the muslim quarters of the towns. The first explanation I would offer for this lies in the fact that only families headed by white-collar workers, or persons employed in the service industries, have enough influence or money to obtain a European flat in a modern district, and these people are not, by definition, poor. Secondly, all urban dwellers are excluded from the benefits of relatively well-paid branches of agriculture, particularly cotton-growing and market gardening. This generalisation applies only to irrigated, arable areas. I know nothing of the life-styles of rural population in isolated or barren areas. It would, however, appear that people are much poorer in such areas, and that in this respect the rural periphery of Central Asia may be considered second only to the rural areas of northern Russia (in particular Leningrad oblast and the Karelian Autonomous Republic).

The urban poor of Central Asia have evidently been excluded from enrichment stemming from the association of Central Asia with the RSFSR. This mechanism lies in the so-called second economy, and the unregistered export of valuable agricultural products to the RSFSR (especially Siberia), the Urals and Volga region. The difficulties of the urban poor are exacerbated by the lack of garden plots to cover their own basic needs. This problem is in turn exacerbated by the failings of the state trade network, which is no better, and perhaps worse, than in the RSFSR. For example, I never saw meat or potatoes for sale in state shops during all my visits to Central Asia. Milk products were also very difficult to come by. The poor have to purchase these foods in the markets, or in cooperative networks, where prices are extremely high, and for most of the year comparable with those in Russia. In April 1976, apples cost two to three roubles a kilo in the Tashkent market, and 1.5 to 2.5 roubles in Samarkand. Beef and lamb cost between six and eight roubles in cooperative shops. Potatoes cost between one and 1.2 roubles a kilo, and may be brought in from Russia.

Bad living conditions are, in my view, an outstanding characteristic of poverty in Central Asia. Muslims traditionally live in their own separate houses, which may at first glance appear to be very big. They may indeed have up to 50% more space than houses in North Russia, but the presence of numerous children evidently reduces the per capita allotment, and co-habitation by three generations is common. Furthermore, the quality is poor. Houses usually lack running water and sanitation, while bathrooms are out of the question. Home-made showers may be found, but they are a novelty, and the fittings for plumbing are simply not on sale. It must not be forgotten that most towns in Central Asia suffer from water shortages. In Bukhara I saw posters warning of infectious diseases, and a local doctor informed me that dysentery was still extremely common.

Of course, it may happen that the traditional Muslim dwelling looks poor only from the outside. Sometimes, behind the clay wall of the courtyard, one finds a well-appointed modern villa. But that is an exception, for the wealthier families do not stay in the traditional districts. Such districts seem to be inhabited exclusively by poor people, and are exceedingly homogeneous in this respect.

The people living in them are dressed very carelessly and poorly. It is possible to meet, not only in the streets, but in the tea-houses as well, people – especially old men – in very worn traditional dress. But this, too, is a local tradition, with a basis in Muslim ideology. I am convinced that this carelessness (predetermined though it may be by social norms) is simply a way of economising in circumstances of extreme poverty. Poverty has, after all, existed in these parts for centuries, and has itself moulded popular culture. It is noteworthy that in other districts of large towns (as in the Caucasus) young people love to show off, and wear prestigious clothing particularly of

foreign manufacture, regardless of how functional it is. This indicates great
instability of taste.

Poverty is reflected in a rather specific manner in demonstrative expenditure
and saving. Marriages are a typical example of the former: the number of
guests may reach one hundred or more, and the feasting last two or three days.
But critical articles in the press suggest that by no means all families can afford
it, and many run up huge debts in the process. That may be so in some cases,
but I believe that there is a deeper explanation. It may be that the married
couple gets, in the form of gifts, far more than their parents spend on the
wedding, and that this is the only way they can acquire sufficient household
goods in conditions of extreme poverty. Demonstrative savings are common:
a room in the traditional house usually contains piles of coats, blankets, cloth
and crockery, set out for view. The careful preservation of such 'wealth',
collected by previous generations, illustrates an inability to replace traditional
forms of wealth with modern ones, thereby masking existing poverty.

The local people realise that they are poor, and struggle against it with all
the means at their disposal. I think that the large family in urban surroundings
may be interpreted as a preliminary reaction to the threat of poverty:
unwillingness to migrate from the area may also be explained by a fear of
poverty linked with proletarianisation. In the countryside resources are
greater, more accessible and a large family is a much more effective
instrument for averting impoverishment.

Many observers agree that Central Asian society is now profoundly
secularised. The retention of many customs and characteristics which are
normally regarded as concomitants of profound religiosity is therefore all the
more striking.

It is our belief that the hierarchisation of society according to wealth is
greater in Central Asia than in the RSFSR. The poorest sections of society
are concentrated in the towns. The quality of their way of life is scarcely better
than that of the poorest people in the RSFSR, though cultural differences
complicate comparison.

DOCUMENT 8. *Poverty and political persecution*

The following document illustrates, in a singularly graphic manner, some of
the ways in which a family may suffer economically if any member becomes
actively engaged in dissident politics. It also gives a glimpse of difficulties
encountered by dissatisfied representatives of national minorities or religious
groups.

Mrs Velikanova, a woman of outstanding bravery, suffered not only the
loss of her husband for this reason, but was herself arrested and sentenced to
four years in a corrective labour camp followed by five years of internal exile.
Had they been younger, her children would have been placed in an
orphanage.

Vol'noe slovo, Vypusk 38: 'Zhenshchina i Rossia' Frankfurt, 1980, p. 57.

A great tragedy has overtaken our family. Tatyana Mikhailovna Velikanova, our mother and the grandmother of our children, has been arrested...We found out that she has been interned in Lefortovo prison by the KGB. For two months now they have not told us what she has been accused of, how she is, or when we will be able to see her. All our requests over the telephone are met by a categorical refusal to give any formal explanation whatever. 'She is a state criminal', says the investigator who is handling her case.

In 1968 the KGB separated us from our father Konstantin Babitski when they threw him into prison, and then sent him into exile in the north, for his participation in a Red Square demonstration against the intervention of Soviet troops in Czechoslovakia. Our mother reared the three of us, alone, on an engineer's modest income which is scarcely enough for one.

Our mother is forty-seven. She has a degree in mathematics, and when she became one of the first women programmists in the country she worked in that field for more than twenty years. But under pressure from the KGB she was obliged to leaver her specialist work and become a night nurse in a children's hospital. But she lost that work as well after a year and more recently has looked after her baby grandchildren at home...We, her children, work or study in the daytime, and there is hardly anyone except her to look after them.

"Blessed are those persecuted for truth".

We know why our mother was arrested. She is one of the founders and an active participant in the Movement for Civil, Religious and National Rights in the USSR. She is a close associate of the academician A. Sakharov...

Our mother slept no more than four of five hours per day, and got up before everyone else, in order to read the letters which had come from people interned in concentration camps, prisons and psychiatric hospitals, from people who were persecuted for their religious faith and convictions, or their desire to emigrate. She had to check everything carefully and compare all the facts, so that there should not be a single suspect work, so that these at times horrifying facts could be made public in a responsible manner, so that she could make a (perhaps almost hopeless) complaint or a request to Soviet administrative organs regarding some new case of violation of human rights. She might have to send a letter to a person who had himself suffered, or to his relatives, to inspire them with hope, and get all the necessary details. It might be necessary to collect clothes and send them to children in need...

People start coming to see her from early in the morning. Here, for example, is a Tatar who was audacious enough to return to his homeland in the Crimea. He bought a hut with his last money, but a few days later the militia and soldiers threw him out onto the street, together with his six children and his elderly parents. His house was razed by a bulldozer. Next comes a woman on her way to see her husband, a Lithuanian who has languished in a prison camp for many years because he dreamed of cultural autonomy for Lithuania. She is followed by a delegation of religious believers who are members of an unregistered Christian commune. Their preacher has just been arrested and they face an enormous fine: their children are persecuted by teachers and beaten by other pupils who are also encouraged by the teachers. Some of the children have been permanently removed by court order and put into children's homes to knock any belief in God out of their heads...

People keep on coming to see her. but apart from all that, our mother has her small grandchildren, who have to be fed, clothed, taken out for walks and put to bed. She has an immense amount to do and has no minute of free time. While she is busy with the children, or talking to one of her visitors, other people who need her help or advice wait in the kitchen, or in the adjoining room of our little flat (which contains, incidentally, only thirty eight square metres for nine of us). Our mother finds a moment to write down what she has heard with difficulty. The telephone rings constantly...

Only in the evening does she free herself of the children, but she goes on caring and sets off, sometimes to the other end of the town, regardless of the weather, to visit somebody who is persecuted, to take to heart, again and again, floods of grief, wipe away other people's tears and give them hope. She is closely followed by KGB agents and cannot rid herself of this humiliating surveillance.

"Blessed are those who forgive, for they will themselves be forgiven."

Our mother is devoted to the cause and a lover of truth. We, and all who have met her, are convinced of it. Whatever accusation the authorities may make against her, we firmly know that she is guilty only of carrying out the will of her Saviour; 'There is no love greater than that which makes somebody lay down his soul for his friends.'

Family signatures and
address. Moscow, December
1979.

DOCUMENT 9. *Infringement of social and economic rights*

Poverty in the Soviet Union is provoked not only by low wages and shortages of consumer goods, but also by indifference of managements to workers' rights, and deprivation of benefits to which they are legally entitled. This exposition of the problem is taken from an April 1979 Declaration by the Moscow Group for Assisting the Implementation of the Helsinki Agreements in the USSR. Some of the signatories (Elena Bronner, Sofia Kalistratova, Malva Landa, Naum Meiman, Viktor Nekipelov and Tatyana Osipova) are well known in the west for their dissident activities. Though our own analysis of Soviet poverty was made before this document came to our attention, there are many points of correspondence.

(MS 3671. No. 27, 1979.) Translation with permission from 'A Chronicle of Human Rights in the USSR', April–June, 1979, p. 29.

A report on social and economic rights in the USSR

Soviet propaganda has persistently maintained that so-called social and economic rights take precedence over civil and political rights. It has also maintained that in the USSR, in contrast to the countries of the 'Free World', social and economic rights are fully secured...

The absence of unemployment in the USSR is cited as the main indicator of universal prosperity. But this and other such claims are merely propagandistic camouflage. Actually, the right to work, the right to favorable conditions of work, and the right to just remuneration for work, are by no means universally secured in the USSR...

The wages of both blue- and white-collar workers are extremely low. The official average wage in the USSR, 161 roubles per month, is a mere statistic. But given the present rate of inflation and the increase in prices, even that figure scarcely ensures 'an existence worthy of human dignity'. And what can we say of the minimum wage which is 70 roubles per month and, in some areas, 60 roubles? The low wage-level is further confirmed by the fact that, as a rule, all members of a Soviet family must work, including persons eligible for old-age pensions. And also by the widespread 'rip-offs' and thefts from places of employment. One worker will take home milk and cream from a dairy; another will take home a bottle of vodka from a distillery; and still another boards from a lumber mill. A situation in which workers are compelled to 'scrounge' what the State does not provide them with, undermines ethical standards, causes a serious morale problem and encourages the spread of lies and hypocrisy throughout society.

The seemingly adequate income enjoyed by a certain percentage of workers' families is often derived from sources other than wages. For the great majority of blue- and white-collar workers, the level of 'take-home' pay is so low that they can barely make ends meet. This may well be the chief cause of the drop in the birth-rate.

Income distribution in the USSR is very arbitrary. There is an immense gap between the minimal wages paid to a considerable part of the population and the high salaries paid to certain people: higher Party and government officials, generals, academicians, etc. Their salaries can reach or even exceed twenty times the minimum wage...

The inequality in wages is aggravated by the inadequate food supply in outlying regions. Whereas the Muscovite buys most of his foodstuffs from State trade outlets, people living in the provinces must buy them at the local market which offers limited selections at exorbitant prices. As a result, feelings of envy and hostility toward the residents of the 'Communist city' of Moscow have become widespread.

Lowest on the pay scale are persons employed in the non-industrial sector: government office workers, employees of utilities, salesclerks, medical personnel, teachers, writers, artists and so forth. And the pensions paid for old age, disability, or loss of a breadwinner are not sufficient for 'an existence worthy of human dignity'.

Although the word is never spoken aloud, genuine *poverty* persists among a considerable part of the population. One cannot arrive at an accurate figure for the number of families that should be classified as poor, since the poverty line in the USSR has never been specified officially. Quasi-officially, the minimum subsistence level has been set at 50 roubles per capita per month (if one assumes that a supplementary allowance of 12 roubles for each child below the age of eight is given only to those families in which the per capita income is less than 50 roubles per month), although in fact that figure represents the threshold not of poverty but of *destitution*. Many pensioners, single mothers and large families live on far less than that 50 roubles per capita.

The piece-rate system, long discredited in the developed countries as 'antediluvian' and vigorously opposed by trade unions in the West, is common in the USSR. Not only that, but it is popular among workers, since they think that they can earn more than with an hourly wage.

At Soviet plants and factories – with a few possible exceptions involving defence plants, 'model factories' and some other key enterprises – the work is poorly organized, health and safety measures are inadequate, and on-the-job accidents are frequent. Also, accidents are concealed by management and accident reports are filed only with reluctance. Management even goes so far as to credit the victim with imaginary 'working hours,' in order to avoid listing him as injured on the job.

Many jobs that involve heavy physical labor (construction, road-building, etc.) are performed mostly by women – because of the low pay and 'lack of prestige'. Women pushing wheelbarrows full of cement on construction scaffolds, and women in orange uniforms with shovels and crowbars in their hands working on railroad gradings, are among the most ugly sights in the Soviet world.

Labor laws are grossly violated at Soviet plants and factories. It is a common practice, especially on the days when the pressure is on to meet the monthly production plan, to make employees work overtime that is not recorded – a violation of the law limiting the length of the work week. Workers are often not paid for this overtime, since they supposedly have an alternate material incentive: 'If we fulfill the plan, we'll get bonuses.'

Common forms of unpaid labor are the nationwide and local 'Subbotniks' (unpaid work on usual days off) and sending people (including schoolchildren and pensioners) to temporary work on collective and state farms, at vegetable storehouses, etc.

The working day for collective farm workers is not regulated at all. And such workers have no paid vacations. Since it is extremely difficult for members to leave a collective farm and settle elsewhere, they have in fact become State serfs.

Any conflict between a worker and management – any criticism or attempt to defend one's rights – is fraught with serious consequences. Management can exert pressure on a worker in many ways: withholding production bonuses, withholding the traditional year-end bonus, taking him off the list of those in line for an apartment, withholding his pass to a health resort and, finally, dismissal. (Management has wide latitude in firing workers since permissible reasons for dismissal are not spelled out in the labor law.)*

In the USSR, one's choice of employment is severely limited. One means of discriminating against workers and turning them into virtual serfs, is the compulsory work-book system (one unknown in the West), which is basically an extension of the internal passport system. Since the entries in the work-book include the reasons for dismissal which may be prejudicial to the worker (e.g., dismissal by reason of conviction for a crime), the work-book constitutes a kind of blacklist. And yet one cannot get a job without a work-book.

One's choice of employment is also limited by the shameful system of residence permits, which makes it impossible for a Soviet citizen to choose his place of residence freely.

Despite such formal indicators of full employment as the apparent shortage of manpower and the 'Help Wanted' ads., functional unemployment does exist in the Soviet Union; i.e., cases where owing to the acute housing shortage, restrictions on place of residence, or a lack of savings, a person is compelled to take work that suits neither his preferences, his education, nor his skills. This compulsion is aggravated by the immoral article on 'parasitism' in the Criminal Code: the obligation, under threat of imprisonment, to seek and accept any kind of work.

Moreover, along with functional [i.e., concealed] unemployment, actual unemployment also exists in the USSR. In Western countries a person who has not worked for two weeks is considered to be unemployed; in the USSR there is always a huge if uncounted number of people who have not worked for many months (if only for those four months 'permitted' by the law on parasitism). At the same time, there is no unemployment compensation in the USSR. Thus a person dismissed from a plant or factory because of a reduction in work force or similar reason, receives severance pay equivalent to two weeks' wages, and nothing more.

If one were to apply to the USSR those concepts of unemployment elaborated during the long history of the labor movement and used in the West, the myth that the Soviet Union is a country with no unemployment would be dissipated.

The most serious violation of the rights of workers is their lack of any effective means of defending their interests. The right to strike is not recognized in Soviet legislation, and any attempt at collective bargaining is harshly put down. The trade unions in the USSR are essentially Party–State agencies rather than workers' organizations to secure a better living standard and improved working conditions...

* On this point see our discussion p. 107.

APPENDIX 2

THE EMIGRE SURVEY

———————— ∽ ————————

The lack of information on many aspects of poverty in the Soviet Union, and impossibility of on-the-spot investigation, prompted us to launch a survey of the former life-styles of Soviet emigres who were, by measures discussed in Chapter One, poor when they resided in the USSR. Since the results of this work are referred to at several points in the foregoing study, some account of its conduct is apposite here. The sources of funding were named in the preface.

The first interviews were conducted in July 1982, in the form of a pilot study of twenty-five families of former Soviet citizens living mostly in the New York, Chicago and San Francisco areas. The text of the questionnaire was all but finalised in the course of this work, only minor additions being effected later. Systematic interviewing began in the USA in September 1982, and was extended to Israel in January 1983, so as to expedite data collection. It was completed everywhere by the end of May 1984, when the sample comprised 348 families and 442 working members.

All the interviewers, of whom there were nine, were former Soviet citizens known to myself or colleagues. All had considerable experience of such work, and were either involved in other research projects, or had connections with some of the more respectable university departments. The interviewers were paid pro rata for locating families (through friends or personal acquaintances), conducting the interviews, and making additional enquiries. The respondents participated voluntarily, without payment. Assurances of anonymity were given in every case, though interviewers were asked to keep a confidential note of families' names and addresses, should clarification of answers be needed. This arrangement worked quite well. The results obtained from the questionnaires were computerised and analyzed by means of numerous SPSS programmes.

The full questionnaire was a document of eighty-seven pages, divided into three parts. Part 'A', completed on behalf of all 348 families, contained sections on family composition, income, housing, food consumption, selected expenses, possessions, holiday patterns, household goods, and childrens' education. Parts 'B' and 'C', which were identical, were applied to 442 working members of the same families, in most cases husband or wife, as available for interviewing. These parts covered problems of employment, social mobility, further education, marriage, clothing, and some time uses, and elicited respondents' opinions on the extent and causes of urban poverty in the USSR. Information was sought on destitute people observed in public places. Most of the questions were formulated in accordance with our own understanding of Soviet reality, after due consultation with former and present Soviet citizens. The section on income owes much to the work of Professors G. Grossman and V. Treml.

The great majority of the families interviewed left the Soviet Union between 1978 and 1982, and reported on their experiences in the years 1977–9. We decided to focus analysis as far as possible on 'full' families with three to five members, since these are numerically preponderant in the European parts of the USSR. The average family size in the sample came out at 3.9 persons. 'Family' was understood as persons who were related, or closely associated, and who shared the same residence. In 323 cases the head of the household was a man (the husband), all families contained a mother and at least one working member, and 322 had at least one resident child. Pensioners and other adults appeared only as members of a given family unit.

The lowest acceptable age for the head of family (or principal earner) was thirty years in the last normal year of residence in the USSR (i.e., before the decision to emigrate affected life-style). This limitation was introduced so as to exclude persons whose earnings were likely to be low through youth or professional immaturity. The average age of women was lower than that of their spouses, but even so nearly 80 % of them were thirty or over. The sample contained 31 grandfathers, 114 grandmothers, 480 minors and 65 adults, totalling 1,361 persons altogether.

Income is central to any definition of poverty, so the parameters set were in this respect particularly stringent. For reasons explained in Chapter One, families were sought with a per capita 'official' income of up to 70 roubles a month. Working members were generally to have a gross 'official' wage or salary of not more than 150 roubles a month, and side, or 'secondary' earnings were not to amount to more than 25 roubles a month per capita. Our wage limit of 150 roubles was thus significantly lower than officially published average for 1979 (163.3 roubles), but high enough to make the location of respondents practicable. The permitted ceiling for secondary earnings, on the other hand, had to be low enough not to affect the presumed 'poverty' life-style.

The median 'net official income' came out at only 54.0 roubles per capita, and 36.8 % of the families failed to reach even the 51.4 rouble threshold proposed by Soviet scholars for the early sixties. Official earnings were, however, supplemented by 14.8 roubles of secondary income per employee over the whole sample, due allowance being made for sporadic involvement. Total per capita income thus reached 60.9 roubles, by which measure only 17.5% of the families surpassed a 70 rouble per capita threshold.*

As for the occupational categories, no responsible managerial staff, army, police or agricultural employees were included. Of the working respondents (regardless of sex), 11.7% were in the least skilled occupations, manual and non-manual. The jobs most commonly held by men at this level were 'labourer' and 'packer': by women – 'checker' and 'sorter', 'store guardian' and the like. Most respondents (69.3%) were semi, or highly skilled manuals, and what we might term middle or high-grade service personnel. The great majority of manuals at these levels were men, by far the most common occupations being fitter, drivers of various kinds, lathe and other machine operators, mechanic, electrician, plasterer, painter and repairer, and welder. The women, who predominated among the non-manuals, were mostly nurses, book-keepers, secretaries and other office staff, laboratory and various technical assistants, kindergarten attendants, etc. The female manuals were mainly in garment production.

The remaining respondents (19.1%) held specialists' jobs normally re-quiring a degree. About two-thirds of these were men; the most common occupations (for both sexes) were engineer, teacher, cultural worker, or doctor. The sample was therefore occupationally somewhat heterogeneous, but since poverty embraces many socio-occupational groups, we did not consider this to be entirely disadvantageous for analysis.

The educational achievements of the adults reflected both the considerable advances made by the USSR in this sphere, and the occupational configuration of the sample. Just over one-third of both husbands and wives had completed the ten-year school, while 38% of the men and 44% of the women had some form of secondary special education. The figures for higher education were about 12% and 7% respectively. Noteworthy were the relatively high levels of achievement of parents as compared with grandparents, and the divergent distribution of men and women (the latter being rather more likely to have completed general or secondary special education, but less likely to have gone on to full-time higher education).

The fact that the overwhelming majority of respondents (86%) were Jews did not, in our opinion, significantly affect their perception of those aspects of Soviet reality which primarily concerned us. Most were thoroughly sovietised, and had experienced no other culture. Resentment against the Soviet system did not surface in accounts of daily living and, indeed, did not

* We retained rouble fractions, as produced by our calculations, though given the nature of the variables they imply rather too high a degree of accuracy. Most of the estimates of secondary income, as averaged out, are best thought of as being indicative to within one or two roubles.

seem to be particularly pervasive. In any case the questionnaire avoided specific political and ethnic problems. The few rather specific instances in which ethnicity might significantly have affected the generality of our argument were commented upon when occasion demanded.

As for geographical location, nearly all the families interviewed lived in European areas of the RSRSR, the Ukraine, White Russia and Moldavia. Fifty-eight per cent lived in towns of over half a million inhabitants, mainly the republican capitals; Chernovtsy (228,000) and Beltsy (135,000), both in the Ukraine, together provided fifty-three families, or 15 % of the sample. Forty-two families, or 12 % of the sample, came from small, or very small towns.

The degree to which the 348 families were representative of the 'Soviet poor' was a matter of central importance to the interpretation of the responses. It was not, however, easily assessed, if only because of the diversity of socio-occupational groups involved. The respondents had earnings which were much below average. The proportion of skilled workers, medium-grade service personnel, and specialists, however, was higher than one would expect in any random sample of poor people. On the other hand we would argue that this discrepancy by no means invalidated the usefulness of the exercise, for we did, at least, reach the upper and middle layers of the urban poor. Many important categories were well represented, and a mixed sample is not without its advantages. Families from the smaller and economically neglected towns were prominent among respondents.

Our central aim was to describe and assess the life-styles and attitudes of people who themselves experienced material hardship, and the sample would appear to have been adequate for that purpose. We wish to conclude with a word of thanks to those who supplied information, and to Mr Konstantin Miroshnik, Mr Leonid Khotin, and Mrs Katerina Vlanina for their organisational help.

NOTES

————————— ⌎ —————————

I. IS THERE POVERTY IN THE SOVIET UNION?

1 *Poverty and Human Development*, World Bank Publication, Oxford University Press, 1980, p. 68.
2 *Ibid.*, p. 14.
3 These paragraphs are based on comment in the US 'Measure of Poverty' series, papers XIII–XV and XVIII, see bibliography; also Zarefsky and McClain, Chapter 1.
4 *Statistical Abstract of the United States*, hence *SAUS*. See *SAUS*, 1964, pp. 340, 390–3.
5 *SAUS*, 1981, p. 446; 1985, p. 460.
6 *Journal of the Royal Statistical Society*, London, July 1919, quoted in *SAUS*, 1920, p. 857.
7 J. G. Chapman, p. 153
8 Yu. N. Korshunov, P. Z. Livshits, and M. S. Rumyantseva, p. 202.
9 *Soviet Economic Performance*, 1966–7, p. 92.
10 M. Matthews (1972), p. 88.
11 *Nar. khoz. 1980*, p. 380. This figure presumably includes the income from the private plot.
12 *Nar. khoz. 1980*, p. 422.
13 G. E. Schroeder, p. 370
14 *Nar. khoz.* p. 476. The total deposited in state banks apparently rose from 18.7 milliard roubles in 1965 to no less than 156.5 milliard roubles in 1980, the increase being proportionately greater in the countryside. Since this money cannot be used to produce an income, the growth represents either a yearning for personal security, or unsatisfied demand.
15 G. E. Schroeder and I. Edwards, p. 19. Figures adopted for our purpose.
16 An overview of these developments may be found in C. C. Zimmerman, p. 439ff.
17 S. N. Prokopovicz, p. 374; I. Ya. Matyukha in A. I. Ezhov (ed.) and others (Moscow 1969), p. 411.
18 G. S. Sarkisyan and N. P. Kuznetsova, p. 48.
19 I. Ya. Matyukha, p. 183ff; A. I. Ezhov (1965), p. 315.
20 A. I. Ezhov (1969), p. 416. Food consumption was an integral part of any family budget and warranted separate investigation. The first one-off studies were conducted amongst 3,400 urban families in 1919. By 1926 the sample contained 10,000 urban and 28,000 rural families (I. Ya. Matyukha, pp. 191, 194).

21　A. I. Khryashcheva, p. 93.

22　A. I. Ezhov (1965), pp. 313, 314.

23　See, for example, *Nar. khoz. SSSR v 1972*, p. 562 and subsequent years.

24　A. I. Ezhov (1957), p. 26; Matthews (1972), p. 44.

25　*Family Living Studies*, p. 54; see also A. I. Ezhov (1965), p. 309.

26　Entitled 'The Needs and Income of the Family: Level, Structure, Prospects',
it appeared in an edition of 10,000 copies (see the bibliography for the Russian
details). Details on the institutes involved were taken from pp. 9, 11, 55, 139.

27　The gross average was given as 96.5 roubles in the statistical handbooks. The 1943
tax regulations, still in force, stipulated paymentts (for workers and employees) of
5.9 roubles on the first 81 roubles earned, plus 12% of earnings between 81 and
100 roubles, plus 13% of higher sums. Changes have since been made in the starting
point, and relief granted to some categories of earners, but by the early eighties the
main framework was unchanged (V. A. Tur 1968, p. 16; 1984, p. 13). The steady
growth in wages has, in fact, meant that people have been paying more tax. Most
workers' and peasants' earnings should be further reduced by 1% for trade unions
dues (V. Z. Shchegel'ski, p. 407).

28　M. Matthews (1972), p. 88. We should, perhaps, add that the value of the threshold
in terms of other 'free' currencies is very difficult to establish, given the artificiality
of the official rate of exchange, and different family spending patterns. However,
in 1965 the rouble was quoted at around 2.50 to the pound, and 90 kopecks to the
dollar, giving nominal thresholds of £20–40p or $57–10c. per month in these
currencies. We shall not pursue this excerise beyond our comment in footnote 31
below.

29　G. S. Sarkisyan and N. P. Kuznetsova, pp. 133, 138.

30　T. I. Zaslavskaya, V. A. Kalmyk, *Chast'*, I, p. 153.

31　See p. 5 above. All these figures produced with regard to this problem arouse great
discussion among economists.

　　There is, of course, nothing sacrosanct about any given figure for cut-off levels.
More detailed discussion may be found in 'The Measure of Poverty' Technical
Paper XIII, *Relative Poverty*, by Jack McNeil, US Bureau of the Census (1975), p.5.

　　Any comparison of Soviet and US poverty levels is fraught with great difficulty,
but the following points are closely relevant.

　　(1) The US poverty 'cut-off' level for a non-farm family of four in 1979 was said
to be an annual money income of $7,412, which for present purposes may be
understood as equalling a net wage of $3,706 for each of two earners (*SAUS*, 1981,
p. 445).

　　(2) The Soviet poverty threshold of 70 roubles per head monthly for an urban
family of four (as adopted here) translates into an annual income of 3,336 roubles,
or two net 'poverty wages' of 1,668 roubles.

　　Two obvious comparisons may be made on this basis.

(a)　*Simple conversion of rouble–dollar sums.* As we have noted, the rouble lacks proper
conversion rates against the dollar, and the patterns of expenditure in Soviet
and American families are very different anyway. However, at the official rate
of exchange (65.9 kopecks to the dollar in 1979) the Soviet family 'poverty
wage' of 3,336 roubles would have converted into $5,062, which was only
68.3% of the US 'cut-off' figure. The free, but illegal exchange rates would
have yielded a considerably less advantageous comparison in rouble
terms.

(b)　*Equating average wages.* In 1976 average real per capita consumption in the
USSR was authoritatively estimated to be 34.4% of that of the USA, and
the gap may actually have widened since (G. E. Schroeder and I. Edwards,
p.v). If the Soviet average wage is equated to 34.4% of the average American

per capita disposable personal income (which was $7,293 in 1979), we arrive at a hypothetical Soviet average wage of $2,509.

The above-mentioned Soviet 'poverty wage' of 1,668 roubles was 95 % of the Soviet average wage in 1979, 95 % of $2,509 would give a putative Soviet poverty wage, in dollars, of $2,384. This is 64.3 % of the US net 'poverty wage' quoted in (1) above.

Both of these comparisons, though rudimentary, indicate that the Soviet poverty threshold was considerably lower than the US 'cut-off level', or to put it another way, that the US definition was much broader. Many people who, in terms of their relative income, came within the state definition of poverty in the US, would be excluded from it in the USSR.

(3) Rouble and dollar figures must be considered not only in relation to the pattern of family expenditure, but also in terms of how much they buy, and the quality of goods and services available. Mr Keith Bush, of the Radio Liberty Research Unit, has estimated that in March 1979, a weekly food basket for a Soviet statistically *average* family of four required 3.4 times as much labour (measured in hours of input) as a comparable American basket (see 'Retail Prices in Moscow and Four Western Cities in March 1979' in L. Schapiro and J. Godson, pp. 251–85). There was also a significant differential for clothing. A 'time' costing of the principal services (housing, transport, education and health) would, however, have favoured the Soviet consumer and tended to redress the balance somewhat. Without venturing further into so conjectural a field, we may conclude that calculations on this basis would also produce a sharp differential in favour of the US.

32 M. Loznevaya, 'Matematicheskie metody v planirovanii zarabotnoi platy', *Sotsialisticheski trud*, No. 10, 1968, p. 27, discussed in Matthews (1972), p. 75. For a more elaborate treatment of distribution figures see P. J. D. Wiles and Stefan Markowski. 'Income Distribution under communism and Capitalism', *Soviet Studies*, No. 4., Vol. 22, 1971.

33 The figure we calculate here is 'x', the sum needed to surpass the threshold, when $(x - \text{deductions} + \text{side earnings} = 139 \text{ roubles})$.

2. WHO ARE THE SOVIET POOR?

1 See, for example. *Planovoe khozyaistvo*, No. 8, 1983, p. 74; *Sottsialisticheski trud*, No. 1, 1984, p. 90.

2 L. E. Kunel'ski, p. 148.

3 *Planovoe khozyaistvo*, No. 9, 1979, p. 46.

4 S. A. Ivanov (ed.), *Trudovoe pravo, entsiklopedicheski slovar'*, p. 230.

5 *Vestnik statistiki*, No. 6, 1983, p. 33.

6 *Itogi vsesoyuzoi perepisi naseleniya*, Vol. 6, p. 20; *Nar. khoz, 1922–82*, p. 400.

7 V. M. Golensov and A. V. Muzyka, p. 184; M. F. V'yaskov, E. A. Mil'ski and A. A. Marushkin, p. 203.

8 *Journal of Comparative Economics*, No. 7, 1983, p. 158. See also M. Matthews (1972), p. 82; A. E. Kotlyar and S. Ya. Turchaninova, p. 139.

9 A. E. Kotlyar and S. Ya. Turchaninova, pp. 67, 75.

10 *Itogi vsesoyuznoi perepisi naseleniya*, 1970 god Vol. 6, p. 166; *Zhenshchiny v SSSR, statisticheskie materialy*, pp. 12–14.

11 A. G. Novitski and G. V. Mil', pp. 185, 188.

12 V. M. Popov, M. I. Sidorova, pp. 154, 155. Aggregate income depends on such things as government policy, location (with regard to growing factors, the proximity of markets, mechanization and transport facilities); the skill of the management; and various social elements, including the nature and availability of manpower.

13 *Ekonomika sel'skogo khozyaistva*, No. 1, 1980, p. 72.

14 T. I. Zaslavskaya and V. A. Kalmyk, *Chast'* I, p. 92; compare also relevant data on pp. 321 and 412 of *Nar. khoz, 1922–82*.

15 For a recent summary of work then done in Novosibirsk, see V. N. Shubkin (1984), p. 73. The attractiveness of professions was also investigated, but the concepts are closely related, and the 'prestige' findings are sufficient for purposes of illustration here.

16 For further reference see Matthews (1972), p. 120.

17 L. E. Kunel'ski, p. 92, earners in worker and employee families, apparently for 1980. It is noteworthy that these figures, if set against the 70-rouble poverty threshold, give income results close to those of the statistical family of four with two earners discussed on p. 26.

18 *Nar. khoz. 1980*, p. 30. *Semiya i Shkola*, No. 9, 1982, p. 44 (I am grateful to Miss S. G. Zayer for this reference). *Chislennost' i sostav naseleniya SSSR*, p. 252. The 7.9 m. figure may include widows with children.

19 *Nar. khoz. 1979*, pp. 409, 439, 557 (namely 30,600 m. roubles over 47.4 m. recipients).

20 V. D. Shapiro, p. 200.

21 *SPR* 1980, p. 303.

22 A. V. Dmitriev, p. 35.

23 A. G. Novitski and G. V. Mil', p. 75.

24 B. Madison (1983), p. 14 and footnote 35; *Trudovoe ustroistvo invalidov v SSSR*, p. 26.

25 *Sovetski entsiklopedicheski slovar'*, p. 384.

26 M. Matthews, 1982, p. 44.

27 A. G. Novitski and G. V. Mil', p. 9.

28 *Nar. khoz. RSFSR 1981*, p. 211.

29 M. Matthews (1982) p. 33. There are widespread misapprehensions about this matter in the West, some encouraged for political ends.

30 For elaboration of these and similar points see M. Matthews (1982), pp. 164, 186.

31 *Sotsiologicheskie issledovaniya*, No. 2, 1981, p. 110.

3. POVERTY LIFE STYLES: FOOD, CLOTHING AND SHELTER

1 G. S. Sarkisyan and N. P. Kuznetsova, p. 58.

2 The national consumption figures must have been calculated across the whole social spectrum, whose needs diverged somewhat from those of the 'statistical family' of two working adults and young children. However, the Soviet authorities are extremely secretive about the compilation of national consumption averages, and assessment of this divergence is difficult. (*Statisticheski slovar'*, p. 452; *Sotsial'no-ekonomicheskaya statistika*, p. 282.) We conclude, however, that the two sets of per capita rates are close enough for some comparative comment. Dietary technicalities do not concern us here.

2 The last officially-admitted round of increases announced in the autumn of 1981, involved 17% to 27% rises in wines, spirits and cigarettes, items much consumed by the poor. A series of luxury goods (jewellery, glass, carpets, fur, woollen goods and some furniture) were subject to price increases of 25% to 30% (*Golos Rodiny*, No. 38, 1981). At the same time, there have been unpublicised rises in the cost of comestibles and durable goods by changing specifications and marketing slightly modified products at a higher price.

4 As it happens, the composition of the sample families by sex and age bears some similarity with the national family pattern, so the level of calory requirements, and potential consumption rates, are possibly more comparable than the Sarkisyan–Kuznetsova basket. Only 8 families out of 348, incidentally, had garden plots, so the average input from this source was negligible.

5 A question to which we have so far found no clear answer concerns the relatively small quantity of bread, potatoes and sugar entered by most respondents. Likely explanations, in our view, are under-reporting – in so far as a high consumption of these items has negative social overtones – and a more carefully chosen diet. Hopefully, this conundrum does not invalidate other responses.

6 *Nar. khoz. 1980*, p. 432.

7 *SPR* 1973, p. 183; B. S. Beisenov, p. 23.

8 Instances of drunkenness among individual Soviet citizens are to be explained [wrote a Soviet lawyer] not by social and economic factors, but by secondary reasons expressing the old moral and ethical attitudes and customs of an overthrown capitalist society... The vitality of such habits is a natural part of the transition from capitalism to socialism... Another source is the negative influence of the capitalist world... Among the internal reasons... for relics of the past in people's minds are shortcomings in our educative work... Managers and social organisations sometimes put up with anti-social acts and do not exert proper influence on violators of public order... The correct and intelligent organisation of workers', and especially young people's, leisure must play an important part in the struggle for the complete removal of these capitalist 'birth marks'. (B. S. Beisenov, p. 13.)

9 *Nar. khoz. 1980*, p. 402.

10 Various family budget figures approved for publication have shown only 3–6% of income to be spent on alcoholic beverages, but such sums must be quite untypical of the public at large. The budgets reproduced in the annual statistical handbooks contain no reference to this matter.

11 Treml, pp. 26, 67–70.

12 Jews (who made up most of the sample) are thought to drink less than other ethnic groups, and those with a desire to emigrate would presumably have had an extra incentive to control drinking habits.

13 *Nar. khoz. 1922–82*, pp. 472, 481.

14 This categorisation (which we shall use below) is distinct from that of 'common useful space' provided in the Soviet statistical abstracts. The latter term is broader, as indicated in the text. On the basis of several Soviet examples we have assumed 'habitable' or 'living' space to be about 60% of 'common useful space'. Though interesting, the tables in Soviet sources rarely provide a breakdown by persons per room; we have seen no serious analysis by socio-economic group; and information on amenities is sparse. Such detail must be winkled out from scholarly treatises or other occasional sources.

15 M. Matthews, 1978, p. 43.

16 *Kratki yuridicheski spravochnik*, p. 410ff.

17 L. V. Kozlovskaya, p. 159.

18 *Nar. khoz. 1980*, pp. 9, 425–7: *SAUS* 1981, p. 760, estimated.

19 *Voprosy ekonomiki*, No. 5, 1981, p. 12; A. V. Baranov, p. 176.

20 Soviet citizens have a constitutional right to housing (Article 44 of the 1977 USSR Constitution) and some degree of security of tenure. However, articles 333 and 334 of the RSFSR Civil Code (matched in the codes of other republics) do give various landlord authorities a specific right of eviction without provision of other living space. The principal justifications are (a) 'systematic violation or spoilage of accommodation, or systematic infringement of the rules of socialist communal living, rendering residence for other people impossible in the same flat or house, after warnings and social pressure have proved ineffective', (b) (when certain enterprises and organisations let accommodation to their own employees) the tenant's voluntary departure from the enterprise or organisation, infringement of labour discipline or criminal activities on his part. It is noteworthy that non-payment of rent is listed as a reason for eviction only in private lettings.

Figures are not, of course, published, so we cannot determine how strictly these rules are applied. It is not unknown for landlord authorities to arrange eviction cases with ulterior motives; while the militia has the right to suspend residence permits for certain violations of the law. For the legal texts see *Grazhdanski kodeks RSFSR* (Moscow 1979); *Grazhdanski kodeks RSFSR, ofitsial'ny tekst* (Moscow 1968) pp. 207–10.

21 G. S. Sarkisyan and N. P. Kuznetsova, p. 161; A. V. Baranov, p. 177.
22 G. S. Sarkisyan and N. P. Kuznetsova, p. 64.
23 See, for example, *Bol'shaya sovetskaya entsiklopedia* (Moscow 1973), Vol. 2, p. 607; Vol. 11, p. 502.
24 *Nar. khoz. 1980*, pp. 7, 430.
25 *Nar. khoz. 1980*, p. 407.

4. POVERTY LIFE STYLES: OTHER ASPECTS

1 *Estimates and Projections of the Population of the USSR*, Table 4; *Nar. khoz, 1922–84*, p. 116.
2 All figures here are quoted in the present day, post-1961, roubles. See M. Matthews (1982), p. 178.
3 M. Matthews (1982) p. 13.
4 M. Matthews (1982), pp. 82, 92, 158, 178.
5 M. Matthews (1982), p. 135ff.
6 M. Matthews (1982), p. 153ff.
7 Although some figures are available for pensioned invalids (who are mostly 'poor' by definition) little or nothing is published on the incidence of many important diseases, or the associated mortality rates, either for the country as a whole, or individual socio-occupational groups. Experience has shown, moreover, that any rise in incidence may halt the publication of a statistical series. Nothing is normally published on accident rates. Since the determination of sickness rates requires access to large samples of the population, there is little to be gleaned from emigre surveys.
8 *SAUS* 1981, p. 871; 1985, pp. 69, 843, 844. Variations of from 17 per thousand in Vilnius (Lithuania) to 51.8 in Dushanbe (Tadzhikistan) were reported in 1974. See C. Davis, Murray Feshbach, *Rising Infant Mortality in the USSR in the 1970's*, pp. 4–6.
9 *Dekrety Sovetskoi vlasti*, Vol 3, pp. 55, 481.
10 *Nar. khoz. 1980*, pp. 496–8; *SAUS* 1985, pp. 102, 106.
11 Mark Field, April 1984; 1976, p. 236ff; C. Davis, p. 240ff.
12 M. Ryan and R. Prentice, p. 1494.
13 C. Davis, p. 253; M. Field, April 1984, p.22.
14 Most of the details which follow are taken from Mriga, pp. 66–73; *Moskva, Kratkaya adresno-spravochnaya kniga*, p. 135, while the last two paragraphs are based on a conversation with a practising Soviet advocate.
15 Details are provided in Chapter Five. Of course, the working week in some sectors of the economy, particularly transport, communications, and agriculture, has to be much more flexible and is governed by special instructions. *Nar. khoz, 1980*, p. 396
16 B. T. Kolpakov and V. D. Patrushev, p. 99.
17 D. I. Dumnov, V. M. Rutgauzer, A. I. Shmarov, p. 96; E. B. Gruzdeva, E. S. Chertikhina, p. 212.
18 M. Matthews (1972) p. 99ff, p. 138; E. B. Gruzdeva, E. S. Chertikhina, p. 178.
19 V. A. Chulanov, p. 34.
20 See Chapter Six below; also M. T. Yovchuk, L. N. Kogan, p. 174ff.

21 See article in T. I. Zaslavskaya, L. A. Khakhulina, op. cit. p. 74.
22 M. Deza and M. Matthews in *Slavic Review*, December 1975, p. 720.
23 *Nar. khoz, 1980*, pp. 414, 461; M. L. Zakharov, V. M. Piskov (1972) pp. 157, 158.

5. WORK AND SOCIAL SECURITY

1 *Kommentarii k zakonodatelstvu o trude*, p. 71.
2 *Ibid.*
3 Blair Ruble, in his interesting book *Soviet Trade Unions* (p. 68) supports this view.
4 S. M. Schwarz, p. 50.
5 S. A. Ivanov, p. 306; decrees of December, 1959 and December, 1966.
6 A. M. Rekunov and K. S. Pavlishchev, p. 296; Rules of 29 Sept. 1972.
7 S. M. Schwarz, p. 103.
8 M. Matthews (1974) Parts IV and V.
9 V. M. Chkhikvadze, p. 472; *Druzhinniku, sbornik materialov*, p. 135.
10 *SPR* 1979, p. 368.
11 A listing of the relevant decrees in the late seventies and early eighties may be found in Puginski, p. 611.
12 'As result of analysing the data on crime, and material from censuses of workers' trade skills in several districts (which vary in their degree of urbanisation, industrialisation, population movement and other characteristics) it is possible to conclude that there is an inverse statistical relationship between the technical and organisational content of mainly physical labour, and the criminal activities of the workers who do it. Thus, in the most urbanised and industrially developed districts studied, the criminal activities of persons engaged in manual work is 3.2 times higher than that of persons working with the help of machines and mechanisms, and 26 times higher than that of persons involved in repair and adjustment. In the least urbanised district the relationship was 1:2.4:7.1. Analogous data were obtained from another study.' *Sotsiologicheskie issledovaniya*, No. 2, 1983, p. 118 (see also p. 120).

   V. M. Kogan, the writer of these lines, is a well-known Soviet authority on crime.
   Numerous explanations of the heinous phenomenon are available, but a particularly succinct one (which does not refer to poverty, of course) may be found in N. P. Grabovskaya, *Ugolovno-pravovaya bor'ba s prestupleniyami nesovershenoletnikh v SSSR*, Leningrad 1961, p. 8.
13 M. L. Zakharov, V. M. Piskov (1972), p. 179ff.
14 V. V. Mriga and others, p. 327.
15 *Zabota partii*...Vol. 2, pp. 665–73.
16 Matthews (1974) p. 343.
17 *Naselenie SSSR*...p. 31.
18 M. L. Zakharov, V. M. Piskov (1972) p. 182.
19 *Zabota partii*, Vol. 2, p. 311.
20 Standard payments were 50% of earnings up to 50 roubles, and 25% of the excess in group one, with a figure of 40% of earnings for group two. The minimum rates were 18 and 14.4 roubles for the two groups of work-related disablement, and 15 or 12 roubles for other types. (*SPR* 1966, p. 271).
21 *Zabota partii*, Vol. 1, p. 277; Ukaz of September 1967.
22 The final sum paid at each level was also affected by: the cause of death (whether it was work-related or not); and if work-related, by the wage the deceased person had received; the nature of the work performed; and the number of years of service.
23 M. L. Zakharov, V. M. Piskov (1979) p. 306.
24 *Zabota partii*, Vol 1, p. 504; M. L. Zakharov, V. M. Piskov (1979) pp. 306ff.

25 M. L. Zakharov, V. M. Piskov (1979) p. 286.

26 Matthews (1972) pp. 452, 453.

27 *Sbornik zakonodatel'nykh aktov o trude*, p. 552; *Kratki yuridicheski slovar'-spravochnik dlya naseleniya*, p. 341.

28 V. V. Mriga, pp. 323, 408.

29 This is an official weekly sent free of charge, mostly for propaganda purposes. Residence outside the socialist motherland is officially categorized as a sad necessity, or error of judgment. *Pravda* has on occasion referred to voluntary emigres or non-returnees in very unflattering terms.

30 B. Madison (1981).

6. POVERTY, POLITICS AND CHARITY

1 See (as a starting point) the Hearings before the Subcommittee on the 'War on Poverty Program,' House of Representatives, 89th Congress, April 12–30, 1965; the Encyclopedia of Associations (1985), Vol. 1; *SAUS* 1985, p. 385; *Voluntary Organisations, an NCVO Directory*.

2 *Problems of Communism*, May–June 1981, p. 12.

3 In 1967 the old republican 'Committees for Resettlement and Recruitment' which had been used to effect labour transfers were turned into 'Committees for the Use of Labor Resources', and in September 1976, into 'Committees for Labour;' but they continued to concern themselves with hiring and labour direction, rather than with social problems.

4 *Trudovoe pravo, entsiklopedicheski slovar'*, 1979, p. 97.

5 *Vedomosti Verkhovnogo Soveta*, No. 14, 1980, p. 258.

6 The hierarchy of soviets as of early 1982, in fact comprised 15 union republics, 20 autonomous republics, 8 autonomous oblasts (or provinces) 10 autonomous districts 128 ('ordinary') oblasts and territories, 3,199 districts and 41,677 rural settlements. The 'autonomous' units were not truly autonomous, but so called to emphasize their ethnic identity.

7 *Moskva, kratkaya adresno-spravochnaya kniga*, p. 95ff; D. N. Nikitin, p. 39ff. Not surprisingly, the procuracy, courts and KGB lie outside the competence of the local soviets.

8 C. W. Lewis in E. M. Jacobs, p. 50.

9 *Itogi vyborov i sostav deputatov*...pp. 13, 207–15.

10 G. V. Barabashev, K. F. Sheremet, p. 250.

11 See, for example, the discussions in B. Ruble; see also L. Schapiro and J. Godson.

12 Carol W. Lewis, Stephen Sternheimer, pp. 150–9.

13 *Rules of the Communist Party of the Soviet Union*, p. 5.

14 Although the same qualites are sought, election to deputy status is obviously a much more serious business. In 1980, 43.1% of the local deputies (i.e. those below the republican level) were party members anyway (*KPSS Naglyadnoe posobie*...p. 211).

15 M. I. Khaldeev, G. I. Krivoshein, p. 208: V. D. Vetrov, p. 124.

16 V. A. Chulanov, p. 181.

17 A good summary of the system is to be found in Harasymiw (1969) though several subsequent treatments are available.

18 M. Matthews (1972), p. 135. The professor thereby became the centre of a minor scandal, and his later published work was less specific. The average ages of the groups, incidentally, were fairly close.

19 *SPR* 1979, pp. 366ff.

20 F. A. Brokgauz and S. P. Efron, Vol. 25, p. 175.

21 K. Zinov'ev, p. 16.

22 *Dekrety sovetskoi vlasti*, Vol. 3, p. 644 (indexed references).

23 E. H. Carr, Vol. 2, p. 284.
24 In practice the vast majority of voluntary societies in the USSR have highly standardised statutes, and fall into a dozen or so general categories remote from charity as we understand it. They include scientific societies; educational and cultural groups; historical associations; numerous strictly controlled societies for cultural contacts with foreign lands; nature, fire-fighting, stamp-collecting societies, etc. The defence and sports organisations are massive and virtually part of the state structure. In 1932 a model set of statutes, issued for all registered 'social' organisations, stipulated that they were to ensure the active participation of the toiling masses in socialist construction, and strengthen national defence. They were also to function on the Marxist-Leninist basis of democratic centralism, and be guided by the principles of Soviet law and their own statutes (*BSE*, Vol. 8, p. 372).
25 S. I. Ozhegov (1952) p. 41; this definition may be compared with the 'neutral' definition in Dal's dictionary of 1880 (regarded as the standard work of pre-revolutionary usage) Vol. 1, p. 94 (republished Moscow 1955); and with the Ozhegov edition of 1964 (p. 48) where the term was still defined as 'bourgeois' but without the 'demeaning' annotation. The lexigraphic history of many such politically sensitive words must be fascinating, and still awaits serious analysis.
26 I. P. Mashkovtsev, G. V., Shcheglov, p. 160.
27 N. S. Malein, p. 238.
28 *Komsomol i podrostki*, p. 260.
29 Two such associations, linked with the name of the imprisoned mineworker, Aleksandr Klebanov, were quickly suppressed. A third, known as SMOT, the Free Inter-Trade (Professional) Union of Toilers, at the time of writing enjoys a precarious existence.

7. SOME FURTHER DIMENSIONS

1 We have discussed its relevance to Soviet society in Matthews, (1978), Chapter Five, so we shall eschew repetition of commonly recognised principles here.
2 M. Matthews (1972), p. 35.
3 Khrushchev claimed to have started work as a shepherd at the age of nine, and Brezhnev as a worker at fifteen.
4 M. Matthews (1972) p. 205.
5 Of course, the matter of simple probability must also be kept in mind. If, at the beginning of the 1980s, a large proportion of the population was still below an accepted poverty threshold, then a complete turnover of the entire group would take a considerable time; the possibility of individuals re-entering it would remain great; and many members of it would be destined never to leave.
6 407 respondents out of 442 completed this section.
7 The figures were, respectively, 11%, 16% and 11%. It is gratifying, incidentally, that the sample apparently contained so few people whose opposition to the political and economic system affected their life styles. This implies a fair balance of opinion in other questions.
8 T. P. Alton, and others, p. 8, Table 3.
9 J. L. Porket, p. 213.
10 I am grateful to Dr J. L. Porket for locating these figures. See: J. Kučerák and A. Kukulová, in *Odbory a společnost*, 1971, Nos. 5–6, pp. 95–110; Jiři Linhart in *Sociologický časopis*, Vol. 16, 1980, No. 3, p. 281, n. 8.
11 *Voice of Solidarity* (Bulletin) Nos. 55, 58, 1983; *RFE Polish Situation Report*, 10 March 1982; p. 8; 21 September 1983, p. 15.
12 *Voice of Solidarity*, No. 75, 26 November, 1983; No. 58, 1 April 1983; No. 67, 12 August 1983.

13 *Voice of Solidarity*, No. 67, 12 August 1983.
14 *RFE Hungarian Situation Report*, 2 March 1978, p. 4.
15 Zsuzsa Ferge, 'Main Trends in Hungarian Social Policy', *New Hungarian Quarterly*, Vol. 23, No. 86, 1982.
16 Interview by Sasza Malko, *Kontakt*, No. 3 (23) March 1984, P. 58.
17 *RFE Hungarian Situation Report*, 13 January 1981.
18 Particularly under the terms of the 'Food Programme', discussed below, and the July 1981 decree 'On Increasing the Output of Consumer Goods, Improving their Quality and Range', in *SPR* 1982, p. 485.
19 Text of the Eleventh Five-year Plan, Section VIII, *SPR* 1982, p. 446 for coal industry; p. 462 for second jobs (sovmeshchenie); *SPR* 1983 p. 317 for extractive and building materials industry; and *SPR* 1983, pp. 51, 75, 78, 71, 87, 283, for agriculture.
20 See, in particular, the decrees of 22 January, 23 February, 2 September 1981 in *SPR* 1982, pp. 475, 477, 492.
21 The measures of the 22 January, 25 August, 2 September and the 5 Octoboer 1981, in *SPR* 1982, pp. 467, 485, 488, 490, 493, 496.
22 *SPR* 1982, p. 471.
23 The deposit was in fact lowered from 42% (Matthews, 1978, p. 44) to 30% in most parts of the USSR, and 20% in peripheral areas. Encouraged in the post-war years, and again under Khrushchev, private house-building was restricted in urban areas after the early sixties, because it impeded comprehensive urban planning, tended to be of inadequate quality, or was thought to promote individualism. The construction of 'co-operative' flats for private ownership also fell into disfavour, though the reasons for that are less clear. Overall, the proportion of privately-built or owned living space in town and country fell from 54% of annual increments in 1960 to 20% of those of 1980 (*Nar. khoz.* 1922–82, p. 426). After 1981 there was another upturn.
24 The major enactments which we shall consider here are listed in 'Prodovol'stvennaya programma SSSR na period do 1990 goda', and 'Ob ulushchenii upravleniya sel'skim khozyaistvom i drugimi otrasliyami agropromyshlennogo kompleska', 24 May 1982, in *SPR* 1983, pp. 23–87: See, in particular, pp. 48, 69, 71, 77, 84–6
25 See decrees of 14 September 1977, 8 January 1981 (*SPR* 1982, p. 314) and 14 January, 1981. A great deal of economic and sociological investigation followed.
26 *SPR* 1983, p. 83.
27 *Nar. khoz.*, *1922–82*, p. 427.

BIBLIOGRAPHY

———— ∽ ————

This bibliography contains those items (books and journals) which are mentioned in the text, together with a few pertinent titles which are not.

We decided that given the flood of writing on poverty, there was no point in attempting to be more inclusive. The length of some Soviet titles causes difficulty when they need to be quoted. Collections of documents, and some well-known reference books are therefore entered under the names of their editors.

In our opinion, no really satisfactory system of transliteration from the Russian Cyrillic has yet been devised. Here we have used commonly accepted spellings, with some simplification of the use of letters indicating palatals ('i' and 'y'), since these are rarely essential to comprehension.

BOOKS

Aivazyan, S. A., Rimashevskaya, N. M., *Tipologia potrebleniya*, Moscow 1978.

Alton, T. P., Bass, E. M., Lazarcik, G., Znayenko, W. (eds.), *Research Project on National Income in East Central Europe, Occasional Papers*, No. OP-70, 'Economic Growth in Eastern Europe, 1965, 1970, 1975–81.' 1982 (L. W. International Financial Research, Inc. New York).

Antosenkova, E. G., Kalmyk, V. A., *Otnoshenie k trudu i tekuchest' kadrov, s prilozheniyami*, Novosibirsk 1970.

Aralov, V. A., Gintsburg, L. Ya. (et al., eds.), *Trudovoe ustroistvo invalidov v SSSR (sbornik normativnykh aktov i metodicheskikh materialov)*, Moscow 1963.

Artemov, V. A., *Problemy sotsialno-ekonomicheskogo razvitiya zapadno-sibirskoi derevni*, Novosibirsk 1981.

Barabashev, G. V., Sheremet, K. F. *Sovetski stroi*, Moscow 1981.

Baranov, A. V., *Sotsial'no-demograficheskoe razvitie krupnogo goroda*, Moscow 1981.

217

Beisenov, B. S., *Alkogolizm – ugolovno-pravovye i kriminologicheskie problemy*, Moscow 1981.

Boiko, V. I. and others, *Sotsiologicheskie kharakteristiki gorodskogo naseleniya Tuvinskoi ASSR*, Novosibirsk 1982.

Bol'shaya sovetskaya entsiklopediya (3rd edition), Moscow 1969–78 (30 volumes).

Borodanov, M. N. and others, *Kolkhoznoe pravo*, Moscow 1970.

Brokgauz, F. A., Efron, S. P. (eds.), *Entsiklopedicheski slovar'* (82 volumes), St Petersburg 1880–1907.

BSE see *Bol'shaya sovetskaya entsiklopediya*.

Carr, E. H., *The Bolshevik Revolution, 1917–1923* (3 volumes), London, 1950-3.

Chapman, J. G., *Real Wages in Soviet Russia Since 1928*, Cambridge: Harvard University Press 1963.

Chayanov, V., *Byudzhetnye issledovaniya – istoriya i metody*, Moscow 1929.

Chernenko, K. U., Smirtyukov, M. S., Bogolyubov, K. M. (eds.), see *Zabota partii i pravitel'stva o blage naroda* below.

Chislennost' i sostav naseleniya po dannym Vsesoyuznoi peripisi naseleniya, Moscow 1984.

Chulanov, V. A., *Sovremennye sovetskie rabochie*, Moscow 1980.

Davis, C., 'The Economics of the Soviet Health System', in *Soviet Economy in the 1980s: Problems and Prospects* (US Congress, Joint Economic Committee) Part 2, US Government Printing Office, Washington, DC, December, 1982, p. 228.

Davis, C. Feshbach, M., *Rising Infant Mortality in the USSR in the 1970s*, International Population Reports, Series P. 95, No. 74, US Dept. of Commerce, Bureau of the Census, Washington, Sept. 1980.

DDR Handbuch, Köln 1979.

Dekrety sovetskoi vlasti, Vols 1–9 Moscow 1957–78.

Dmitriev, A. V., *Sotsialnye problemy ludei pozhilogo vozrasta*, Moscow 1980.

Druzhinniku, sbornik zakonodatel'nykh i inikh materialov, Moscow 1963.

Dumnov, D. I., Rutgauzer, V. M., Shmarov, A. I. *Byudzhet vremeni naseleniya*, Moscow 1984.

Encyclopedia of Associations, Vols. 1, 2, 1985, Gale Research Company, Detroit, Michigan.

Entsiklopedicheski slovar' pravovykh znanii (Chkhikvadze, V. M. and others, eds.) Moscow 1965.

Ershov, A. N., Yurchenko, A. F. *Spravochnik rukovoditeliya predpriyatiya obshchestvennogo pitaniya*, Moscow 1981.

Estimates and Projections of the Population of the USSR (cyclostyled): Prepared by the Foreign Demographic Analysis Division, Bureau of the Census, US Department of Commerce, March 1977, Washington DC, USA.

Ezhov, A. I., *Organizatsiya gosudarstvennoi statistiki v SSSR*, Moscow 1957.

Ezhov, A. I., *Sistema i metodolgia pokazatelei sovetskoi statistiki*, Moscow 1965.

Ezhov, A. I. and others (eds.), *Istoriya sovetskoi gosudarstvennoi statistiki*, Moscow 1969.

Family Living Studies, International Labour Organisation, Geneva 1961.

Ferge, Z. 'Main Trends in Hungarian Social Policy', *New Hungarian Quarterly*, Vol. 33, No. 86, 1982, p. 137.

Field, M. (ed.), *Social Consequences of Modernisation in Communist Societies*, Baltimore 1976.

Field, M., *Medical Care in the Soviet Union; Promises and Reality* (Cyclostyled Report, Kennan Institute), Washington, April 1984.

George, V. *Poverty and Inequality in Common Market Countries*, London 1980.

George, V., and Manning, N., *Socialism, Social Welfare and the Soviet Union*, London 1980.

Glushkov, N. T. and others (eds.), *Spravochnik po tsenoobrazovaniyu*, Moscow 1985.

Golensov, V. M., Muzyka, A. V., *Oplata truda v stroitel'stve*, Kiev 1980.

Grazhdanski kodeks RSFSR, s izmeneniyami i dopolneniyami na 1 oktyabrya 1978, Moscow 1979.

Grazhdanski kodeks RSFSR, ofitsial'ny tekst, Moscow 1968.

Gruzdeva, E. B., Chertikhina, E. S., *Trud i byt sovetskikh zhenshchin*, Moscow 1983.

Harasymiw, B., 'Nomenklatura; the Soviet Communist Party's Leadership Recruitment System', *Canadian Journal of Political Science*, December 1969, No. 4, p. 493.

Höremann, H. H., *Die Wirtschaft OstEuropas und der V. R. China zum Beginn der 80 Jahre*, Verlag Kohlhammer, Stuttgart 1983.

Itogi vsesoyuznoi perepisi naseleniya 1970 goda, Raspredelenie naseleniya SSSR po zanyatiyam, Moscow 1973.

Itogi vyborov i sostav deputatov mestnykh sovetov narodnykh deputatov, statisticheski sbornik, Moscow 1977.

Ivanov, S. A. (ed.), *Trudovoe pravo, entsiklopedicheski slovar'*, Moscow 1977.

Jacobs, E. M., *Soviet Local Government and Politics*, London 1983.

Kabo, E. O., 'Byudzhetny indeks (istoricheski ocherk)', in *Sovetskaya statistika za polveka (1917–67)*, Akademia Nauk SSSR, Moscow 1970.

Kelam, A. A., 'Razvitie sotsial'noi struktury sovetskogo obshchestva' in Filippov, F. P. (and others, eds.), *O formirovanii sotsial'noi odnorodnosti*, Tallin 1981.

Khaldeev, M. I., Krivoshein, G. I. (compilers), *Pervichnaya partiinaya organizatsiya; opyt, formy i metody raboty*, Moscow 1979.

Kheinman, S. A. (and others, eds.), *Stroitel'stvo materialno-tekhnicheskoi bazy kommunizma* (2 vols.) Moscow 1982.

Khryashcheva, A. I., *Gruppy i klassy v krest'yanstve*, Moscow 1926.

Kolpakov, B. T., Patrushev, V. D., (eds.), *Byudzhet vremeni gorodskogo naseleniya*, Moscow 1971.

Kommentarii k zakonodatelstvu o trude (V. I. Trebilov, and others, eds.), Moscow 1975.

Komsomol i podrostki, dokumenty i materialy s'ezdov komsomola (B. Myshenkov, V. Shmitkov, eds.) Moscow 1971.

Korshunov, Yu. N., Livshits, P. Z., Rumyantseva, M. S. (eds.), *Sovetskoe zakonodatelstvo o trude*, Moscow 1980.

Kotlyar, A. E., Turchaninova, S. Ya., *Zanyatost' zhenshchin v proizvodstve*, Moscow 1975.

Kozlovskaya, L. V., *Sotsial'nye aspekty razmeshcheniya promyshlennosti*, Minsk, 1977.

K.P.S.S., *Naglyadnoe posobie po partiinomy stroitel'stvu*, Moscow 1980.

Kratki yuridicheski slovar'-spravochnik dlya naseleniya (I. A. Azovkin and others, eds.), Moscow 1962.

Kratki yuridicheski spravochnik v pomoshch' profaktivu (R. Z. Livshits and others, eds.), Moscow 1975.

Kunel'ski, L. E., *Zarabotnaya plata i stimulirovanie truda, sotsial'no-ekonomicheski aspekt*.

Lewis, C. W., Sternheimer, S., *Soviet Urban Management: with comparisons to the United States*, New York 1979.

McAuley, A., Economic Welfare in the Soviet Union, London 1979.

Madison, B., '*Social Welfare in the Soviet Union*', Stanford 1968.

Madison, B., *The Soviet Social Welfare System as Experienced and Evaluated by Consumers and Personnel* (Cyclostyled, National Council for Soviet and East European Research) Washington D.C., September 1981.

Malein, N. S., *Sbornik normativnykh aktov po khozyaistvennomu zakonodatel'stvu*, Moscow 1979.

Malov, N. I., Churakov, V. I., *Sovremennye osnovy i metody planirovaniya razvitiya zdravookhraneniya*, Moscow 1981.

Mashkovtsev, I. P., Shcheglov, G. V., eds,, *Organizatsionno-massovaya rabota profsoyuzov, Sbornik ofitsial'nykh materialov*, Moscow 1983.

Matthews, M. *Class and Society in Soviet Russia*, London 1972.

Matthews, M., *Education in the Soviet Union, Policies and Institutions since Stalin*, London 1982.

Matthews, M., *Privilege in the Soviet Union, A Study of Elite Life Styles under Communism*, London 1978.

Matthews, M. (ed.) *Soviet Government – A Selection of Official Documents on Internal Policies*, London 1974.

Matyukha, I. Ya., *Statistika byudzhetov naseleniya*, Moscow 1967.

'The Measure of Poverty', a series of Technical Papers produced under the auspices of the US Department of Health, Education, and Welfare by the Poverty Studies Task Force, Washington, DC 1974– .

Michev, D., *35 godini – Sotsialisticheska Bulgariya*, Sofia 1979.

Moskva, kratkaya adresno-spravochnaya kniga, Moscow 1977.

Mriga, V. V., Monastyrski, E. A., Lisnichenko, T. N., *Yuridicheski spravochnik dlya naseleniya, – 600 voprosov i otvetov po sovetskomu zakonodatel'stvu*, Kiev 1974.

Nalaev, Sh. M, (ed.), *Kalmytskaya ASSR, statisticheski sbornik*, Kalmytskaya knizhnoe izdatelstvo, Kalmyk ASSR 1981.

Nar. khoz. see '*Narodnoe khozyaistvo*'

Narodnoe khozyaistvo RSFSR, statisticheski ezhegodnik, Moscow (Various years).

Narodnoe khozyaistvo SSSR, statisticheski ezhegodnik, Moscow (Various years).

Naselenie SSSR po dannym vsesoyuznoi perepisi naseleniya 1979 goda (brochure, 32pp.) Moscow 1980.

Nazarov, M. G., *Sotsialno-ekonomicheski statisticheski slovar'*, Moscow 1981.

Nikitin, D. N., *Sovety narodnykh deputatov, status, kompetentsiya, organizatsiya, deyatel'nost'*, *sbornik dokumentov*, Moscow 1980.

Novitski, A. G., Mil', G. V., *Zanyatost' pensionerov*, Moscow 1981.

Osborn, R. J., *Soviet Social Policies*, Illinois 1970.

Osipov, G. V. and Szczepańsky, Jan, *Sotsial'nye problemy truda i proizvodstva*, Moscow 1969.

Ozhegov, S. I. (ed.), *Slovar' russkogo yazyka*, Moscow 1952; 1964.

Peterkin, B., 'Food Plans for Poverty Measurement', *Technical Paper XII*, 'The Measure of Poverty' (q.v.), November 1976.

Pohorille, M., 'Social Welfare Distribution and Social Equality', *Oeconomica Polonia*, Vol. 6, No. 3, 1979, p. 295.

Poland, Statistical Data, 1983, Warsaw 1983.

Popov, V. M., Sidorova, M. I., *Sotsial'no-ekonomicheskie problemy prozvoditel'nosti truda i vosproizvodstva rabochei sily v sel'skom khozyaistve*, Moscow 1979.

'Inequalities in Eastern Europe: the Case of Old-Age Pensioners' *Papers in East European Economics*, No. 64, Oxford, 1980 (cyclostyled).

'Retired Workers in Poland', *Osteuropa-Wirtschaft*, No. 4, 1981, p. 294.

Porket, J. L., 'Sex-Related Differences in Income under Soviet-Type Socialism', *Osteuropa-Wirtschaft* No. 3, 1982, p. 213.

Poverty and Human Development, World Bank Publication, Oxford University Press, 1980.

Prokopovicz, S. N., *Histoire Economique de l'URSS*, Au Portulan chez Flammarion, Paris, 1952.

Puginksi, B. I., and others (eds.) *Nastol'naya kniga khozyaistvennogo rukovoditelya po zakonodatel'stvu*, Moscow 1985.

Rekunov, A. M., Pavlishchev, K. S., *Gosudarstvennaya ditsiplina*, Moscow 1978.

Rocznik Statisticzny, 1983, Warsaw, 1983.

Rubinov, A. Z., *Lestnitsa prestizha*, Moscow 1976.

Ruble, B., *Soviet Trade Unions*, Cambridge University Press 1981.

Rules of the Communist Party of the Soviet Union, Moscow 1977.

Ryan, M., Prentice, R., 'Spatial variations in the Soviet health service,' *British Medical Journal*, p. 1494, 7 May 1983.

Ryvkina, R. V., *Obraz zhizni sel'skogo naseleniya*, Novosibirsk 1979.

Sarkisyan, G. S. and Kuznetsova, N. P., *Potrebnosti i dokhod sem'i, uroven', struktura, perspektivy*, Moscow 1967.

SAUS, see '*Statistical Abstract of the United States*'.

Savinov, N. P. (ed.), *Finansovaya rabota profsoyuzov – Sbornik ofitsial'nykh materialov*, Moscow 1979.

Sbornik zakonodatel'nykh aktov o trude, Moscow 1960.

Sbytova, L. S., *Struktura zanyatosti i effektivnost' proizvodstva* Moscow 1982.

Schapiro, L., Godson, J. (eds.), *The Soviet Worker, Illusions and Realities*, MacMillan, London, 1981.

Schroeder, G. E., 'Soviet Living Standards – Achievements and Prospects' in *Soviet Economy in the 1980s: Problems and Prospects* (US Congress, Joint Economic Committee) Part 2, US Government Printing Office, Washington, DC, December 1982.

Schroeder, G. E., Denton, M. E., *An Index of Consumption in the USSR*, Washington 1982.

Schroeder, G. E. and Edwards, I., *Consumption in the USSR: an International Comparison*, US Government Printing Office, Washington, 1981.

Schwarz, S. M., *Labor in the Soviet Union*, Cresset Press, 1953.

Shapiro, V. D., *Chelovek na pensii*, Moscow 1980.

Shchegel'ski, V. Z., *Spravochnik profsoyuznogo rabotnika*, Moscow 1975.

Shubkin, V. N., *Trudyashchayasya molodezh': obrazovanie, professia, mobil'nost'*, Moscow 1984.

Shustov, A. I., Budarin, V. I., *Spravochnik direktora shkoly*, Moscow 1971.

Sorokin, P. A., Zimmermann, C. C., Galpin, C. J. (eds.), *A Source book in Rural Sociology* (Vol. 2), Minneapolis, 1931.

Sotsial'noe strakhovanie v SSSR – Sbornik ofitsial'nykh materialov, (Simonenko, G. S., ed.), Moscow 1976.

Sotsial'no-ekonomicheskaya statistika; slovar', N. G. Nazarov (ed.), Moscow 1981.

Sovetski entsiklopedicheski slovar' (Prokhorov, A. M. and others, eds.), Moscow 1979.

Soviet Economic Performance 1966–7, US Government Printing Office, Washington, 1968 (Joint Economic Committee).

SPR, see *Spravochnik partiinogo rabotnika.*

Spravochnik partiinogo rabotnika, Moscow (Various years).

Statistical Abstract of the United States (*SAUS*) (Various years), US Dept of Commerce, Bureau of the Census, Washington.

Statisticheski slovar', A. I. Ezhov and others (eds.), Moscow 1965.

Statistisches Jahrbuch der DDR, East Berlin, 1984.

Statisticheski ezhegodnik stran-chlenov soveta ekonomicheskoi vazimopomoschi, Moscow 1982.

Stroitel'stvo material'no-tekhnicheskoi bazy kommunizma (2 vol.) Kheinman, S. A. and others (eds.), Moscow 1982.

Townsend, P., *Poverty in the United Kingdom* (Penguin, 1979).

Treml, V., *Alcohol in the USSR, A Statistical Study*, Durham, N.C. 1982.

Tsogoev, N. V. (ed.) *Ekonomicheskoe i sotsialnoe razvitie Stavropolya v 10 desyatiletke*, Stavropolski Krai, Stavopol', 1981.

Tur, V. A., *Spravochnik po nalogam i sboram s naseleniya*, Moscow 1968; Moscow 1984.

Vasiliev, V. I., Lukyanov, A. I. eds., *Kommentarii k zakonu o statuse narodnykh deputatov v SSSR*, Moscow 1981.

Vetrov, V. D. and others, eds., *Raionny komitet partii*, Moscow 1972.

Voluntary Organisations, An NCVO Directory 1985/86, Bedford Square Press, 1985.

V'yaskov, M. F., Mil'ski, E. A., Marushkin, A. A., *Oplata truda rabotnikov predpriyatii, organiszatsii i uchrezhdenii, obsluzhivayushchikh selskoe khozyaistvo*, Moscow 1981.

Yovchuk, M. T., Kogan, L. N., *Dukhovny mir sovetskogo rabochego*, Moscow 1972.

Zabota partii i pravitel'stva o blage naroda, Sbornik dokumentov, Vol. 1, Chernenko, K. U. and Smirtyukov, M. S., (eds.) Moscow 1974; Vol. 2, Smirtyukov, M. S. and Bogolyubov, K. M., (eds.), Moscow 1980.

Zakharov, M. L., Piskov, V. M., *Sotsial'noe obespechenie i strakhovanie v SSSR, Sbornik ofitsial'nykh dokumentov s kommentariyami*, Moscow 1972; *Sbornik normativnykh aktov*, Moscow 1979.

Zarejsky, D., McClain, T. B., '*Poverty in the United States, a reference Manual for Debates*' National Textbook Co., Skokie, Illinois, 1973.

Zaslavskaya, T. I., Kalmyk, V. A., *Sovremennaya sibirskaya derevnya* (Chasti I, II), Novosibirsk 1975.

Zaslavskaya, T. I., Khakhulina, L. A., *Sotsialnoe razvitie sela: analiz i modelirovanie*, Novosibirsk 1980.

Zhenshchiny v SSSR, statisticheskie materialy, Moscow 1983.

Zimmerman, C. C., *Consumption and Standards of Living*, New York, 1976.

Zinov'ev, K. (FitzLyon), *Rossiya nakanune revolyutsii*, London, 1983.

XXVI S'ezd KPSS, Stenograficheski otchet, 2 vols, Moscow 1981.

JOURNALS

Byulleten' goskomiteta po trudu i sotsial'nym voprosam

Religion in Communist Lands

Ekonomika sel'skogo khozyaistva

Golos Rodiny

Problems of Communism

Materialy samizdata (Cyclostyled), RFE–RL Archiv samizdata, Munich

Planovoe khozyaistvo

RFE Hungarian Situation Reports (Cyclostyled) Munich

RFE Polish Situation Reports (Cyclostyled), Munich

RFE–RL Soviet Area Audience and Opinion Research (Bulletin, Cyclostyled)

Sem'ya i Shkola

Slavic Review

Sotsialisticheski trud

Sotsial'noe obespechenie

Sotsiologicheskie issledovaniya

Vedomosti Verkhovnogo Soveta

Vestnik statistiki
Voice of Solidarity (Bulletin)
Vol'noe slovo
Voprosy ekonomiki

INDEX